Lecture Notes in Computer Science

2009

Edited by G. Goos, J. Hartmanis and J. van L

T0230314

Springer
Berlin
Heidelberg
New York
Barcelona
Hong Kong
London
Milan
Paris
Singapore
Tokyo

Hannes Federrath (Ed.)

Designing Privacy Enhancing Technologies

International Workshop on Design Issues
in Anonymity and Unobservability
Berkeley, CA, USA, July 25-26, 2000
Proceedings

Springer

Series Editors

Gerhard Goos, Karlsruhe University, Germany
Juris Hartmanis, Cornell University, NY, USA
Jan van Leeuwen, Utrecht University, The Netherlands

Volume Editor

Hannes Federrath
FU Berlin, Institut Informatik
Takustr. 9, 14195 Berlin, Germany
E-mail: federrath@inf.tu-dresden.de

Cataloging-in-Publication Data applied for

Die Deutsche Bibliothek - CIP-Einheitsaufnahme

Designing privacy enhancing technologies : proceedings / International
Workshop on Design Issues in Anonymity and Unobservability, Berkeley,
CA, USA, July 25 - 26, 2000. Hannes Federrath (ed.). - Berlin ;
Heidelberg ; New York ; Barcelona ; Hong Kong ; London ; Milan ; Paris ;
Singapore ; Tokyo : Springer, 2001
    (Lecture notes in computer science ; Vol. 2009)
    ISBN 3-540-41724-9

CR Subject Classification (1998): C.2, D.4.6, E.3, H.3, H.4, I.7, K.4, K.6.5

ISSN 0302-9743
ISBN 3-540-41724-9 Springer-Verlag Berlin Heidelberg New York

Springer-Verlag Berlin Heidelberg New York
a member of BertelsmannSpringer Science+Business Media GmbH

http://www.springer.de

© Springer-Verlag Berlin Heidelberg 2001
Printed in Germany

Typesetting: Camera-ready by author, data conversion by PTP Berlin, Stefan Sossna
Printed on acid-free paper   SPIN 10782052   06/3142   5 4 3 2 1 0

Preface

This workshop addresses the design and realization of anonymity services for the Internet and other communication networks. The main topics of the workshop are

- Attacks on Systems,
- Anonymous Publishing,
- Mix Systems,
- Identity Management, and
- Pseudonyms and Remailers.

Anonymity and unobservability have become "hot topics" on the Internet. Services that provide anonymous and unobservable access to the Internet are useful for electronic commerce applications (obviously with the need for strong authenticity and integrity of data) as well as for services where the user wants to remain anonymous (e.g. web-based advisory services or consultancy).

I would like to thank the other members of the program committee John Borking, Marit Köhntopp, Andreas Pfitzmann, Avi Rubin, Adam Shostack, Michael Waidner, and Sonja Zwissler for their helpful hints, for doing the reviews, and for their patience. A special thanks is dedicated to Lila Finhill of ICSI for her help in all administrative and financial concerns, and Christian Schindelhauer for his support on LaTeX.

July 2000   Hannes Federrath

Organization

This workshop was held at the International Computer Science Institute (ICSI), Berkeley, California, July 25-26, 2000.

Program Committee

John Borking	Registratiekamer Netherlands
Hannes Federrath	ICSI, Berkeley
Marit Köhntopp	Privacy Commissioner Schleswig-Holstein, Germany
Andreas Pfitzmann	Dresden University of Technology, Germany
Avi Rubin	AT&T Research
Adam Shostack	Zero-Knowledge Systems, Montreal, Canada
Michael Waidner	IBM Zurich Research Lab
Sonja Zwissler	ICSI, Berkeley

Sponsoring Institutions

International Computer Science Institute, Berkeley, USA
Zero-Knowledge Systems, Montreal, Canada

Table of Contents

Terminology

Attacks on Systems

Anonymous Publishing

Mix Systems

Identity Management

Pseudonyms and Remailers

Anonymity, Unobservability, and Pseudonymity – A Proposal for Terminology

Andreas Pfitzmann[1] and Marit Köhntopp[2]

[1] Dresden University of Technology, Department of Computer Science, D-01062
Dresden, Germany
`pfitza@inf.tu-dresden.de`
[2] Independent Centre for Privacy Protection Schleswig-Holstein, Germany;
Unabhängiges Landeszentrum für Datenschutz Schleswig-Holstein, Postfach 71 21,
D-24171 Kiel, Germany
`marit@koehntopp.de`

Abstract. Based on the nomenclature of the early papers in the field,
we propose a set of terminology which is both expressive and precise.
More particularly, we define *anonymity, unlinkability, unobservability,*
and *pseudonymity* (*pseudonyms* and *digital pseudonyms*, and their attributes).

We hope that the adoption of this terminology might help to achieve
better progress in the field by avoiding that each researcher invents a
language of his/her own from scratch. Of course, each paper will need
additional vocabulary, which might be added consistently to the terms
defined here.

1 Setting

We develop this terminology in the usual setting that *senders* send *messages* to
recipients using a communication network. For other settings, e.g. users querying
a database, customers shopping in an e-commerce shop, the same terminology
can be derived by abstracting away the special names "sender", "recipient", and
"message". But for ease of explanation, we use the specific setting here.

All statements are made from the perspective of an attacker who may be
interested in monitoring what communication is occurring, what patterns of
communication exist, or even in manipulating the communication.

We assume that the attacker is not able to get information on the sender or
recipient from the message content. Therefore, we do not mention the message
content in the sequel.

2 Anonymity

To enable anonymity of a subject, there always has to be an appropriate set of
subjects with potentially the same attributes.

H. Federrath (Ed.): Anonymity 2000, LNCS 2009, pp. 1–9, 2001.

> **Anonymity** is the state of being not identifiable within a set
> of subjects, the **anonymity set**.

The *anonymity set* is the set of all possible subjects who might cause an action. Therefore, a sender may be anonymous only within a set of potential senders, his/her *sender anonymity set*, which itself may be a subset of all subjects worldwide who may send messages from time to time. The same is true for the recipient, who may be anonymous within a set of potential recipients, which form his/her *recipient anonymity set*. Both anonymity sets may be disjoint, be the same, or they may overlap.

Anonymity is the stronger, the larger the respective anonymity set is and the more evenly distributed the sending or receiving, respectively, of the subjects within that set is.[1]

3   Unlinkability

With respect to the system of which we want to describe anonymity, unobservability, or pseudonymity properties, *unlinkability* of two or more items means that within this system, these items are no more and no less related than they are related concerning the a-priori knowledge.

This means that the probability of those items being related stays the same before (a-priori knowledge) and after the run within the system (a-posteriori knowledge of the attacker).[2]

E.g. two messages are unlinkable if the probability that they are sent by the same sender and/or received by the same recipient is the same as those imposed by the a-priori knowledge.

4   Anonymity in Terms of Unlinkability

If we consider the sending and receiving of messages as the items of interest (IOIs), *anonymity* may be defined as unlinkability of an IOI and an identifier of a subject (ID). More specifically, we can describe the anonymity of an IOI

---

[1] One might differentiate between the term anonymity and the term indistinguishability, which is the state of being indistinguishable from other elements of a set. Indistinguishability is stronger than anonymity as defined in this text. Even against outside attackers, indistinguishability does not seem to be achievable without dummy traffic. Against recipients of messages, it does not seem to be achievable at all. Therefore, the authors see a greater practical relevance in defining anonymity independent of indistinguishability. The definition of anonymity is an analog to the definition of "perfect secrecy" by Claude E. Shannon [9], whose definition takes into account that no security mechanism whatsoever can take away knowledge from the attacker which he already has.

[2] Normally, the attacker's knowledge can only increase (analogously to Shannon's definition of "perfect secrecy", see above).

such that it is not linkable to any ID, and the anonymity of an ID as not being linkable to any IOI.

So we have *sender anonymity* as the properties that a particular message is not linkable to any sender and that to a particular sender, no message is linkable.

The same is true concerning *recipient anonymity*, which signifies that a particular message cannot be linked to any recipient and that to a particular recipient, no message is linkable.

A weaker property than each of sender anonymity and recipient anonymity is *relationship anonymity*, i.e. it may be traceable who sends which messages and it may also be possible to trace who receives which messages, but it is untraceable who communicates to whom. In other words, sender and recipient (or recipients in case of multicast) are unlinkable.

5   Unobservability

In contrast to anonymity and unlinkability, where not the IOI, but only its relationship to IDs or other IOIs is protected, for unobservability, the IOIs are protected as such.[3]

> ***Unobservability* is the state of IOIs being indistinguishable**
> **from any IOI at all.**

This means that messages are not discernible from "random noise".

As we had anonymity sets with respect to anonymity, we have *unobservability sets* with respect to unobservability.

Sender unobservability then means that it is not noticeable whether any sender within the unobservability set sends.

Recipient unobservability then means that it is not noticeable whether any recipient within the unobservability set receives.

Relationship unobservability then means that it is not noticeable whether anything is sent out of a set of could-be senders to a set of could-be recipients.

6   Relationships between Terms

With respect to the same attacker, unobservability reveals always only a true subset of the information anonymity reveals. We might use the shorthand notation

---

[3] Unobservability can be regarded as a possible and desirable property of steganographic systems (see "Known mechanisms"). Therefore it matches the information hiding terminology [6], [12]. In contrast, anonymity, describing the relationship to *IDs*, does not directly fit into that terminology, but independently represents a different dimension of properties.

$$\text{unobservability} \to \text{anonymity}$$

for that. Using the same argument and notation, we have

$$\text{sender unobservability} \to \text{sender anonymity}$$
$$\text{recipient unobservability} \to \text{recipient anonymity}$$
$$\text{relationship unobservability} \to \text{relationship anonymity}$$

As noted above, we have

$$\text{sender anonymity} \to \text{relationship anonymity}$$
$$\text{recipient anonymity} \to \text{relationship anonymity}$$

$$\text{sender unobservability} \to \text{relationship unobservability}$$
$$\text{recipient unobservability} \to \text{relationship unobservability}$$

7   Known Mechanisms for Anonymity and Unobservability

DC-net [2] [3] and MIX-net [1]are mechanisms to achieve sender anonymity and relationship anonymity, respectively, both against strong attackers. If we add dummy traffic, both provide for the corresponding unobservability [7].

Broadcast [2] [8] [11] and anonymous information retrieval [5] are mechanisms to achieve recipient anonymity against strong attackers. If we add dummy traffic, both provide for recipient unobservability.

Of course, dummy traffic alone can be used to make the number and/or length of sent messages unobservable by everybody except for the recipients; respectively, dummy traffic can be used to make the number and/or length of received messages unobservable by everybody except for the senders. As a side remark, we mention steganography and spread spectrum as two other well-known unobservability mechanisms.

8   Pseudonymity

Pseudonyms are identifiers of subjects, in our setting of sender and recipient. (If we would like to, we could easily generalize pseudonyms to be identifiers of sets of subjects, but we do not need this in our setting.) The subject that may be identified by the pseudonym is the *holder* of the pseudonym[4].

Pseudonymity is the use of pseudonyms as IDs.

---

[4] We prefer the term "holder" over "owner" of a pseudonym because it seems to make no sense to "own" IDs, e.g. bit strings. Furthermore, the term "holder" sounds more neutral than the term "owner", which is associated with an assumed autonomy of the subject's will.

So *sender pseudonymity* is defined by the sender's use of a pseudonym, *recipient pseudonymity* is defined by the recipient's use of a pseudonym.

A *digital pseudonym* is a bit string which is

- unique as ID and
- suitable to be used to authenticate the holder and his/her IOIs, e.g. messages.

9   Pseudonymity with Respect to Linkability

Whereas anonymity and accountability are the extremes with respect to linkability[5] to subjects, pseudonymity is the entire field between and including these extremes. Thus, pseudonymity comprises all degrees of linkability to a subject. Using the same pseudonym more than once, the holder may establish a reputation. Moreover, accountability can be realized with pseudonyms. Some kinds of pseudonyms enable dealing with claims in case of abuse of unlinkability to holders: Firstly, third parties may have the possibility to reveal the identity of the holder in order to provide means for investigation or prosecution. Secondly, third parties may act as liability brokers of the holder to clear a debt or settle a claim.

There are many properties of pseudonyms which may be of importance in specific application contexts. In order to describe the properties of pseudonyms with respect to anonymity, we limit our view to two dimensions and give some typical examples:

1. Initial knowledge of the linking between the pseudonym and its holder The knowledge of the linking may not be a constant but change over time for some or even all people. Normally, the knowledge of the linking only increases.
   - *public pseudonym:*
     The linking between a public pseudonym and its holder may be publicly known even from the very beginning. E.g. the linking could be listed in public directories such as the entry of a phone number in combination with its owner.
   - *initially non-public pseudonym:*
     The linking between an initially non-public pseudonym and its holder may be known by certain parties, but is not public at least initially. E.g. a bank account where the bank can look up the linking may serve as a non-public pseudonym. For some specific non-public pseudonyms, certification authorities could reveal the identity of the holder in case of abuse.
   - *initially unlinkable pseudonym:*
     The linking between an initially unlinkable pseudonym and its holder is – at least initially – not known to anybody with the possible exception of the holder himself/herself. Examples for unlinkable pseudonyms are

---

[5] Linkability is the negation of unlinkability, i.e. items are either more or are either less related than they are related concerning the a-priori knowledge.

(non-public) biometrics like DNA information unless stored in databases including the linking to the holders.

Public pseudonyms and initially unlinkable pseudonyms can be seen as extremes of the described pseudonym dimension whereas initially non-public pseudonyms characterize the continuum in between.

Anonymity is the stronger, the less is known about the linking to a subject. The strength of anonymity decreases with increasing knowledge of the pseudonym linking. In particular, under the assumption that no gained knowledge on the linking of a pseudonym will be forgotten, a public pseudonym never can become an unlinkable pseudonym. In each specific case, the strength of anonymity depends on the knowledge of certain parties about the linking relative to the chosen attacker model.

2. Linkability due to the use of a pseudonym in different contexts

- *person pseudonym:*
  A person pseudonym is a substitute for the holder's name which is regarded as representation for the holder's civil identity. It may be used in all contexts, e.g. a nickname, the pseudonym of an actor, or a phone number.

- *role pseudonym:*
  The use of role pseudonyms is limited to specific roles, e.g. a customer pseudonym or an Internet account used for many instantiations of the same role "Internet user". The same role pseudonym may be used with different communication partners. Roles might be assigned by other parties, e.g. a company, but they might be chosen by the subject himself/herself as well.

- *relationship pseudonym:*
  For each communication partner, a different relationship pseudonym is used. The same relationship pseudonym may be used in different roles for communicating with the same partner. Examples are distinct nicknames for each communication partner.

- *role-relationship pseudonym:*
  For each role and for each communication partner, a different role-relationship pseudonym is used. This means that the communication partner need not be aware that two pseudonyms used in different roles belong to the same holder.

- *transaction pseudonym[6]:*
  For each transaction, a different transaction pseudonym is used, e.g. randomly generated transaction numbers for online-banking. Thus, there is at least no possibility to link different transactions by equality of pseudonyms. Therefore, transaction pseudonyms can be used to realize as strong anonymity as possible.[7]

---

[6] Apart from "transaction pseudonym" some employ the term "one-time-use pseudonym", taking the naming from "one-time pad".

[7] In fact, the strongest anonymity ("transaction anonymity") is given when there is no identifying information at all, i.e. information that would allow linking of anonymous

The strength of the anonymity of these pseudonyms can be represented as the lattice that is illustrated in the following diagram. The arrows point in direction of increasing anonymity, i.e. A → B stands for "B enables stronger anonymity than A".

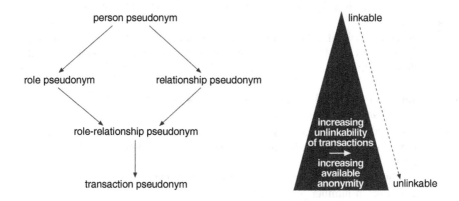

In general, anonymity of both role pseudonyms and relationship pseudonyms is stronger than anonymity of person pseudonyms. The strength of anonymity increases with the application of role-relationship pseudonyms, the use of which is restricted to both the same role and the same relationship. Ultimate strength of anonymity is obtained with transaction pseudonyms.

Anonymity is the stronger, ...

- ... the less often and the less context-spanning pseudonyms are used and therefore the less data about the holder can be linked.
- ... the more often pseudonyms are changed over time.

10 Known Mechanisms and Other Properties of Pseudonyms

A digital pseudonym could be realized as a public key to test digital signatures where the holder of the pseudonym can prove holdership by forming a digital signature which is created using the corresponding private key [1]. The most prominent example for digital pseudonyms are public keys generated by the user himself/herself, e.g. using PGP[8].

___

entities, thus transforming the anonymous transaction into a pseudonymous one. If the transaction pseudonym is used exactly once, we have the same degree of anonymity as if no pseudonym is used at all.

[8] In using PGP, each user may create an unlimited number of key pairs by himself/herself, bind each of them to an e-mail address, self-certify each public key by using his/her digital signature or asking another introducer to do so, and circulate it.

A *public key certificate* bears a digital signature of a so-called *certification authority* and pertains to the binding of a public key to a subject. An *attribute certificate* is a digital certificate which contains further information (*attributes*) and clearly refers to a specific public key certificate. Independent of certificates, attributes may be used as identifiers of sets of subjects as well. Normally, attributes refer to sets of subjects (i.e. the anonymity set), not to one specific subject.

There are several other properties of pseudonyms which should only be shortly mentioned but not discussed in detail in this text. They comprise different degrees of, e.g.,

- limitation to a fixed number of pseudonyms per subject[9] [1] [2] [4],
- guaranteed uniqueness[10] [1] [10],
- transferability to other subjects,
- convertability, i.e. transferability of attributes of one pseudonym to another[11] [2] [4],
- possibility and frequency of pseudonym changeover,
- limitation in number of uses,
- validity (e.g. time limit, restriction to a specific application),
- possibility of revocation or blocking, or
- participation of users or other parties in forming the pseudonyms.

In addition, there may be some properties for specific applications (e.g. addressable pseudonyms serve as a communication address) or due to the participation of third parties (e.g. in order to circulate the pseudonyms, to reveal identities in case of abuse, or to cover claims).

Some of the properties can easily be realized by extending a digital pseudonym by attributes of some kind, e.g. a communication address, and specifying the appropriate semantics. The binding of attributes to a pseudonym can be documented in an attribute certificate produced either by the holder himself/herself or by a certification authority. If the attribute certificate is dated, anybody can spot the currently valid one among different certificates which are inconsistent with one another.

11   Concluding Remark

This text is a first proposal for terminology in the field "anonymity, unobservability, and pseudonymity". The authors hope to get feedback to improve this text and to come to a more precise terminology. Everybody is invited to participate in the process of defining an essential set of terms.

---

[9] For pseudonyms issued by an agency that guarantees the limitation of at most one pseudonym per individual, the term "is-a-person pseudonym" is used.

[10] E.g. "globally unique pseudonyms".

[11] This is a property of convertible credentials.

References

1. David Chaum: Untraceable Electronic Mail, Return Addresses, and Digital Pseudonyms; Communications of the ACM 24/2 (1981) 84-88.
2. David Chaum: Security without Identification: Transaction Systems to make Big Brother Obsolete; Communications of the ACM 28/10 (1985) 1030-1044.
3. David Chaum: The Dining Cryptographers Problem: Unconditional Sender and Recipient Untraceability; Journal of Cryptology 1/1 (1988) 65-75.
4. David Chaum: Showing credentials without identification: Transferring signatures between unconditionally unlinkable pseudonyms; Auscrypt '90, LNCS 453, Springer-Verlag, Berlin 1990, 246-264.
5. David A. Cooper, Kenneth P. Birman: Preserving Privacy in a Network of Mobile Computers; 1995 IEEE Symposium on Research in Security and Privacy, IEEE Computer Society Press, Los Alamitos 1995, 26-38.
6. Birgit Pfitzmann (collected by): Information Hiding Terminology – Results of an informal plenary meeting and additional proposals; Information Hiding, LNCS 1174, Springer-Verlag, Berlin 1996, 347-350.
7. Andreas Pfitzmann, Birgit Pfitzmann, Michael Waidner: ISDN-MIXes – Untraceable Communication with Very Small Bandwidth Overhead; 7th IFIP International Conference on Information Security (IFIP/Sec '91), Elsevier, Amsterdam 1991, 245-258.
8. Andreas Pfitzmann, Michael Waidner: Networks without user observability – design options; Eurocrypt '85, LNCS 219, Springer-Verlag, Berlin 1986, 245-253; revised and extended version in: Computers & Security 6/2 (1987) 158-166.
9. C. E. Shannon: Communication Theory of Secrecy Systems; The Bell System Technical Journal 28/4 (1949) 656-715.
10. Stuart Stubblebine, Paul Syverson: Authentic Attributes with Fine-Grained Anonymity Protection; Financial Cryptography 2000, LNCS Series, Springer-Verlag, Berlin 2000.
11. Michael Waidner: Unconditional Sender and Recipient Untraceability in spite of Active Attacks; Eurocrypt '89, LNCS 434, Springer-Verlag, Berlin 1990, 302-319.
12. J. Zöllner, H. Federrath, H. Klimant, A. Pfitzmann, R. Piotraschke, A. Westfeld, G. Wicke, G. Wolf: Modeling the security of steganographic systems; 2nd Workshop on Information Hiding, LNCS 1525, Springer-Verlag, Berlin 1998, 345-355.

Traffic Analysis: Protocols, Attacks, Design Issues, and Open Problems

Jean-François Raymond

Zero-Knowledge Systems, Inc.
`jfr@zeroknowledge.com`

Abstract. We present the traffic analysis problem and expose the most important protocols, attacks and design issues. Afterwards, we propose directions for further research.
As we are mostly interested in efficient and practical Internet based protocols, most of the emphasis is placed on mix based constructions. The presentation is informal in that no complex definitions and proofs are presented, the aim being more to give a thorough introduction than to present deep new insights.

1 Introduction

Privacy is becoming a critical issue on the Internet. Polls constantly remind us that users feel that one of the most important barriers to using the Internet is the fear of having their privacy violated. Unfortunately, this isn't unjustified as marketers and national security agencies have been very aggressive in monitoring user activity [1].

Two things can happen as a result of this lack of privacy: either the Internet's popularity diminishes or, as seems more likely, the Internet becomes the most pervasive surveillance system ever. The problem studied in this text isn't a purely theoretic one, in fact some would argue that it is a crucial one to solve if the online world is to continue expanding and *improving*. In any case, from both theoretical and practical perspectives, it certainly deserves to receive much more attention than it has gotten so far.

1.1 Desirable Properties

Our goal is to protect users against *traffic analysis*. That is, we don't want an adversary that can monitor and/or compromise certain parts of the systems to be able to match a message sender with the recipient (sender-recipient matchings).

A related problem is that of *network unobservability* which attempts to hide all communication patterns. (how many, at what time and to whom/from whom messages are sent and received). Notice that network unobservability implies the ineffectiveness of traffic analysis.

---

[1] See http://www.freedom.net and http://www.inf.tu-dresden.de/~hf2/anon for examples.

H. Federrath (Ed.): Anonymity 2000, LNCS 2009, pp. 10–30, 2001.

Whereas message privacy can be obtained using encryption, it's much harder to protect sender and/or recipient privacy; especially in large open networks. The number of different assumptions and settings is huge which makes it difficult to define and reason about the problem in a rigorous manner.

As with many constructions in cryptography, there are efficiency, practicality/security tradeoffs to be made. For example, if efficiency and practicality weren't issues, we could broadcast messages in order to protect recipient privacy.

Notice that the problem definition isn't entirely trivial. We can't provide "perfect" privacy since the number of possible senders and recipients is bounded. So, for example, if there are only two parties on the network, an attacker having access to this information can trivially determine who is communicating with whom ... The best we can hope for is to make all possible sender-recipient matchings look equally likely. That is, the attacker's $view^2$'s statistical distribution should be independent from the actual sender-recipient matchings. The protocol of subsection 2.2 has this strong property whereas those of subsection 2.3 usually don't. Unfortunately, there are no satisfactory definitions/methods providing a solid framework in which to analyze protocols that fall short of the optimal performance[3] and we usually need to rely on more or less ad-hoc arguments.

1.2   Overview

A concise literature review can be found in section 2. A comprehensive listing of attacks against mix-networks is presented in section 3. Design issues related to large mix based networks are given in section 4. We propose directions for further research in section 5 and conclude in section 6.

2   Literature Review

Before delving more deeply into the problem, we briefly review some privacy protecting mechanisms. Although the link between these and sender-recipient privacy can be tenuous in certain instances, we believe that some of the ideas used in these techniques might be useful.

2.1   Related Problems

- *Secure Multi Party Computations (SMPC)[14]* : A group of users, each having a private input, want to securely compute a function of their private inputs. At the end of the protocol, all users should know only the value of the function. That is, each user will not have gained any information about the other users' private inputs apart from what can be deduced from the function's value.

---

[2] By *view*, we mean all the information available to the attacker.

[3] i.e. protocols in which traffic analysis can help in obtaining *some* non-trivial information about sender-recipient matchings.

- *Oblivious RAM [22]:* Code privacy can be protected by using a tamper resistant cryptographic processor. The protocol is such than an outside party looking at the memory accesses (reads and writes) can't gain any information about what is being computed and how it is being computed. The code's privacy is protected which could be useful to prevent reverse engineering and software piracy.
- *Private Information Retrieval(PIR) [10,11,12]* : A user privately queries one or many disjoint databases. By privately, we mean that the database(s) will not have any information about what element the user has queried.
- *Oblivious Transfers [36]:* This problem has many versions which are equivalent in that one implies the other. We mention a flavor which is related to PIRs and is referred to as 1 out of n oblivious transfer. These protocols have very similar properties as PIRs, the major difference being that the database privacy is also protected: the user doesn't gain any information about the other entries in the database.
- *Steganography [27]* : Steganography is the branch of information privacy that attempts to hide information within publicly observable data (e.g. using digital watermarking [42], subliminal channels [41], etc.).

2.2 Chaum's Dining-Cryptographer Networks (Dc-Nets)[7,43]

The goal here is to have one participant anonymously broadcast a message. If the message is aimed at one user, the sender can encrypt the message by, for example, using an asymmetric crypto-system. Since the message is received by all parties, recipient anonymity is trivially maintained.

Let $P = \{P_1, P_2, \ldots, P_n\}$ be the set of participants and let $(F, \oplus)$ be a finite Abelian (commutative) group (for example $(\mathbb{Z}_m, +)$) in which all computations will be carried out. The protocol goes as follows:

1. **Initialization:** Each participant securely shares secret keys (chosen at random from F) with *some* other participants. We denote the secret key shared by P_y and P_z by $K_{y,z}(= K_{z,y})$ and define the set G composed of all pairs (P_y, P_z) such that P_y and P_z share a secret key. Notice that if $(P_y, P_z) \in G$ then $(P_z, P_y) \in G$.
2. **Message Transmission:** In order to send a message M, P_i broadcasts:

$$M \oplus \sum_{\forall j \text{ s.t. } \{P_i, P_j\} \in G} sign(i - j) \cdot K_{i,j}$$

Where $sign(x) = 1$ if $x > 1$ and -1 otherwise.
3. **"Noise" Transmission:** All other participants, P_j, broadcast:

$$\sum_{\forall k \text{ s.t. } \{P_j, P_k\} \in G} sign(j - k) \cdot K_{j,k}$$

4. **Computing the Message:** All interested participants can obtain M by adding ($\oplus$) all broadcasted messages. The fact that the sum of all broadcasted message equals M can be seen by noting that all terms except M cancel out because of $sign()$. (i.e. for each term of the form $sign(j - l) \cdot K_{j,l}$ we have $sign(l - j) \cdot K_{l,j} = sign(l - j) \cdot K_{j,l} = -sign(j - l) \cdot K_{j,l}$.)

In order to quantify the scheme's security, we define a graph having n vertices, labelled by $1, 2, \ldots, n$ (each representing a participant), with edges between nodes i and j if and only if P_i and P_j share a secret key. For example, if all participants share a secret key, the graph will be fully connected.

Fact 1 *If the graph obtained by removing the vertices corresponding to the participants controlled by an adversary is connected then the protocol protects sender anonymity. (Note that we assume that the broadcasted values are known to the attacker.)*

This analysis is tight in that if the graph isn't connected, an attacker can determine from which of the disconnected parts of the graph the sender is from.

Drawbacks. Unfortunately, the protocol has serious drawbacks:

1. *Secure and reliable broadcast channel:* To protect against active adversaries[4], we need to rely on physical devices because secure and reliable broadcast mechanisms can't be constructed by algorithmic means. This problem can be partially fixed by the technique of Waidner [43] that uses a fail-stop broadcast.
2. *Channel jamming:* If many participants try to send a message at the same time, all is lost as the sum of all broadcasted values will equal the sum of the messages (e.g. $M_1 \oplus M_2 \oplus \ldots \oplus M_j$). An even bigger problem is if a participant acts maliciously and deliberately sends channel jamming messages; this allows him to compute the legitimate message while the other users can't gain any information.
3. *Number of messages:* Every user needs to participate every time a message is broadcasted which is a problem both in terms of efficiency and robustness. This is an unrealistic constraint in large networks.
4. *Shared secret keys:* The number of keys to share could be too large for practical purposes (need a new key for each transmission). Note that pseudo-random numbers can be used as keys to alleviate this problem. The fact that many users need to share secret keys with (possibly many) participants is also a serious problem in terms of practicality.

Despite these problems, dc-nets are useful in many situations (e.g [19]), and, as far as efficiency is concerned, for certain underlying network topologies (e.g. rings), the complexity is acceptable. Also note that dc-nets can be used in conjunction with other sender-recipient privacy protecting mechanisms such as mix

---

[4] adversaries capable of adding and removing messages from the communication channels.

networks. For example, a certain number of users can transmit information to a mix network using a dc-net. In this setting, even if the mix network security is violated, the attacker can only ascertain that the sender of a given message is one of the parties using the dc-net[5].

2.3   Chaum's Mixes

A mix node is a processor that takes as input a certain number of messages which it modifies and outputs in a random order. The messages are modified and reordered in such a way that it is nearly impossible to correlate a message that "comes in" with a message that "goes out". The mix nodes can be used to prevent traffic analysis in roughly the following manner:

1. The message will be sent through a series of mix nodes (a route), say $i_1, i_2, \ldots, i_d$. The user encrypts the message with node i_d's key, encrypts the result with node i_{d-1}'s key and so on with the remaining keys.
2. The mix nodes receive a certain number of these messages which they decrypt[6], randomly reorder and send to the next nodes in the routes.

Note that each mix node knows only the previous and next node in a received message's route. (The entry and exit node know the source (sender) and destination (recipient) of the message respectively.) Hence, unless the route only goes through a single node, compromising a mix node doesn't trivially enable an attacker to violate sender-recipient privacy.

Different Approaches to Route Selection. The route that a message will follow can be determined in a few ways:

- *Cascade [24,23]:* The route can be constant, that is, it doesn't change. In this setting, the attacker knows the entry, exit and intermediate nodes. This kind of mix network is usually referred to as "mix-cascade". Although they are easier to implement and manage, mix-cascades are *much* easier to traffic analyze.
- *Random Order:* The routes can also be chosen at random, that is, the user chooses $i_1, i_2, \ldots, i_d$ uniformly at random. This type of mix network is usually referred to as "mix-net".
- *Other Methods:* One can think of many other ways of choosing routes, for example: A) part of the route could be fixed B) the route could be chosen at random from a set of pre-determined choices C) the route could be chosen at random subject to some restriction (e.g. mixes not all in the same legal jurisdiction).

In the following, we consider only mix-nets although some comments/attacks will apply to other route selection mechanisms.

---

[5] Assuming that the dc-net's security hasn't been compromised.
[6] They remove a layer of encryption.

Different Approaches to Flushing Mix Nodes. Many approaches to "flushing" messages can be used:

- *Message threshold:* The mix nodes wait until they receive a certain number of messages before "releasing" all of them at the same time.
- *Message Pool [13]:* The flushing algorithm for mixmaster [13] has two parameters: the pool size n and the probability of sending p. The nodes wait until they have n messages in their pool at which time, they shuffle the messages and send each one with probability p (e.g. if $p = 1$ the scheme is identical to the message threshold approach). Note that unsent and newly received messages are placed in the pool.
- *Stop and Go [29]:* Kesdogan et al. give an interesting scheme in which messages wait random times at a nodes before being released (note that the waiting period is determined by the sender). In this setting, the attacker has a probability of success: If an empty node (i.e. one not currently processing any message) receives a message and does not receive another one before sending the decrypted message, the attacker can easily "follow" the message – routing the message through this node doesn't "help". Perhaps the most interesting contribution of this paper is that a statistical analysis is used to determine the probability of this happening.
- *Other :* There are many other reasonable algorithms for doing this, for example mix nodes could receive a random number of messages and output a constant number of them (using dummy messages to fill the gaps).

Mix Networks in Other Settings. Many researchers have studied how mixes can be used within existing networks such as ISDN, Internet and GSM (see for example [32,33,34,31]).

Although these are very interesting papers, they don't provide any deep insights about traffic analysis.

Robust Mixes. Very recently, researchers [1,2,17,25,30] have invented robust mixes, in which messages are properly delivered to the recipient even if a certain number of mix nodes are *misbehaving*. Unfortunately, the constructions don't seem practical for most real-world situations since a large number of the mix nodes, a bulletin board and a public key crypto-system are required.

We note that a mix network that works even if a certain number of nodes *are not forwarding the messages* was proposed in [33,31]. This construction, although it doesn't have many of the nice properties of robust mixes, can be very attractive as it works with classical mix networks (don't need bulletin board, public key crypto-system).

2.4 Rackoff and Simon's Analysis

In [39], Rackoff and Simon provide a solid theoretic framework in which we can reason about sender-recipient privacy. Using complex arguments about rapidly converging Markov processes, they are able to prove that an attacker can't successfully traffic analyze a specific type of mix network (with constrained user behavior). Unfortunately, the setting is of limited practical interest: it's synchronous, all participants need to send a message, mix-nodes process at most two messages at a time and the routes are constrained. Furthermore, although the constructions are efficient (from a complexity theorist's point of view), they do not seem amenable to real-world implementation. In spite of these shortcomings, their work provides the only known solid theoretic foundation for reasoning about traffic analysis.

2.5   Rubin and Reiter's Crowds

Rubin and Reiter propose an lighter weight alternative to mixes and dc-nets in [37,38]. Their system can be seen as a P2P (peer-to-peer) relaying network in which all participants forward messages. The messages are forwarded to the final destination with probability p and to some other participants (chosen at random) with probability $1 - p$. The authors provide a fairly detailed security analysis but, unfortunately, the system does not protect against very powerful adversaries and so we will not discuss it further.

3   Attacks

The attacks mentioned in this section aren't based on any specific implementation[7], instead, we give attacks that can be mounted on the high level descriptions of the schemes. We assume there are no implementation weaknesses, for example, we assume that messages coming in a mix node can't be correlated with a message going out (by a passive external adversary). Note that securely implementing cryptographic protocols is an extremely difficult task even for protocols that seem very simple like the Diffie-Hellman key exchange [18] and so will not be discussed as it is beyond the scope of this work.

In order to give a list of attacks, it is important to solidly define what assumption are made about the attacker's power. We consider the following attacker properties:

- *Internal-External:* An adversary can compromise communication mediums (external) and mix nodes, recipients and senders (internal).
- *Passive-Active:* An active adversary can arbitrarily modify the computations and messages (adding and deleting) whereas a passive adversary can only listen. For example, an external active adversary can remove and add messages from the wire(s) he controls and a passive internal adversary can easily correlate messages coming in a compromised node with messages going out (but can't modify them).

---

[7] For an attack on an RSA based implementation of a mix see [35].

– *Static-Adaptive:* Static adversaries choose the resources they compromise before the protocol starts and can't change them once the protocol has started. Adaptive adversaries on the other hand are allowed to change the resources they control while the protocol is being executed. They can, for example, "follow" messages.

An adversary can, of course, have any combination of these properties. For example, he could control a mix node in a passive manner and actively control wires. Note that there might be other relevant attacker properties (these are the ones usually considered in theoretical cryptography).

We warn the reader that the immunization mechanisms presented in the following subsections are by no means comprehensive and many details are omitted.

3.1   Brute Force Attack

The brute force attack is very instructive because it can help in determining how much, where and when to use dummy traffic. Dummy messages are messages that are sent through the network in order to complicate the attacker's task. On the Internet, mix network operators sometimes need to pay for each message and so we want to be sure the dummy messages have a good security to cost ratio.

The idea behind this attack is very simple: follow every possible path the message could have taken (*passive external adversary*). If the mix isn't well designed and the attacker is extremely lucky, he can link sender and recipient. In most cases however, the attacker will be able to construct a list of possible recipients.

We present the attack in a setting in which each mix node waits until it receives t messages before flushing them (i.e. sending all t messages). In addition, we assume that each message goes through exactly d mix nodes. The attack can be carried out in any setting however the analysis then becomes a bit more involved.

1. The attacker first follows a message from a sender to a first mix node.
2. The attacker then follows *every* (t) message that the first node releases. The adversary needs to follow messages going to anywhere between t and 1 different nodes. If all messages are sent to either the same mix node or recipients, the attacker only needs to monitor one node. On the other hand, if all t messages are sent to different nodes, the attacker needs to observe t different mix nodes.
3. The process continues like this until messages reach the dth level nodes. The attacker then need only "follow" messages leaving the mix network (i.e. going to recipients).

What can the attacker learn from such an attack ? In the worst case, the attacker only needs to follow one path and can match a sender with a recipient. In the best case, the attacker needs to follow t^{d-1} paths through the mix network and t^d messages to the outside world and so can match one sender with t^d

possible recipients. Although the worst case is unacceptable, by adding dummy traffic intelligently, we can make the worst case scenario as good as needed. We propose adding dummy messages in the following manner:

- We make sure that each mix node "sprays" its message around adequately. That is, the nodes should ensure that at least t' different mix nodes receive one of its messages (dummy or real).
- We make sure that each mix node sends at least t'' messages outside the mix network every time it sends messages. These should be sent to participating users (or content providers).

The attacker now follows, at the very least, t' different paths through the mix network, and, at the last node, follows messages going to $t' \cdot t''$ distinct recipients (assuming that the final destinations are all different). Hence, the attacker can only match one sender with $t' \cdot t''$ recipients. Note that the probability that an attacker only needs to follow $t' \cdot t''$ is extremely small (if $t \gg t', t''$), and will generally be much larger. Furthermore, if the mix nodes collaborate when choosing who receives dummy messages this bound can easily be increased.

In addition (or in replacement of) to dummy traffic, the users can create routes of random length to fool adversaries. If the routes are arbitrarily large, in order to accurately match one sender with a set of possible recipients, the attacker needs to follow an arbitrarily large number of paths.

The attack can be carried out by passive, static, external adversaries, capable of taping the required wires. (If the attacker can't tap a significant number of wires, the probability of him being able to follow all paths is very low.) Note that if the attacker can't tap a relevant wire, he won't be able to produce a complete potential recipient list since the paths going through the missing wires are lost. A passive, external, adaptive adversary is better suited to this problem as he can "follow" the messages, compromising only the relevant channels (wires).

Since the previous scheme is very simple, it's easy to calculate security/practicality tradeoffs and compare mix-networks with respect to their resistance to brute force attacks. For example it allows us to answer questions like:

- Are busy networks with few nodes more resistant to brute force attacks than quiet networks with many nodes ?
- How helpful is dummy traffic if it's used in a particular manner ?

(Note that if the brute force attack is carried out many times, the techniques of subsection 9 can be used.)

3.2 The Node Flushing Attack (a.k.a. Spam Attack, Flooding Attack, n-1 Attack)

First mentioned in [8], the flush attack is very effective and can be mounted by an active external adversary. If the nodes wait till they have t messages before "flushing", an attacker can send $t - 1$ messages and easily associate messages leaving the node with those having entered. This can be seen by noting that the adversary will be able to match his inputs with the messages leaving the node.

Dummy traffic can make things a bit more difficult for the attacker since he can't distinguish them from legitimate messages. Unfortunately, if dummy traffic is only used in specific instances, as proposed in subsection 3.1, an attacker can choose his messages so that dummy traffic isn't used.

Another potential solution is to authenticate each message which allows nodes to detect flushing attempts. Unfortunately, this entails authenticating each message and detecting flushing attempts which could be computationally infeasible. We remark that simple-minded implementations of this solution can be broken by message playback attacks. Authentication and privacy protection are two seemingly contradictory requirements however using Chaumian blinding [9] or Brands credentials [5] we can satisfy both requirements.

Stop-and-Go mix nodes (in which a message waits a random amount of time) can *partially* solve this problem. Unfortunately, they only have "probabilistic" security.

There are some similarities with denial of service attacks [6,15]. Hence, if t is very large, using hashcach [3] or pricing functions [20] might be effective solutions.

Yet another option is to "re-mix" the messages, that is, the mix nodes use the same mechanism as the user to send the messages to the next nodes – "recursive mixing". This feature is implemented in mixmaster[13].

Notice that by encrypting the traffic between mix nodes, the attacker looses the ability to easily recognize *his* messages (the partial ($< t - 1$ spams) node flushing attack isn't as effective).

3.3   Timing Attacks

If the different routes that can be taken require different amounts of time, the system could be vulnerable to timing attacks. Precisely, given the set of messages coming in the network and the set of message going out of the network (as well as the arrival, departure times respectively), route timing information might be useful in correlating the messages in the two sets.

For example, suppose there are two routes, one taking 2 second and the other 4 seconds and assume that the two messages coming in the network arrive at 0:00 and 0:01 and that the two messages leave the network at 0:03 and 0:04. The attacker doesn't need to carry out expensive computations in order to correlate the messages coming in with the messages going out ...

Remark also that an attacker having access to just one of the communicating parties might be able to infer which route is taken by simply computing the *round trip time*. That is, calculating the time it takes to receive a reply. This attack is interesting in that even if one of the parties uses "constant link padding[8]" the attack is still effective.

The attack motivates the use of mix nodes that wait variable amounts of time before flushing messages. We remark that randomly increasing the latency doesn't completely solve the problem since an attacker might be able to rule out

---

[8] The flow of messages between the participant and the first node is constant.

some routes (e.g. if a message exits the mix network faster than the minimum time needed to go through some routes then these routes can be ruled out). Hence, the minimum time needed to go through each route should be the same. (It's not clear if this can be directly used in real-world situations since some routes could be very slow – because of mix node processing speed, speed of the communication wires, number of mix nodes in the route, etc.). This kind of attack is mentioned in [28,40].

3.4   Contextual Attacks

These are the most dangerous attacks and, unfortunately, they are very diffi-cult to model in a rigorous manner. The problem is that real-world users don't behave like those in the idealized model. We remark that this class of attack is particularly effective for real-time interactive communications.

Communication Pattern Attacks. By simply looking at the communication patterns (when users send and receive), one can find out a lot of useful informa-tion. Communicating participants normally don't "talk" at the same time, that is, when one party is sending, the other is usually silent. The longer an attacker can observe this type of communication synchronization, the less likely it's just an uncorrelated random pattern.

This attack can be mounted by a passive adversary that can monitor entry and exit mix nodes. Law enforcement officials might be quite successful mounting this kind of attack as they often have a-priori information: they usually have a hunch that two parties are communicating and just want to confirm their suspicion.

Packet Counting Attacks. These types of attacks are similar to the other contextual attacks in that they exploit the fact that some communications are easy to distinguish from others. If a participant sends a non-standard (i.e. unu-sual) number of messages, a passive external attacker can spot these messages coming out of the mix-network. In fact, unless all users send the same number of messages, this type of attack allows the adversary to gain non-trivial information.

A partial solution is to have parties only send standard numbers of messages but this isn't a viable option in many settings.

The packet counting and communication pattern attacks can be combined to get a "message frequency" attack (this might require more precise timing information).

Communication pattern, packet counting and message frequency attacks are sometimes referred to as traffic shaping attacks and are usually dealt with by im-posing rigid structure[9] on user communications[4]. Notice that protocols achiev-ing "network unobservability" are immune to these attacks.

---

[9] It's not clear whether this is a viable option for large Internet based systems.

Intersection Attack. An attacker having information about what users are active at any given time can, through repeated observations, determine what users communicate with each other. This attack is based on the observation that users typically communicate with a relatively small number of parties. For example, the typical user usually queries the same web sites in different sessions (his queries aren't random). By performing an operation similar to an intersection on the sets of active users at different times it is probable that the attacker can gain interesting information. The intersection attack is a well known open problem and seems extremely difficult to solve in an efficient manner.

3.5   Denial of Service Attacks

By rendering some mix nodes in-operational, an active adversary might obtain some information about the routes used by certain users. It seems highly probable that users that have their routes "destroyed" will behave differently than parties that haven't. Network unobservability or "client challenges[10]" (e.g. [3, 20,26]) might be required to properly solve this problem for real-time interactive communications.

3.6   Active Attacks Exploiting User Reactions

Active adversaries might be able to gain non-trivial sender-recipient matching information by exploiting the fact that user behavior depends on the message received. A variation on the following attack can even be used against dc-nets that don't use a secure broadcast channel (see [43]).

1. The adversary first intercepts a message M just before it enters the mix net.
2. M is then sent to a set of possible recipients. The parties not expecting to receive this message message will probably react in a different manner than a party expecting it.

The attacker can use this to get some sender-recipient matching information. Note that if the nodes in the route authenticate the messages the attack is prevented.

3.7   The "Sting" Attack

If one of the party involved in a dialog is corrupt, he might be able to, in a sense, "encode" information in his messages (see [28]). For example, government agencies might set up a fake "bomb making instruction web sites" and try to find out who accesses it. Many methods for identifying a user querying the web page come to mind: varying the reply latency, sending messages of a specific length, etc.

In some situations, it might be even easier to compromise user privacy. For example, if the sting web site gives fake information pertaining to financial fraud, the user might (non-anonymously) act upon this information at which point he can be arrested.

---

[10] Prevention mechanisms for denial of service attacks.

3.8 The "Send n' Seek" Attack

This attack is, in a sense, the opposite of the "sting" attack of subsection 3.7. Instead of having the recipient try to find the sender's identity, it's the sender that attempts to uncover the recipient's identity. This attack is particularly dangerous against non-interactive processes. For example, privacy protecting e-mail systems (see for example [21]) can be attacked by sending an easily identifiable number of messages and trying to identify these messages at suspect destinations (e.g. POP boxes). Notice that the terms sender and recipient are used very loosely here; the sender refers to the party initiating the connection.

3.9 Attacks Based on the Message's Distinguishing Features

If the user's (unencrypted) messages have distinguishing characteristics, the recipient (and maybe the last node, depending on whether the message is encrypted) might be able to link the message with one or many individuals. For example, analyzing writing styles probably reveals non-trivial information about the sender.

3.10 Message Delaying

The attacker can withhold messages until he can obtain enough resources (i.e. wires, nodes, etc.) or until the network becomes easier to monitor or to see if the possible recipients receive other messages, etc. In view of this attack, it makes sense to have the mix nodes verify authenticated timing information (the authenticated timing information could be inserted in the message by the sender or the nodes).

3.11 Message Tagging [16]

An active internal adversary that has control of the first and last node in a message route, can tag (i.e. slightly modify) messages at the first node in such a way that the exit node can spot them. Since the entry node knows the sender and the exit node the recipient, the system is broken.

A solution to this problem is to make it difficult to tag messages. The techniques that can be used to do this depend on the implementation and so are not discussed here.

A slight variant of this attack can be mounted by an active external adversary if the messages don't have a rigid structure. Remark that this attack has many similarities with subliminal channels [41]; this observation forms the basis of some of the following variations:

- **Shadow Messages:** If an adversary sends messages that follow the same path as the message being followed, it can easily transmit some information to the output. For example, the attacker can just replay the message in such a way that it can spot them leaving the mix network (e.g. varying the message frequency).

- **Message Delaying:** The attacker can delay messages to obtain some information. These delays can presumably detected.
- **Broadcast:** An attacker can broadcast messages notifying his accomplices that a particular message has entered the network. This isn't a particularly powerful attack but it could be virtually impossible to detect.

The message tagging based attacks motivate using extremely rigid message structure and authenticating timing information (in order to prevent message delays and message playbacks).

3.12   Partial or Probabilistic Attacks

Most of the preceding attacks can be carried out partially, that is, the attacker can obtain partial or probabilistic information. For example, he could deduce information of the form:

1. With probability p, A is communicating with B or A is communicating with one of the users in a group.
2. A is not communicating with B,C and D.

These attacks haven't been thoroughly addressed so far and seem very promising, especially when carried out a large number of times.

3.13   Approaches to Modeling Attacks

The previous attacks have assumed that the adversary controlled all the required resources (wires, nodes). When only considering static adversaries, it might make sense to calculate the probability that the required resources are controlled. This approach is especially relevant when the adversary just wants to obtain *a* sender-recipient matching.

Unfortunately, assuming static adversaries doesn't seem helpful for making design decisions (i.e. how much dummy traffic); it might however help us in determining if there is a reasonable threat that the system can be broken.

4   Mix Network Design Issues

In this section, we present issues related to mix-network design.

4.1   Anonymity Versus Pseudonymity

Probably the most important design issue is that of anonymity versus pseudonymity. Note that by pseudonymous, we mean that some node(s) knows the user's pseudonym (it can't link a pseudonym with a real-world identity). Another option is to have the user be anonymous in the mix network but be pseudonymous in its dealings with other users (half-pseudonymity). Half-pseudonymity won't be discussed in any detail because its properties are similar to the pseudonymity ones. Here are the most important advantages of both anonymity and pseudonymity.

- **Anonymity**
    1. Provides better security since if a pseudonym (nym) is linked with a user, all future uses of the nym can be linked to the user.
- **Pseudonymity**
    1. We get the best of both worlds: privacy protection and accountability (and openness). Since pseudonyms (nyms) have a persistent nature, long term relationships and trust can be cultivated. (half pseudonymity also)
    2. Pseudonym based business models (for mix node operators) are more attractive than anonymity based ones.
    3. Abuse control is easier to deal with when nyms are used.
    4. Authentication (verifying that someone has the right to use the network) is easier: either Brands credentials [5] or Chaumian blinding [9] needs to be used [11] when using anonymity.
    5. Allows non-interactive processes (e.g. e-mail).

4.2   Packet Sizes

In many situations, using different message sizes yield substantial performance improvements. For example TCP/IP connections require on average one small control packet for every two (large) data packet. It might be inefficient for small messages to be padded or large packets split up in order to get a message of the correct size. As usual in cryptography, we have a security/performance tradeoff: Using more than one message size gives better performance but worse security. We strongly suspect however that there are techniques which improve the security properties of the multiple packet size option (e.g. randomly expanding small messages.).

4.3   Dummy Messages

Dummy traffic is often used in an unstructured manner and so might not be as effective as it could be, we note the following observations:

1. If a node sends its message to less than t' nodes we suggest sending dummy messages in such a way that t' nodes receive messages. The larger t', the harder it is to mount the brute search attacks.
2. Each node should send messages to at least t'' destinations outside the mix network (dummy messages should be used to fill the gaps). The larger t'', the harder it is to mount the brute search attack. Furthermore, this technique also seems to complicate attacks in which the adversary monitors the exit nodes.
3. In order to randomize the user's communication patterns, we should seriously consider having the user send dummy traffic to the entry node. The challenge here is to have good security and minimize the amount of dummy messages used (see [4]).

---

[11] both of these techniques are patented.

4. Dummy messages could also be used to reduce the amount of time messages stay at a given node. It seems that waiting for c messages to enter a mix node before sending b ($b > c$) has similar security properties as waiting to receive b messages before releasing them. This trick could be used to reduce the time messages wait at nodes.

4.4   Routing

For large Internet based systems especially, having the user choose the nodes in his route randomly doesn't seem like a viable option because:

1. The nodes and users must "know[12]" each other node which might be impractical.
2. Some servers are far from each other and it doesn't make sense from a performance view point to have, for example, a route consisting of nodes in Australia, Canada, South Africa and China.
3. Nodes should be "socially" independent. Ideally, the nodes in a route should belong to different organizations and be located in different legal jurisdiction. The whole idea behind using more than one node is that none of them have enough information to determine sender-recipient matchings. Hence, if all nodes in a route belong to the same organization we might as well just use a single node. The motivation for having nodes in different legal jurisdiction is that more than one subpoena needs to be obtained to legally compromise nodes.

Creating good network topologies and route finding algorithms with respect to security and efficiency doesn't seem entirely trivial.

Note also that in order to limit the number of public key operations executed, some systems (e.g. [21]) use static routes that allows mix nodes to associate each message with a connection identifier which makes some of the attacks mentioned previously a lot easier to carry out.

4.5   Node Flushing Algorithm

As seen in subsection 2.3, there are many different approaches to flushing nodes. Again, there is a security/practicality tradeoff: the longer messages *can* stay in mix-nodes the better the security (in most settings).

4.6   Query Servers and Privacy Protection

In many situations, the user needs to retrieve some information from a query server, for example network configuration information, pseudonym public keys, etc. These queries shouldn't erode privacy: the query servers shouldn't obtain non-trivial information about sender-recipient matchings. The obvious approach

---

[12] e.g. know the IP address, Port number and status.

to this problem is to have the user download the entire databases (the answer to every possible query) but unfortunately, the amount of data to transfer might be too large. We suspect that private information retrieval protocols [10,11] might be very useful in these situations. This design issue illustrates a fundamental security principle:

A system is only as secure as its weakest link.

5   Directions for Further Research

Probably the most important direction for further research in this field is that of attacks. As it seems unlikely that we can obtain Rackoff-Simon [39] type bounds for real-world implementations, it's a good idea to find and rigorously analyze as many attacks as possible and either :

– Try to immunize our protocols against these attacks.
– Detect when the attack is mountable and take the appropriate measures.

The new and clever attacks that will be effective against mix networks will probably be empirical in nature. Mathematical analysis of mix network traffic seems like the most promising avenue for mounting attacks. Perhaps ideas from the field of pattern recognition and measure theory could be used ...

We now give a listing of some other relevant problems (in no particular order):

1. Most of the attacks mentioned are aimed; what about a more general class of attack in which an attacker doesn't require a particular sender-recipient matching but would settle for an arbitrary one ?
2. The best we can hope for is that the attacker's view be independent from the sender-recipient matchings. Is it possible to obtain weaker results in which the view is slightly biased? Such a result would allow us to determine how much information the attacker needs to gather in order to get a "convincing" sender recipient linking (instead of relying on ad-hoc arguments).
3. Another possible avenue of research is formalizing the effectiveness of a given adversary in breaking the protocol. That is working with a more precise adversary descriptions; Instead of active, static and internal adversaries, we could have adversaries taping two specific communication channels, having total control of a particular mix node, etc. It's not clear how this would help us in designing good protocols, however it might be useful when certain parts of the network are thought to be compromised.
4. It's not clear at all what real-world adversary can do. Can they tap wires and compromise nodes at will ? It would be very instructive to know what can be done, the level of sophistication required and the computational resources needed (memory, CPU cycles, network access, etc.).
5. It would be extremely useful to determine when the mix-network is vulnerable or, more generally, what security mix-networks provide in different situations.

6. All issues mentioned in section 4 need to be thoroughly analyzed.

7. Caching popular content would improve security and it's not clear what the best way to go about doing this is.

8. Perhaps the exit nodes can perform some computations for the users. For example, the TCP control messages could be handled by the exit mix node (i.e. the control messages would not be handled by the user).

9. Heaps of security and efficiency problems arise when incorporating privacy protecting mechanisms within existing protocols (e.g. http, telnet, etc.).

10. A detailed specification (e.g. within IETF) could be devised to help mix-network designers. This would protect mix-network operators from known attacks and give attackers a precise model to "study" (thus helping us improve the specification ...)

6   Conclusion

We have given an introduction to the traffic-analysis problem by presenting the most important constructions, attacks, design issues and direction for further research. It is hoped that research addressing some of the problems exposed in this work will allow us to stop using terms such as : "seems", "probably", "I suspect" in our discussions about traffic analysis.

Acknowledgements. We would like to thank Adam Back, Adam Shostack, Anton Stiglic, Frédéric Légaré, Michael Freedman and Ulf Moller for excellent feedback, interesting discussions and for having mentioned many of the attacks presented in this paper. We also wish to thank the anonymous referees for their very helpful comments.

References

1. M Abe. Universally verifiable mix-net with verification work independent of the number of mix-servers. In *Advances in Cryptology – Eurocrypt '98*, volume 1403 of *Lecture Notes in Computer Science*, pages 437–447, Helsinki, Finland, 31 May–4 June 1998. Springer-Verlag.

2. M Abe. Mix-network on permutation networks. In *Advances in cryptology — ASIACRYPT'99*, volume 1716, pages 258–273. Springer-Verlag, 1999.

3. Adam Back. Hashcash. http://www.cypherspace.org/~adam/hashcash/, march 1997.

4. Oliver Berthold, Hannes Federrath, and Marit Kohntopp. Project anonymity and unobservability in the internet. Presented at CFP 2000.

5. Stefan A. Brands. Restrictive blinding of secret-key certificates. Technical Report CS-R9509, CWI - Centrum voor Wiskunde en Informatica, February 28, 1995.

6. CERT. Advisory ca-96.21: Tcp syn flooding and ip spoofing attacks, 24 September 1996.

7. D Chaum. The dining cryptographers problem: Unconditional sender and recipient untraceability. *Journal of Cryptology*, 1:65–75, 1988.

8. David Chaum. Untraceable electronic mail, return addresses and digital pseudonyms. *Communications of the A.C.M.*, 24(2):84–88, February 1981.
9. David Chaum. Blind signatures for untraceable payments. In R. L. Rivest, A. Sherman, and D. Chaum, editors, *Proc. CRYPTO 82*, pages 199–203, New York, 1983. Plenum Press.
10. Benny Chor, Oded Goldreich, Eyal Kushilevitz, and Madhu Sudan. Private information retrieval. In *36th IEEE Conference on the Foundations of Computer Science*, pages 41–50. IEEE Computer Society Press, 1995.
11. Benny Chor, Oded Goldreich, Eyal Kushilevitz, and Madhu Sudan. Private information retrieval. *Journal of the ACM*, 45(6):965–981, 1998.
12. David A. Cooper and Kenneth P. Birman. Preserving privacy in a network of mobile computers. In *1995 IEEE Symposium on Research in Security and Privacy*, pages 26–38. IEEE Computer Society Press, 1995. http://cs-tr.cs.cornell.edu:80/Dienst/UI/1.0/Display/ncstrl.cornell/TR85-1490.
13. Lance Cottrell. Mixmaster. http://www.obscura.com/~loki/.
14. Ronald Cramer. Introduction to secure computation. In *Lectures on data security : modern cryptology in theory and practice*, volume 1561 of *Lecture Notes in Computer Science*, pages 16–62. Springer, 1999.
15. Daemon9. Project neptune. Phrack Magazine, 48(7): File 13 of 18, 8 November 1996. Available at www.fc.net/phrack/files/p48/p48-13.html.
16. Wei Dai. private communication, 1999.
17. Yvo Desmedt and Kaoru Kurosawa. How to break a practical mix and design a new one. To be presented at Eurocrypt 2000.
18. W. Diffie and M. Hellman. New directions in cryptography. *IEEE Transactions on Information Theory*, 22:644–654, 1976.
19. Shlomi Dolev and Rafail Ostrovsky. Efficient anonymous multicast and reception. In Walter Fumy, editor, *Advances in Cryptology – EUROCRYPT ' 97*, Lecture Notes in Computer Science, pages 395–409. Springer-Verlag, Berlin Germany, 1997.
20. Cynthia Dwork and Moni Naor. Pricing via processing or combatting junk mail. In Ernest F. Brickell, editor, *Advances in Cryptology—CRYPTO '92*, volume 740 of *Lecture Notes in Computer Science*, pages 139–147. Springer-Verlag, 1993, 16–20 August 1992.
21. Ian Goldberg and Adam Shostack. Freedom network whitepapers.
22. Oded Goldreich and Rafail Ostrovsky. Software protection and simulation on oblivious RAMs. *Journal of the ACM*, 43(3):431–473, 1996.
23. C. Gulcu and G. Tsudik. Mixing E-mail with BABEL. In *Symposium on Network and Distributed Systems Security (NDSS '96)*, San Diego, California, February 1996. Internet Society. http://www.zurich.ibm.com/ cgu/publications/gt95.ps.gz.
24. Ceki Gulcu. The anonymous E-mail conversation. Master's thesis, Eurecom Institute, 229 route des Cretes, F-06904 Sophia-Antipolis, France, June 1995.
25. Jakobsson. A practical mix. In Kaisa Nyberg, editor, *Advances in Cryptology – EUROCRYPT '98*, volume 1403 of *Lecture Notes in Computer Science*, pages 448–. Springer-Verlag, 1998.
26. A. Juels and J. Brainard. Client puzzles: A cryptographic defense against connection depletion attacks. In S. Kent, editor, *NDSS '99 (Networks and Distributed Security Systems)*, pages 151–165, 2000.
27. D. Kahn. *The Codebreakers*. Macmillan Publishing Company, 1967.
28. John Kelsey. private communication, 1999.

29. Dogan Kesdogan, Jan Egner, and Roland Büschkes. Stop-and-go mixes providing probabilistic security in an open system. In David Aucsmith, editor, *Information Hiding: Second International Workshop*, volume 1525 of *Lecture Notes in Computer Science*, pages 83–98. Springer-Verlag, Berlin, Germany, 1998.

30. W Ogata, K Kurosawa, K Sako, and K Takatani. Fault tolerant anonymous channel. In *Information and Communications Security — First International Conference*, volume 1334 of *Lecture Notes in Computer Science*, pages 440–444, Beijing, China, 11–14 November 1997. Springer-Verlag.

31. A Pfitzmann and M Waidner. Networks without user observability – design options. In *Advances in Cryptology – Eurocrypt '85*, volume 219 of *Lecture Notes in Computer Science*. Spinger-Verlag, 1985.

32. Andreas Pfitzmann. A switched/broadcast ISDN to decrease user observability. 1984 International Zurich Seminar on Digital Communications, Applications of Source Coding, Channel Coding and Secrecy Coding, March 6-8, 1984, Zurich, Switzerland, Swiss Federal Institute of Technology, Proceedings IEEE Catalog no. 84CH1998-4, 183-190, 6–8 March 1984.

33. Andreas Pfitzmann. How to implement ISDNs without user observability–some remarks. Technical report, Institut für Informatik, University of Karlsruhe, Institut für Informatik, University of Karlsruhe, 1985.

34. Andreas Pfitzmann, Birgit Pfitzmann, and Michael Waidner. ISDN-mixes: Untraceable communication with very small bandwidth overhead. In *GI/ITG Conference: Communication in Distributed Systems*, pages 451–463. Springer-Verlag, Heidelberg 1991, February 1991.

35. B Pfitzmann and A Pfitzmann. How to break the direct rsa-implementation of mixes. In *Advances in Cryptology – Eurocrypt '89*, volume 434 of *Lecture Notes in Computer Science*. Springer-Verlag, 1989.

36. M. Rabin. How to exchange secrets by oblivious transfer. Technical Report Technical Memo TR-81, Aiken Computation Laboratory, Harvard University, 1981.

37. Michael K. Reiter and Aviel D. Rubin. Crowds: Anonymity for Web Transactions. ACM Transactions on Information and System Security, volume 1, pages 66–92, 1998.

38. Michael K. Reiter and Aviel D. Rubin. Anonymous Web transactions with crowds. Communications of the ACM, volume 42, number 2, pages 32–48, 1999.

39. Charles Rackoff and Daniel R. Simon. Cryptographic defense against traffic analysis. In *Proceedings of the Twenty-Fifth Annual ACM Symposium on the Theory of Computing*, pages 672–681, San Diego, California, 16–18 May 1993.

40. M G Reed, P F Syverson, and D M Goldschlag. Anonymous connections and onion routing. *IEEE Journal on Special Areas in Communications*, 16(4):482–494, May 1998.

41. G. J. Simmons. The history of subliminal channels. *IEEE Journal on Selected Areas in Communications*, 16(4):452–462, May 1998.

42. L. F. Turner. Digital data security system, 1989. Patent IPN WO 89/08915.

43. M Waidner. Unconditional sender and recipient untraceability in spite of active attacks. In *Advances in Cryptology – Eurocrypt '89*, volume 434 of *Lecture Notes in Computer Science*. Springer-Verlag, 1989.

The Disadvantages of Free MIX Routes and How to Overcome Them

Oliver Berthold[1], Andreas Pfitzmann[1], and Ronny Standtke[2]

[1] Dresden University of Technology, Germany
{ob2,pfitza}@inf.tu-dresden.de
[2] Secunet, Dresden
Ronny.Standtke@gmx.de

Abstract. There are different methods to build an anonymity service using MIXes. A substantial decision for doing so is the method of choosing the MIX route. In this paper we compare two special configurations: a fixed MIX route used by all participants and a network of freely usable MIXes where each participant chooses his own route. The advantages and disadvantages in respect to the freedom of choice are presented and examined. We'll show that some additional attacks are possible in networks with freely chosen MIX routes. After describing these attacks, we estimate their impact on the achievable degree of anonymity. Finally, we evaluate the relevance of the described attacks with respect to existing systems like e.g. Mixmaster, Crowds, and Freedom.

1   Introduction

The concept of MIXes was developed in 1981 by David Chaum [3], in order to enable unobservable communication between users of the internet. A single MIX does nothing else than hiding the correlation between incoming and outgoing messages within a large group of messages.

If participants exclusively use such a MIX for sending messages to each other, their communication relations will be unobservable - even though if the attacker does control all the network connections. Without additional information not even the receiver gets to know the identity of the message's sender.

When using only one MIX, one has to rely upon its security completely. Therefore usually several MIXes are used in a chain. Now, any single MIX does not have all the information which is needed to reveal communication relations. At worst, a MIX may only know either sender or receiver.

According to the attacker model for MIXes, the communication relations have to be kept secret even in case that all but one MIX cooperate with an attacker who taps all lines (called *global attacker*). But a sufficient number of reliable participants is necessary: A single participant can not be anonymous if all or most of the other participants are controlled by the attacker. All possible attacks on a MIX network are to be examined with regard to that attacker model.

H. Federrath (Ed.): Anonymity 2000, LNCS 2009, pp. 30–45, 2001.

There are different possibilities to organise the co-operation of several MIXes. Generally, all MIXes exist independently from each other in the internet. When anybody wants to use a certain MIX, he simply sends his message to it, respectively, he has another MIX send his message to it. This kind of co-operation is further called a *MIX network*.

A special variation is to define a single valid chain of MIXes for a group of participants. This we will call a *MIX cascade* (compare [6]).

Apart of those two concepts there is a high variety of hybrid combinations of MIX network and MIX cascade. For example, possible configurations are:

- **A network of cascades:** The sender chooses a number of defined cascades through which his message is sent sequentially.
- **A network with restricted choice of patches:** Every MIX defines its possible successors to send messages to.
- **Multiple-duplicated cascades:** For every position within the cascade several physical MIXes are defined, such that a user can choose stepwise.
- **Tree structures:** Here a MIX cascade is used which has on some positions duplicated MIXes. A possible scenario may consist of many first-step MIXes and a single last-step MIX. Now, a distribution and acceleration can be reached when the anonymity group is to be quite large and not all the dummy traffic is to be forwarded to the last MIX.

Up to now these combinations were examined only partially. But in contrast to the MIX network some kinds of attacks which we will describe later in this paper, are not possible or may be prevented more easily. We will discuss the advantages of different configurations when describing types of attacks.

As the headline says, compare the MIX cascade with the MIX network with regard to:

- Attacks being possible under one configuration but not under the other.
- Attacks that can only be prevented under one of both configurations (- nowadays).
- Evaluation about the qualification of MIX network and MIX cascade to guarantee anonymity and unobservability with a global attacker as he was described above.

First of all we will check how unobservability and anonymity can be reached by the use of MIXes and how it is possible to evaluate anonymity. In the following section will be examined what kinds of attacks exist in general and how they can be prevented. The final section then deals with the question how these attacks may endanger existing anonymity services.

2   Unobservability and Anonymity by MIXes

As already said in the introduction, a MIX hides the relation between the incoming and outgoing messages. This is done by collecting a number of messages and reorder them before sending them on their way.

Because a particular outgoing message could have been sent by any of the senders of the incoming messages, the sender of this message is unobservable within that group. But on the other hand, it is a fact that the message was certainly sent from within that group. The degree of anonymity can be defined by the size of the group, i.e. the number of possible senders. For example, the anonymity may be measured as

$A = ld(n)$ [bit] where n is the number of senders. Its meaning is the logarithm with base 2 of n.

An attacker who wants to find out the sender of a particular message does reach his aim with the same probability as he may guess the value of a random string of A bits.

When using a MIX cascade, the degree of anonymity stays the same if all messages received by the first MIX are forwarded correctly to the last MIX. This is true even if only one MIX in the cascade doesn't work together with the global attacker. However, the degree of anonymity decreases when messages are lost on their way through the cascade (e.g. because of active attacks on the link between sender and first MIX of the cascade). It decreases in the same amount as the number of those senders decreases whose messages are still existing.

The situation is different in a MIX network. When a MIX is directly receiving messages from a set of MIXes the anonymity group of senders is the union of the anonymity groups of all these MIXes.

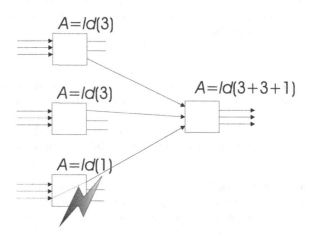

Fig. 1. Anonymity group in a MIX network

Of course, that is only true if all the MIXes are trustworthy. If an attacker is getting to know the way of reordering in a MIX, this particular MIX doesn't contribute any longer to the degree of anonymity. That means, outgoing messages from this MIX have an anonymity group of $n=1$, if this MIX is the first or last one or if the attacker controls all MIXes before or behind it.

Another problem is arising for all combinations of MIXes, when the attacker is able to recognise, that several messages sent at several times can be linked to one and the same sender.

If the participants join and leave the group from time to time, the anonymity of a group of linkable messages is only among those senders who were part of the group for the whole time.

An attacker may easily be able to link messages when the senders do not communicate with each other but rather want to use public services like internet anonymously. The connection to the internet server is usually not encrypted and hold up for a certain time, during which several packets of data are exchanged.

In order to make intersections of anonymity groups more difficult often dummy traffic is used which can not be distinguished from real messages. That proceeding ensures that every active user always is part of the anonymity group.

3   Attacks on a Single MIX

3.1   Message Size

The attacker could distinguish the messages sent by a MIX, if they would be different in size. Because the size of the sent message is the same as the size of the received message, an attacker could correlate them. A solution is, that every message should have exactly the same size. If the data is less than this defined message size, padding is used. In a MIX network each message contains information special for a certain MIX. So this information is extracted from the message and the MIX has to fill the free space using padding, so that the message size remains the same.

This is not necessary at all in a MIX cascade, because all messages take the same way and are shortened to the same size each time.

3.2   Replay

The decryption of a message done by each MIX is deterministic. So if the same message would pass a MIX, the result of the decryption sent by the MIX would also be the same. An attacker who observes the incoming and outgoing messages, could send the same message to the MIX again, and would see which message is sent twice from the MIX. So this MIX is bridged and the conclusion is, that a MIX must not process messages he has already processed.

Usually, this is achieved by using a database in which a MIX stores every processed message. If a new message arrives, he first checks if this message isn't already stored in this database.

3.3   Manipulating of Messages

If an attackers changes only some bits of a message, then if inappropriate cryptography is used he can detect this broken message also after it has passed a trustworthy MIX. This is possible especially if:

- he is the receiver of the message, or
- he controls the server, which would send the decrypted message to the real receiver, or
- a MIX transforms the message in such a way, that the manipulated bit(s) would remain on the same position (i.e. if the MIX uses the stream cipher modus OFB). Assuming that there are a trustworthy MIX followed by an attacking MIX. The attacker changes a bit of that part of the message, which belongs to the message header for the attacking MIX. Now he sends this message to the trustworthy MIX, which will forwards the message to the attacking MIX. If this MIX decrypts the message, he would detect the error in the message header, but restores it (changes the bit again). The attacker now knows the relation between the manipulated incoming message and a correct outgoing message and can trace it to the receiver.

The attacker detects the broken message, because the final decrypted message (which goes to the receiver) usually contains a lot of redundancy or the message header for a MIX has to satisfy a well known format.

To prevent these attacks, each MIX has to verify the integrity of every received message by checking included redundancies. This could be a message hash generated by the sender and included in the message header for each MIX.

3.4   Blocking of Messages

If an attacker blocks some messages, the senders of these messages are excluded from the anonymity group. The same result is achieved, if some messages are manipulated (as described above).

The extreme case is known as "n-1 attack". In this case all messages but one, will be blocked, manipulated or generated by the attacker. So the only message the attacker doesn't know is the message he wants to trace. So the attacker has bridged the trustworthy MIX or has limited the anonymity group of the remaining messages (if there are more than one).

There exists no general applicable method, in order to prevent this attacks. A possible solution is that the MIX must be able to identify each user (sender of messages). The MIX has ensure that the messages he receives are sent by enough different users and so the attacker doesn't control a majority of them.

The next section discusses how this could be done by the MIXes, considering the different possibilities of configuration (network or cascade).

Under certain circumstances it is possible that an attacker could uncover the route of a message, if he only blocks a single message:

If the attacker can find out the plaintext of messages and the user sends many messages, which definitely are related (i.e. the blocked message is part of a bigger data stream) then the attacker could detect in which data stream the message he blocked is missing.

4 Comparison MIX Network - MIX Cascade

4.1 Motivation

There still exists a controversial discussion, which kind of a MIX configuration is the better one. The advocates of the MIX-network are always pointing out that there are the following advantages:

Each user can decide on his own, which MIXes he wants to trust. Because an attacker has the best chance to observe a user, if he controls as many MIXes as possible (or even all MIXes), it seems that a MIX cascade is extremely unsuitable.

1. In this case an attacker knows exactly which MIXes he has to control in order to observe a user successfully. But if the user can choose his own route, he can exclude MIXes, which seem untrustworthy to him and an attacker has to control much more MIXes in order to achieve the same probability to attack successfully. The community of users could publish which MIXes are not trustworthy and so would prevent attacks.
2. Because a MIX network could theoretically grow up to an infinite number of MIXes, the anonymity group could also raise to an infinite size. Every user can choose an arbitrary route of MIXes and so an observer could not detect, messages of which users a MIX currently processes.
3. There exists no structure, so a MIX network is very flexible, scalable and extendable. It could be realised as a fault-tolerant network. The only thing, that must be done, is to publish, when a MIX is inserted into or removed from the network. Such a system would be predestined for usage in the Internet.

The advocates of the MIX cascade oppose, that the security of the MIX network can't really be proven up to now. For instance the facts of the 2nd point - as explained above - are only true, if all MIXes are trustworthy. When assuming an attacker model, where only one MIX of a route is trustworthy, the anonymity group wouldn't become bigger than the batch size of this MIX.

In the next section we will describe additional attacks and show, that the level of anonymity is much smaller in reality. Nevertheless, a MIX network is much more flexible compared to a MIX cascade. But it's possible to construct a fault-tolerant MIX cascade, too [5]. And there would be more than one cascade world-wide, so the advantage described in point 1 could be applied to cascades as well: a user chooses the cascade, he trusts. Adding new cascades extends the system as far as needed (Point 3). Compared to the MIX network, an unbalanced load sharing wouldn't have negative impacts on the performance. Only users of a cascade, which is insufficiently used compared to its capacity, would achieve a lower level of anonymity. If the load of a MIX network is non-uniform, then on the one hand some MIX could be temporarily overloaded. On the other hand a MIX with little load would have to wait for a long time to gather enough incoming message or would send many dummies, which would produce additional traffic.

The most important reason, why you shouldn't use a MIX network is the low level of security. This is the conclusion of the authors of this paper, after they found a number of attacks against a MIX network. The following sections describes these attacks and show why they occur especially in a MIX network and why it's hard to prevent them.

4.2   Achievable Level of Anonymity

If we assume that there exists a single trustworthy MIX only, then the achievable level of anonymity could not be higher than the size of the batch of this MIX.

In the following sections we describe attacks, which parts this input batch and so decreases the size of the anonymity group.

Position in MIX route. Based on our attacker model, each user should be anonymous, even if his messages only pass one trustworthy MIX. In a MIX network a certain MIX may be on different positions on the individual routes of the messages he receives. In comparison a MIX of a cascade will always have the same position because the route is static as long as the cascade exists.

The question is: is a MIX of a MIX network able to detect his position in a route of a certain message and if so, can he use this knowledge to partition the input batch?

If the attacker controls all other MIXes, which this message passes through, then it's easy to detect the position of the trustworthy MIX. He simply counts the number of passed MIXes for every message.

Now the attacker knows the composition of the incoming batch: He knows the routing position for each user's message.

If we assume, that every user sends his messages using the same number of MIXes (e. g. sets the route length to the maximum allowed for by the message format used in order to get maximal anonymity), then the attacker also knows, how many MIXes each user's message yet already passed.

Because he controls all following MIXes of each route, he can determine, how many MIXes each sent message has yet to pass. Because all routes have the same length, incoming messages can only have been transformed into outgoing messages if the route lengths would match.

Eventually, a message is only unobservable in that group of messages which have this MIX on the same routing position. So the attacker successfully partitioned the input batch and decreased the level of anonymity of each user. Figure 2 illustrates this attack.

In order to prevent this attack, each user has to choose a different route length for each of his/her messages or they only use each MIX for a particular position within routes. But this particular position within routes would be in contrast to the flexibility of the MIX network and in fact results in a MIX cascade with possibly duplicated MIXes.

The first method, that the user should choose the length of the route, would only partly be a solution: There still exists a constant maximum of the length

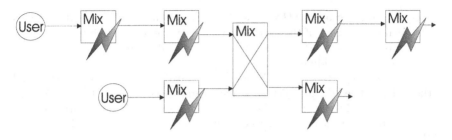

Fig. 2. Routing position of a trusted MIX

of a route, and so it's possible to calculate intersections, using the procedure explained above.

The only advantage is that a bigger number of neighbouring route positions are building a common anonymity group. Nevertheless, the probability that there are different anonymity groups in one batch is still very high. Building only one anonymity group is only achievable, if the route could have an infinite length, because in this case every message could still pass any number of MIXes. But because a message header is needed for each MIX and all messages should have the same size, there always exists a maximum length of routes.

Additionally, it may be possible, that the attacker knows the plaintext of the message. In this case the attacker could calculate how many MIXes a message could have passed at most, even if the quota of the message header is different in order to allow different route lengths. To prevent this, each message header should have the same size. But this implies another restriction on the maximum of the length of a route, because a message should be able to transport as many data as possible and so a short message header, allowing only short routes, would be chosen.

If an attacker can assume, that a user would normally send more than one message to a certain receiver, then the probability of calculating small intersections increases.

If the user chooses a different MIX route for each of these messages, different anonymity groups arise each time. So the attacker could calculate the intersection of all these anonymity groups. Even if all users would always choose the same route, the anonymity groups wouldn't be identical, because the MIX network doesn't work synchronously.

Conclusion: If only one MIX of a route is trustworthy, then the achievable anonymity is distinctly lower in a MIX network compared to a synchronously working MIX cascade.

Using a configuration of MIXes which allows only a fixed routing position for each MIX for all messages it processes prevents the partitioning of the batches and so prevents this attack.

MIX cascades, duplicated MIX cascades and tree structures as explained in the introduction are working in that way.

Determining the next MIX. The previous section describes an attack which is especially successful, if the users select different routes for each message. Now we want to explain an attack, which could be done, if the users send all messages using the same individual route.

A trustworthy MIX of a MIX network receives messages sent by users and other MIXes. The MIX forwards these messages either to users or to other MIXes.

An attacker knows the senders of all messages, which came directly from users. Additionally, he knows all senders of messages which passed only attacking MIXes.

Because a MIX forwards the messages only to some other MIXes or users, only they could be possible receivers of an incoming message.

If there are only a few trustworthy MIXes, only those users which are connected by the described graph, are members of the anonymity group of a received message. This is illustrated in Figure 3.

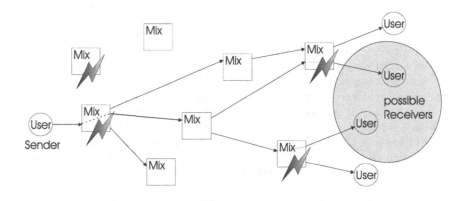

Fig. 3. Intersection set of anonymity group

If the users send their messages, using always the same route, an attacker only needs to observe a trustworthy MIX at those times, when this MIX forwards a message of a sender the attacker is interested in.

A MIX network doesn't work synchronously, so the batches always generate different anonymity groups. So if the attacker would calculate the intersection of these anonymity groups, then after a finite time he knows which MIX has received the message, he is interested in.

The attacker repeats this procedure sequentially attacking the following MIX on the route and so on until he attacks the last MIX.

So the anonymity group of the sent message would become the group of receivers addressed from the last trustworthy MIX on the route. It is assumed, that for all messages there exists a maximal route length known by the attacker.

If a user sends more than one message to the same receiver, then the attacker has a good chance to determine this receiver.

If the attacker is able to observe the whole network and could store all communication relations of all MIXes for a long period of time, he could attack all users and all trustworthy MIXes simultaneously.

A possible solution would be that each MIX has to send at least one message to each other MIX. These messages could be dummies.

If the number of MIXes increases, many dummies have to be sent. All these dummies have to pass more than one MIX, because if they would be sent only to the next MIX, this MIX could be an attacking one and detect that this message was only a dummy. The problem is that all these dummies would dramatically increase the network traffic.

On the other hand, the achievable security is uncertain: Based on the attacker model only one MIX of a route is trustworthy, so that the following variations are possible:

- *The generator of dummies is a trustworthy MIX:* All other MIXes of the route are controlled by the attacker, so he knows which messages are dummies.
- *The trustworthy MIX is somewhere else on the route:* The attacker controls the generator of dummies, so he knows which MIX gets dummies and which one gets real messages.

So the attacker would detect to which MIX or participant the observed MIX forwards the received messages, although dummies were sent.

We think, that sending dummies in this way isn't practicable.

Another solution for this problem could be, that the user has to choose his MIX route with regard to some rules.

For each MIX, some neighbouring MIXes are defined. So the MIX has to send dummies only to these MIXes, what reduces the expenditure. In this case the explained attack wouldn't be possible.

We described this configuration in the introduction as an alternative to the completely freely chosen MIX network. Other configurations are possible, too - like tree structured networks, with the last MIX as root or a MIX cascade. They would prevent the attack, because each MIX has only one successor.

4.3   Probability of Unobservability

If we use a MIX cascade, then we optimize for the case that only one MIX is trustworthy. Based on the functionality of each MIX, also in this case the transported messages are unobservable, at least if no active attacks occur.

In the following section, we calculate the probability, that at least one MIX of a randomly selected route of a MIX network is trustworthy.

Because each user chooses only some MIXes for his route, the probability that he chooses at least one trustworthy MIX is:

$$p = 1 - a^l$$

(a is the quota of attacking MIXes and l is the length of the route)

This formula is only true, if each MIX could be selected more then once for each route. But this isn't very clever, because if a MIX is selected repeatedly, then the probability decreases, that at least one trustworthy MIX is passed by the message. The conclusion is that each message should pass each MIX at most once. For this case the formula for calculating the probability p is as follows:

$$p = 1 - \frac{M_A! \cdot (M_A + M_G - l)!}{(M_A - l)! \cdot (M_A + M_G)!}$$

(M_A is the number of attacking MIXes, M_G is the number of trustworthy MIXes and l is the length of the route.)

If a user during the time sends many messages, which belong together (this means, that an attacker knows, that these message are sent from the same user), then we have to raise the probability p to the power of the number of messages k. So the probability to observe a user is:

$$1 - p^k$$

Example (comparison MIX cascade - MIX network):
length of cascade (route): 4 MIXes
Based on our attacking model 3 MIXes of this cascade could be attackers. That are 75% attacking MIXes.

If we assume that 20 MIXes are building a MIX network and that 75% of these MIXes are attacking ones, too, then a randomly chosen route contains at least one trustworthy MIX with a probability of 71.8%.

4.4   Active Attacks

In Sections 3.3 and 3.4 we described active attacks on a single MIX. We showed that an attacker who manipulates messages (Section 3.3) wouldn't be successfully, if each MIX verifies the integrity of each message.

But this solution nevertheless doesn't prevent all effects of this attack. It only changes this attack in an attack, which blocks messages (Section 3.4) because broken messages would be deleted.

It's not easy to prevent these message blocking attacks and especially these attacks are very dangerous:

If the attacker knows the plaintext of the message, then he can use active attacks, in order to achieve the following:

- If he blocks the messages of some users, he can decrease the anonymity group of a certain user. If he can also link some messages of this user, then blocking only few messages could be enough to detect the sender.
- The attacker may detect, that he doesn't receive a message, he is waiting for. This is possible if this message is part of a larger data stream, that would be broken without this message. So in an extreme case blocking one message could be enough to uncover the communication relation.

A possible solution to prevent these active attacks, results in deleting all messages of the whole MIX network if one is blocked.

A fundamental problem in detecting these attacks is the following:

If an attacker only blocks some messages, a MIX would wait until he gets enough messages. So an attacker will generate some own messages and will send them to the MIX.

How should a MIX decide, if an incoming message comes either from the attacker or from a real user? He has to know this, in order to recognise the attack.

There exist several different basic approaches for the MIX cascade, in order to solve this problem.

Users verifying the MIXes. In this case all messages a MIX receives are sent to all users. So each user can check that his message has arrived at the MIX. If that's true, he sends an acknowledgement to the MIX. The MIX forwards the batch only to the following MIX, if he receives these acknowledgements from all users.

The problem is, that the MIX must know, which users have sent messages and the MIX has to ensure, that a certain acknowledgement was really sent by one of these participants.

So each user has to own a digital certificate and authenticates himself (and the acknowledgement he has sent) to the MIX.

In the case of a MIX network, this could be a problem, because:

- The attacker shouldn't know, who has sent a message to which MIX, because this would extremely reduce the achievable anonymity and the attacks explained in Section 4.2 could be done much easier. In order to prevent this, each user has to send acknowledgements to all MIXes of the network, even if he hasn't used them. And he also has to receive all messages published by each MIX. Of course this would dramatically decrease the efficiency.
- But now an acknowledgement sent by a user doesn't mean in every case that one of his messages is currently processed and so the acknowledgements tell nothing about the number of real messages in a batch. When using big MIX networks there always exists the risk that the anonymity group could be very small.
- A MIX network doesn't work synchronically, so the user has to decide, if his message has been blocked or if it only arrived late for being processed in the current batch. A successful attack could be to delay $n - 1$ messages for one batch.

Ticket-method. A new idea developed by our group is, that the MIX only accepts messages which come verifiable from the group of registered participants. Each registered participant gets exactly one ticket from every MIX, which is only valid for a certain batch. If a MIX processes a batch, he verifies, that every message contains such a valid ticket. Because each participant gets only one ticket for each batch, he can only send one message. So the attacker could only generate as many messages as the number of users he controls. A MIX couldn't link a ticket to the belonging user, because we use blind signatures. The whole procedure is explained in detail in [2] (contained in this book).

This procedure is only badly applicable in a MIX network, because:

- The user has to request tickets from every MIX in the world, whereas in a cascade, the user only has to request tickets from each MIX in the cascade he/she intents to use.
- The user doesn't know exactly, which batch will contain his message. Therefore, the user has to request tickets from every MIX for many batches and include many tickets for each step.
- And finally only a part of these ticket would be used so that a MIX could only ensure, that no additional messages sent by an attacker would be processed. But the attacker could decrease the anonymity group by blocking some messages. in the cascade, the number of tickets issued could exactly match the batch size.

Summarising, the described methods to prevent active attacks are very expensive. A user of a MIX network couldn't use every MIX at every time, so:

- the expenditure grows up excessively, because nevertheless, the user has to execute these methods with every MIX.
- These procedures wouldn't achieve an acceptable level of security

As a result, we think, that it isn't possible to protect a MIX network against such attacks with justifiable expenses. So an active attacker could easily observe at least a certain user.

5   Classification of Existing Architectures

In this section we discuss, how the described attacks are related to existing and used services.

But we have to say that these services are developed assuming that there are only substantial weaker attackers in comparison to our assumption about strong attackers.

5.1   Remailer

Anonymous remailers, like for instance Mixmaster have the advantage that they need not to work real-time.

Because of that Remailer-MIXes could use a different method for building an anonymity group. They collect incoming messages in a pool. Outgoing messages are selected casually out of this pool. Because a message theoretically can remain in the pool for an unlimited amount of time, none of the already received messages can be excluded of the anonymity group. Because of that the described attacks (Section 4.2) that limit the size of the anonymity group can rarely be used successfully.

It can be assumed that the messages are atomic and unlinkable because the recipients are many different users, who can be trusted in most cases according to the attacker model. But the attacks as described in Section 4.2 and 4.4 are especially successful if messages can be linked. Attacks by using the length of messages (Section 3.1) and the replay of messages (3.2) are at least prevented by the Mixmaster. The attack by manipulating messages (3.3) is not possible because it is assumed that the attacker gets the plaintext of messages.

It is possible to block messages and a MIX can be flooded with messages by the attacker because the remailer can not check the origin of a message (4.4). The attacker doesn't know the number of messages stored in the pool, because the delay of a message in the MIX is unknown for it.

This attack for remailers is only possible with a certain probability in contrast to MIXes that work in a deterministic way. It increases with expenditure. The attack by choice of MIX routes (4.3) can't be prevented, because it is a net of remailers similar to the MIX network.

Result: Some of the described attacks are theoretically possible. Because the remailers don't work in a deterministic way the attacks are complicated. Because of that pool mixes cannot be used for real-time services. The Mixmaster remailer in comparison to other anonymity services as described in Section 5 offers the best protection against observation.

5.2   Onion-Routing/Freedom

Zero Knowledge offers the commercial system "Freedom" [4]. This is a MIX network that provides unobservable and anonymous real-time connections between network nodes. So it provides access to different internet services. The way how it works is very similar with the service Onion-Routing [7].

To achieve little delay for every user an anonymous route across the MIX network is provided. The advantage of this routes is that the data must only be encrypted or decrypted via a symmetrical cryptographic system. Of course all data transmitted over one route are linkable. Because these routes can be generated every time and the users send different amounts of data at different times via the route an attack by using the length of messages (3.1) is possible.

Also a replay attack (3.2) is possible. There is no checking of message replay in the MIXes. Instead of that Freedom uses link encryption between neighbouring MIXes.

Because of that an external attacker that controls none of the MIXes can't achieve much:

- Via the use of streaming cipher even identical messages result in a different representation of bits.
- The external attacker can't add messages because he does not know the key needed.

– Because of dummy traffic there exists a permanent traffic load between the
  mixes. That prevents successful attacks by traffic analysis.

But if the attacker controls part of the MIXes specific attacks via message
blocking (3.4, 4.4) or traffic analysis (4.2) are possible: an attacking MIX knows
its own key used for link encryption and can divide dummy traffic from real
messages.

The Freedom network only accepts registered users, that identify themselves
via tokens. This check is only done by the last MIX of the chosen route. Because
of this the attacker can generate messages on its own, which are accepted by
MIXes.

Even if only authenticated messages would be accepted by MIXes this attack
could not be prevented because ever user theoretically can own an unlimited
amount of tokens.

The attack explained in Section 4.2.2 which would determine the route of
a message is only partly realisable. To each MIX per definition belong some
neighbouring MIXes. This decreases the number of possible routes and this in
fact increases the size of the anonymity group.

Each MIX reorders the messages only in a very limited amount. So if an
attacker controls neighbouring MIXes, the anonymity groups would become very
small.

Conclusion: The Freedom network only prevents attacks from external observers and isolated attacking MIXes. If some MIXes of a route cooperate with
the attacker, the attacker has a very good chance to observe a user.

5.3   Crowds

The Crowds system is based on a very different principle. A participant sends
a message only with a certain probability directly into the internet. Otherwise
he forwards the message to an other randomly selected user. This user does the
same and so on.

A message passes several users and all these users get knowledge of the plaintext. An external attacker wouldn't get the plaintext, because the connections
between the users are encrypted.

Based on the attacking model explained above, this isn't a problem, because
most participants are trustworthy ones. Eventually no user knows if a request
he receives from another user really comes from this user.

An assumption is that the attacker isn't able to observe the whole network.
Otherwise he could detect, if a user receives a message from an other one. If
a user sends a message and hadn't received one, this message must come from
himself.

Conclusion: Crowds protect only against observations done by the communication partner (i.e. the WEB-server) or done by an other, isolated participant.

The described attacks are not applicable, because Crowds are based on a different principle. On the other hand all attacks assume a much stronger attacker
than the designer of Crowds expected.

6 Summary

Based on the described attacks and their high probability of success the Conclusion is that a MIX network can't be realised securely, especially when we think of the well known attacking model defined by David Chaum. The theoretical anonymity group of a very big MIX network, that contains all users, is practically not achievable, even if all MIXes are trustworthy ones.

In Section 4.4 we described attacks, which block messages. These attacks in principle apply to MIX cascades, too. But for this case promising basic approaches have been developed in order to prevent these attacks [1] [2].

If a service is to be constructed, which is secure against global attackers, a MIX cascade or any other of the described configurations should be chosen instead of a MIX network. This would prevent at least some of the illustrated attacks.

A disadvantage of the MIX cascade is that the cascade consists of default MIXes which have to be used. A user cannot express his trust in certain MIXes by using them or his distrust by not using them. But a user may choose that cascade he wants to use and trust in.

References

1. Oliver Berthold, Hannes Federrath, Marit Köhntopp: Project "Anonymity and Unobservability in the Internet"; Workshop on Freedom and Privacy by Design; in: Proceedings of the Tenth Conference on Computers, Freedom & Privacy; CFP 2000: Challenging the Assumptions; Toronto/Canada, April 4-7, 2000; ACM, New York 2000; 57-65; http://www.inf.tu-dresden.de/ hf2/publ/2000/BeFK2000cfp2000/.
2. Oliver Berthold, Hannes Federrath, Stefan Köpsell: Web MIXes: A system for anonymous and unobservable Internet access. Proceedings of Workshop on Design Issues in Anonymity and Unobservability, July 25-26, 2000 in Berkeley.
3. David Chaum: Untraceable Electronic Mail, Return Addresses, and Digital Pseudonyms. Communications of the ACM 24/2 (1981) 84-88.
4. The Freedom Network Architecture. Zero-Knowledge-Systems, Inc., 1998. http://www.freedom.net/
5. Andreas Pfitzmann: Diensteintegrierende Kommunikationsnetze mit teilnehmerüberprüfbarem Datenschutz; University Karlsruhe, Department of computer science, Dissertation, Feb. 1989, IFB 234, Springer-Verlag, Heidelberg 1990.
6. Andreas Pfitzmann, Birgit Pfitzmann, Michael Waidner: ISDN-MIXes - Untraceable Communication with Very Small Bandwidth Overhead. Proc. Kommunikation in verteilten Systemen, IFB 267, Springer-Verlag, Berlin 1991, 451-463.
7. M. G. Reed, P. F. Syverson, D. Goldschlag: Anonymous Connections and Onion Routing. IEEE Journal on Selected Areas in Communication. Spezial Issue on Copyright and Privacy Protection, 1998. http://www.onion-router.net/Publications/JSAC-1998.ps

Freenet: A Distributed Anonymous Information Storage and Retrieval System

Ian Clarke[1], Oskar Sandberg[2], Brandon Wiley[3], and Theodore W. Hong[4]*

[1] Uprizer, Inc., 1007 Montana Avenue #323, Santa Monica, CA 90403, USA
ian@octayne.com
[2] Mörbydalen 12, 18252 Stockholm, Sweden
md98-osa@nada.kth.se
[3] 2305 Rio Grande Street, Austin, TX 78705, USA
blanu@uts.cc.utexas.edu
[4] Department of Computing, Imperial College of Science, Technology and Medicine,
180 Queen's Gate, London SW7 2BZ, United Kingdom
t.hong@doc.ic.ac.uk

Abstract. We describe Freenet, an adaptive peer-to-peer network application that permits the publication, replication, and retrieval of data while protecting the anonymity of both authors and readers. Freenet operates as a network of identical nodes that collectively pool their storage space to store data files and cooperate to route requests to the most likely physical location of data. No broadcast search or centralized location index is employed. Files are referred to in a location-independent manner, and are dynamically replicated in locations near requestors and deleted from locations where there is no interest. It is infeasible to discover the true origin or destination of a file passing through the network, and difficult for a node operator to determine or be held responsible for the actual physical contents of her own node.

1 Introduction

Networked computer systems are rapidly growing in importance as the medium of choice for the storage and exchange of information. However, current systems afford little privacy to their users, and typically store any given data item in only one or a few fixed places, creating a central point of failure. Because of a continued desire among individuals to protect the privacy of their authorship or readership of various types of sensitive information[28], and the undesirability of central points of failure which can be attacked by opponents wishing to remove data from the system[11,27] or simply overloaded by too much interest[1], systems offering greater security and reliability are needed.

We are developing Freenet, a distributed information storage and retrieval system designed to address these concerns of privacy and availability. The system operates as a location-independent distributed file system across many individual

---

* Work of Theodore W. Hong was supported by grants from the Marshall Aid Commemoration Commission and the National Science Foundation.

H. Federrath (Ed.): Anonymity 2000, LNCS 2009, pp. 46–66, 2001.

computers that allows files to be inserted, stored, and requested anonymously. There are five main design goals:

- Anonymity for both producers and consumers of information
- Deniability for storers of information
- Resistance to attempts by third parties to deny access to information
- Efficient dynamic storage and routing of information
- Decentralization of all network functions

The system is designed to respond adaptively to usage patterns, transparently moving, replicating, and deleting files as necessary to provide efficient service without resorting to broadcast searches or centralized location indexes. It is not intended to guarantee permanent file storage, although it is hoped that a sufficient number of nodes will join with enough storage capacity that most files will be able to remain indefinitely. In addition, the system operates at the application layer and assumes the existence of a secure transport layer, although it is transport-independent. It does not seek to provide anonymity for general network usage, only for Freenet file transactions.

Freenet is currently being developed as a free software project on Sourceforge, and a preliminary implementation can be downloaded from `http://www.free-netproject.org/`. It grew out of work originally done by the first author at the University of Edinburgh[12].

2   Related Work

Several strands of related work in this area can be distinguished. Anonymous point-to-point channels based on Chaum's mix-net scheme[8] have been implemented for email by the Mixmaster remailer[13] and for general TCP/IP traffic by onion routing[19] and Freedom[32]. Such channels are not in themselves easily suited to one-to-many publication, however, and are best viewed as a complement to Freenet since they do not provide file access and storage.

Anonymity for consumers of information in the web context is provided by browser proxy services such as the Anonymizer[6], although they provide no protection for producers of information and do not protect consumers against logs kept by the services themselves. Private information retrieval schemes[10] provide much stronger guarantees for information consumers, but only to the extent of hiding which piece of information was retrieved from a particular server. In many cases, the fact of contacting a particular server in itself can reveal much about the information retrieved, which can only be counteracted by having every server hold all information (naturally this scales poorly). The closest work to our own is Reiter and Rubin's Crowds system[25], which uses a similar method of proxying requests for consumers, although Crowds does not itself store information and does not protect information producers. Berthold *et al.* propose Web MIXes[7], a stronger system that uses message padding and reordering and dummy messages to increase security, but again does not protect information producers.

The Rewebber[26] provides a measure of anonymity for producers of web information by means of an encrypted URL service that is essentially the inverse of an anonymizing browser proxy, but has the same difficulty of providing no protection against the operator of the service itself. TAZ[18] extends this idea by using chains of nested encrypted URLs that successively point to different rewebber servers to be contacted, although this is vulnerable to traffic analysis using replay. Both rely on a single server as the ultimate source of information. Publius[30] enhances availability by distributing files as redundant shares among n webservers, only k of which are needed to reconstruct a file; however, since the identity of the servers themselves is not anonymized, an attacker might remove information by forcing the closure of $n-k+1$ servers. The Eternity proposal[5] seeks to archive information permanently and anonymously, although it lacks specifics on how to efficiently locate stored files, making it more akin to an anonymous backup service. Free Haven[14] is an interesting anonymous publication system that uses a trust network and file trading mechanism to provide greater server accountability while maintaining anonymity.

distributed.net[15] demonstrated the concept of pooling computer resources among multiple users on a large scale for CPU cycles; other systems which do the same for disk space are Napster[24] and Gnutella[17], although the former relies on a central server to locate files and the latter employs an inefficient broadcast search. Neither one replicates files. Intermemory[9] and India[16] are cooperative distributed fileserver systems intended for long-term archival storage along the lines of Eternity, in which files are split into redundant shares and distributed among many participants. Akamai[2] provides a service that replicates files at locations near information consumers, but is not suitable for producers who are individuals (as opposed to corporations). None of these systems attempt to provide anonymity.

3 Architecture

Freenet is implemented as an adaptive peer-to-peer network of nodes that query one another to store and retrieve data files, which are named by location-independent keys. Each node maintains its own local datastore which it makes available to the network for reading and writing, as well as a dynamic routing table containing addresses of other nodes and the keys that they are thought to hold. It is intended that most users of the system will run nodes, both to provide security guarantees against inadvertently using a hostile foreign node and to increase the storage capacity available to the network as a whole.

The system can be regarded as a cooperative distributed filesystem incorporating location independence and transparent lazy replication. Just as systems such as distributed.net[15] enable ordinary users to share unused CPU cycles on their machines, Freenet enables users to share unused disk space. However, where distributed.net uses those CPU cycles for its own purposes, Freenet is directly useful to users themselves, acting as an extension to their own hard drives.

The basic model is that requests for keys are passed along from node to node through a chain of proxy requests in which each node makes a local decision about where to send the request next, in the style of IP (Internet Protocol) routing. Depending on the key requested, routes will vary. The routing algorithms for storing and retrieving data described in the following sections are designed to adaptively adjust routes over time to provide efficient performance while using only local, rather than global, knowledge. This is necessary since nodes only have knowledge of their immediate upstream and downstream neighbors in the proxy chain, to maintain privacy.

Each request is given a *hops-to-live* limit, analogous to IP's time-to-live, which is decremented at each node to prevent infinite chains. Each request is also assigned a pseudo-unique random identifier, so that nodes can prevent loops by rejecting requests they have seen before. When this happens, the immediately-preceding node simply chooses a different node to forward to. This process continues until the request is either satisfied or exceeds its hops-to-live limit. Then the success or failure result is passed back up the chain to the sending node.

No node is privileged over any other node, so no hierarchy or central point of failure exists. Joining the network is simply a matter of first discovering the address of one or more existing nodes through out-of-band means, then starting to send messages.

3.1   Keys and Searching

Files in Freenet are identified by binary file keys obtained by applying a hash function. Currently we use the 160-bit SHA-1[4] function as our hash. Three different types of file keys are used, which vary in purpose and in the specifics of how they are constructed.

The simplest type of file key is the *keyword-signed key* (KSK), which is derived from a short descriptive text string chosen by the user when storing a file in the network. For example, a user inserting a treatise on warfare might assign it the description, text/philosophy/sun-tzu/art-of-war. This string is used as input to deterministically generate a public/private key pair. The public half is then hashed to yield the file key.

The private half of the asymmetric key pair is used to sign the file, providing a minimal integrity check that a retrieved file matches its file key. Note however that an attacker can use a dictionary attack against this signature by compiling a list of descriptive strings. The file is also encrypted using the descriptive string itself as a key, for reasons to be explained in section 3.4.

To allow others to retrieve the file, the user need only publish the descriptive string. This makes keyword-signed keys easy to remember and communicate to others. However, they form a flat global namespace, which is problematic. Nothing prevents two users from independently choosing the same descriptive string for different files, for example, or from engaging in "key-squatting"—inserting junk files under popular descriptions.

These problems are addressed by the *signed-subspace key* (SSK), which enables personal namespaces. A user creates a namespace by randomly generating a public/private key pair which will serve to identify her namespace. To insert a file, she chooses a short descriptive text string as before. The public namespace key and the descriptive string are hashed independently, XOR'ed together, and then hashed again to yield the file key.

As with the keyword-signed key, the private half of the asymmetric key pair is used to sign the file. This signature, generated from a random key pair, is more secure than the signatures used for keyword-signed keys. The file is also encrypted by the descriptive string as before.

To allow others to retrieve the file, the user publishes the descriptive string together with her subspace's public key. Storing data requires the private key, however, so only the owner of a subspace can add files to it.

The owner now has the ability to manage her own namespace. For example, she could simulate a hierarchical structure by creating directory-like files containing hypertext pointers to other files. A directory under the key text/philosophy could contain a list of keys such as text/philosophy/sun-tzu/art-of-war, text/philosophy/confucius/analects, and text/philosophy/nozick/anarchy-state-utopia, using appropriate syntax interpretable by a client. Directories can also recursively point to other directories.

The third type of key is the *content-hash key* (CHK), which is useful for implementing updating and splitting. A content-hash key is simply derived by directly hashing the contents of the corresponding file. This gives every file a pseudo-unique file key. Files are also encrypted by a randomly-generated encryption key. To allow others to retrieve the file, the user publishes the content-hash key itself together with the decryption key. Note that the decryption key is never stored with the file but is only published with the file key, for reasons to be explained in section 3.4.

Content-hash keys are most useful in conjunction with signed-subspace keys using an indirection mechanism. To store an updatable file, a user first inserts it under its content-hash key. She then inserts an indirect file under a signed-subspace key whose contents are the content-hash key. This enables others to retrieve the file in two steps, given the signed-subspace key.

To update a file, the owner first inserts a new version under its content-hash key, which should be different from the old version's content hash. She then inserts a new indirect file under the original signed-subspace key pointing to the updated version. When the insert reaches a node which possesses the old version, a key collision will occur. The node will check the signature on the new version, verify that it is both valid and more recent, and replace the old version. Thus the signed-subspace key will lead to the most recent version of the file, while old versions can continue to be accessed directly by content-hash key if desired. (If not requested, however, these old versions will eventually be removed from the network—see section 3.4.) This mechanism can be used to manage directories as well as regular files.

Content-hash keys can also be used for splitting files into multiple parts. For large files, splitting can be desirable because of storage and bandwidth limitations. Splitting even medium-sized files into standard-sized parts (e.g. 2^n kilobytes) also has advantages in combating traffic analysis. This is easily accomplished by inserting each part separately under a content-hash key, and creating an indirect file (or multiple levels of indirect files) to point to the individual parts.

All of this still leaves the problem of finding keys in the first place. The most straightforward way to add a search capability to Freenet is to run a hypertext spider such as those used to search the web. While an attractive solution in many ways, this conflicts with the design goal of avoiding centralization. A possible alternative is to create a special class of lightweight indirect files. When a real file is inserted, the author could also insert a number of indirect files each containing a pointer to the real file, named according to search keywords chosen by her. These indirect files would differ from normal files in that multiple files with the same key (i.e. search keyword) would be permitted to exist, and requests for such keys would keep going until a specified number of results were accumulated instead of stopping at the first file found. Managing the likely large volume of such indirect files is an open problem.

An alternative mechanism is to encourage individuals to create their own compilations of favorite keys and publicize the keys of these compilations. This is an approach also in common use on the world-wide web.

3.2   Retrieving Data

To retrieve a file, a user must first obtain or calculate its binary file key. She then sends a request message to her own node specifying that key and a hops-to-live value. When a node receives a request, it first checks its own store for the data and returns it if found, together with a note saying it was the source of the data. If not found, it looks up the nearest key in its routing table to the key requested and forwards the request to the corresponding node. If that request is ultimately successful and returns with the data, the node will pass the data back to the upstream requestor, cache the file in its own datastore, and create a new entry in its routing table associating the actual data source with the requested key. A subsequent request for the same key will be immediately satisfied from the local cache; a request for a "similar" key (determined by lexicographic distance) will be forwarded to the previously successful data source. Because maintaining a table of data sources is a potential security concern, any node along the way can unilaterally decide to change the reply message to claim itself or another arbitrarily-chosen node as the data source.

If a node cannot forward a request to its preferred downstream node because the target is down or a loop would be created, the node having the second-nearest key will be tried, then the third-nearest, and so on. If a node runs out of candidates to try, it reports failure back to its upstream neighbor, which will then try *its* second choice, etc. In this way, a request operates as a steepest-ascent hill-climbing search with backtracking. If the hops-to-live limit is exceeded, a failure result is propagated back to the original requestor without any further nodes being tried. Nodes may unilaterally curtail excessive hops-to-live values to reduce network load. They may also forget about pending requests after a period of time to keep message memory free.

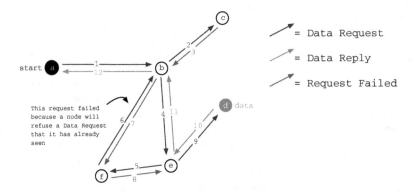

Fig. 1. A typical request sequence.

Figure 1 depicts a typical sequence of request messages. The user initiates a request at node a. Node a forwards the request to node b, which forwards it to node c. Node c is unable to contact any other nodes and returns a backtracking "request failed" message to b. Node b then tries its second choice, e, which forwards the request to f. Node f forwards the request to b, which detects the loop and returns a backtracking failure message. Node f is unable to contact any other nodes and backtracks one step further back to e. Node e forwards the request to its second choice, d, which has the data. The data is returned from d via e and b back to a, which sends it back to the user. The data is also cached on e, b, and a.

This mechanism has a number of effects. Most importantly, we hypothesize that the quality of the routing should improve over time, for two reasons. First, nodes should come to specialize in locating sets of similar keys. If a node is listed in routing tables under a particular key, it will tend to receive mostly requests for keys similar to that key. It is therefore likely to gain more "experience" in answering those queries and become better informed in its routing tables about which other nodes carry those keys. Second, nodes should become similarly specialized in storing clusters of files having similar keys. Because forwarding a request successfully will result in the node itself gaining a copy of the requested file, and most requests will be for similar keys, the node will mostly acquire files with similar keys. Taken together, these two effects should improve the efficiency of future requests in a self-reinforcing cycle, as nodes build up routing tables and datastores focusing on particular sets of keys, which will be precisely those keys that they are asked about.

In addition, the request mechanism will cause popular data to be transparently replicated by the system and mirrored closer to requestors. For example, if a file that is originally located in London is requested in Berkeley, it will become cached locally and provide faster response to subsequent Berkeley requests. It also becomes copied onto each computer along the way, providing redundancy if the London node fails or is shut down. (Note that "along the way" is determined by key closeness and does not necessarily have geographic relevance.)

Finally, as nodes process requests, they create new routing table entries for previously-unknown nodes that supply files, increasing connectivity. This helps new nodes to discover more of the network (although it does not help the rest of the network to discover *them*; for that, the announcement mechanism described in section 3.5 is necessary). Note that direct links to data sources are created, bypassing the intermediate nodes used. Thus, nodes that successfully supply data will gain routing table entries and be contacted more often than nodes that do not.

Since keys are derived from hashes, lexicographic closeness of keys does not imply any closeness of the original descriptive strings and presumably, no closeness of subject matter of the corresponding files. This lack of semantic closeness is not important, however, as the routing algorithm is based on knowing here keys are located, not where subjects are located. That is, supposing a string such as text/philosophy/sun-tzu/art-of-war yields a file key AH5JK2, requests for this file can be routed more effectively by creating clusters containing AH5JK1, AH5JK2, and AH5JK3, not by creating clusters for works of philosophy. Indeed, the use of hashes is desirable precisely because philosophical works will be scattered across the network, lessening the chances that failure of a single node will make all philosophy unavailable. The same is true for personal subspaces—files belonging to the same subspace will be scattered across different nodes.

3.3   Storing Data

Inserts follow a parallel strategy to requests. To insert a file, a user first calculates a binary file key for it, using one of the procedures described in section 3.1. She then sends an insert message to her own node specifying the proposed key and a hops-to-live value (this will determine the number of nodes to store it on). When a node receives an insert proposal, it first checks its own store to see if the key is already taken. If the key is found, the node returns the pre-existing file as if a request had been made for it. The user will thus know that a collision was encountered and can try again using a different key. If the key is not found, the node looks up the nearest key in its routing table to the key proposed and forwards the insert to the corresponding node. If that insert causes a collision and returns with the data, the node will pass the data back to the upstream inserter and again behave as if a request had been made (i.e. cache the file locally and create a routing table entry for the data source).

If the hops-to-live limit is reached without a key collision being detected, an "all clear" result will be propagated back to the original inserter. Note that for inserts, this is a successful result, in contrast to situation for requests. The user then sends the data to insert, which will be propagated along the path established by the initial query and stored in each node along the way. Each node will also create an entry in its routing table associating the inserter (as the data source) with the new key. To avoid the obvious security problem, any node along the way can unilaterally decide to change the insert message to claim itself or another arbitrarily-chosen node as the data source.

If a node cannot forward an insert to its preferred downstream node because the target is down or a loop would be created, the insert backtracks to the second-nearest key, then the third-nearest, and so on in the same way as for requests. If the backtracking returns all the way back to the original inserter, it indicates that fewer nodes than asked for could be contacted. As with requests, nodes may curtail excessive hops-to-live values and/or forget about pending inserts after a period of time.

This mechanism has three effects. First, newly inserted files are selectively placed on nodes already possessing files with similar keys. This reinforces the clustering of keys set up by the request mechanism. Second, new nodes can use inserts as a supplementary means of announcing their existence to the rest of the network. Third, attempts by attackers to supplant existing files by inserting junk files under existing keys are likely to simply spread the real files further, since the originals are propagated on collision. (Note, however, that this is mostly only relevant to keyword-signed keys, as the other types of keys are more strongly verifiable.)

3.4 Managing Data

All information storage systems must deal with the problem of finite storage capacity. Individual Freenet node operators can configure the amount of storage to dedicate to their datastores. Node storage is managed as an LRU (Least Recently Used) cache[29] in which data items are kept sorted in decreasing order by time of most recent request (or time of insert, if an item has never been requested). When a new file arrives (from either a new insert or a successful request) which would cause the datastore to exceed the designated size, the least recently used files are evicted in order until there is room. The resulting impact on availability is mitigated by the fact that the routing table entries created when the evicted files first arrived will remain for a time, potentially allowing the node to later get new copies from the original data sources. (Routing table entries are also eventually deleted in a similar fashion as the table fills up, although they will be retained longer since they are smaller.)

Strictly speaking, the datastore is not a cache, since the set of datastores is all the storage that there is. That is, there is no "permanent" copy which is being replicated in a cache. Once all the nodes have decided, collectively speaking, to drop a particular file, it will no longer be available to the network. In this respect, Freenet differs from systems such as Eternity and Free Haven which seek to provide guarantees of file lifetimes.

The expiration mechanism has an advantageous aspect, however, in that it allows outdated documents to fade away naturally after being superseded by newer documents. If an outdated document is still used and considered valuable for historical reasons, it will stay alive precisely as long as it continues to be requested.

For political or legal reasons, it may be desirable for node operators not to explicitly know the contents of their datastores. This is why all stored files are encrypted. The encryption procedures used are not intended to secure the file—that would be impossible since a requestor (potentially anyone) must be capable of decrypting the file once retrieved. Rather, the objective is that the node operator can plausibly deny any knowledge of the contents of her datastore, since all she knows *a priori* is the file key, not the encryption key. The encryption keys for keyword-signed and signed-subspace data can only be obtained by reversing a hash, and the encryption keys for content-hash data are completely unrelated. With effort, of course, a dictionary attack will reveal which keys are present—as it must in order for requests to work at all—but the burden such an effort would require is intended to provide a measure of cover for node operators.

3.5   Adding Nodes

A new node can join the network by discovering the address of one or more existing nodes through out-of-band means, then starting to send messages. As mentioned previously, the request mechanism naturally enables new nodes to learn about more of the network over time. However, in order for existing nodes to discover *them*, new nodes must somehow announce their presence. This process is complicated by two somewhat conflicting requirements. On one hand, to promote efficient routing, we would like all the existing nodes to be consistent in deciding which keys to send a new node (i.e. what key to assign it in their routing tables). On the other hand, it would cause a security problem if any one node could choose the routing key, which rules out the most straightforward way of achieving consistency.

We use a cryptographic protocol to satisfy both of these requirements. A new node joining the network chooses a random seed and sends an announcement message containing its address and the hash of that seed to some existing node. When a node receives a new-node announcement, it generates a random seed, XOR's that with the hash it received and hashes the result again to create a commitment. It then forwards the new hash to some node chosen randomly from its routing table. This process continues until the hops-to-live of the announcement runs out. The last node to receive the announcement just generates a seed. Now all nodes in the chain reveal their seeds and the key for the new node is assigned as the XOR of all the seeds. Checking the commitments enables each node to confirm that everyone revealed their seeds truthfully. This yields a consistent random key which cannot be influenced by a malicious participant. Each node then adds an entry for the new node in its routing table under that key.

4   Protocol Details

The Freenet protocol is packet-oriented and uses self-contained messages. Each message includes a transaction ID so that nodes can track the state of inserts and requests. This design is intended to permit flexibility in the choice of transport mechanisms for messages, whether they be TCP, UDP, or other technologies such as packet radio. For efficiency, nodes using a persistent channel such as a TCP connection may also send multiple messages over the same connection. Node addresses consist of a transport method plus a transport-specific identifier such as an IP address and port number, e.g. tcp/192.168.1.1:19114. Nodes which change addresses frequently may also use virtual addresses stored under *address-resolution keys* (ARK's), which are signed-subspace keys updated to contain the current real address.

A Freenet transaction begins with a Request.Handshake message from one node to another, specifying the desired return address of the sending[1] node. (The sender's return address may be impossible to determine automatically from the transport layer, or the sender may wish to receive replies at a different address from that used to send the message.) If the remote node is active and responding to requests, it will reply with a Reply.Handshake specifying the protocol version number that it understands. Handshakes are remembered for a few hours, and subsequent transactions between the same nodes during this time may omit this step.

All messages contain a randomly-generated 64-bit transaction ID, a hops-to-live limit, and a depth counter. Although the ID cannot be guaranteed to be unique, the likelihood of a collision occurring during the transaction lifetime among the limited set of nodes that it sees is extremely low. Hops-to-live is set by the originator of a message and is decremented at each hop to prevent messages being forwarded indefinitely. To reduce the information that an attacker can obtain from the hops-to-live value, messages do not automatically terminate after hops-to-live reaches 1 but are forwarded on with finite probability (with hops-to-live again 1). Depth is incremented at each hop and is used by a replying node to set hops-to-live high enough to reach a requestor. Requestors should initialize it to a small random value to obscure their location. As with hops-to-live, a depth of 1 is not automatically incremented but is passed unchanged with finite probability.

To request data, the sending node sends a Request.Data message specifying a transaction ID, initial hops-to-live and depth, and a search key. The remote node will check its datastore for the key and if not found, will forward the request to another node as described in section 3.2. Using the chosen hops-to-live limit, the sending node starts a timer for the expected amount of time it should take to contact that many nodes, after which it will assume failure. While the request is being processed, the remote node may periodically send back Reply.Restart messages indicating that messages were stalled waiting on network timeouts, so that the sending node knows to extend its timer.

If the request is ultimately successful, the remote node will reply with a Send.Data message containing the data requested and the address of the node which supplied it (possibly faked). If the request is ultimately unsuccessful and its hops-to-live are completely used up trying to satisfy it, the remote node

---

[1] Remember that the sending node may or may not be the original requestor.

will reply with a Reply.NotFound. The sending node will then decrement the hops-to-live of the Send.Data (or Reply.NotFound) and pass it along upstream, unless it is the actual originator of the request. Both of these messages terminate the transaction and release any resources held. However, if there are still hops-to-live remaining, usually because the request ran into a dead end where no viable non-looping paths could be found, the remote node will reply with a Request.Continue giving the number of hops-to-live left. The sending node will then try to contact the next-most likely node from its routing table. It will also send a Reply.Restart upstream.

To insert data, the sending node sends a Request.Insert message specifying a randomly-generated transaction ID, an initial hops-to-live and depth, and a proposed key. The remote node will check its datastore for the key and if not found, forward the insert to another node as described in section 3.3. Timers and Reply.Restart messages are also used in the same way as for requests.

If the insert ultimately results in a key collision, the remote node will reply with either a Send.Data message containing the existing data or a Reply.NotFound (if existing data was not actually found, but routing table references to it were). If the insert does not encounter a collision, yet runs out of nodes with nonzero hops-to-live remaining, the remote node will reply with a Request.Continue. In this case, Request.Continue is a failure result meaning that not as many nodes could be contacted as asked for. These messages will be passed along upstream as in the request case. Both messages terminate the transaction and release any resources held. However, if the insert expires without encountering a collision, the remote node will reply with a Reply.Insert, indicating that the insert can go ahead. The sending node will pass along the Reply.Insert upstream and wait for its predecessor to send a Send.Insert containing the data. When it receives the data, it will store it locally and forward the Send.Insert downstream, concluding the transaction.

5   Performance Analysis

We performed simulations on a model of this system to give some indications about its performance. Here we summarize the most important results; for full details, see [21].

5.1   Network Convergence

To test the adaptivity of the network routing, we created a test network of 1000 nodes. Each node had a datastore size of 50 items and a routing table size of 250 addresses. The datastores were initialized to be empty, and the routing tables were initialized to connect the network in a regular ring-lattice topology in which each node had routing entries for its two nearest neighbors on either side. The keys associated with these routing entries were set to be hashes of the destination nodes' addresses. Using hashes has the useful property that the resulting keys

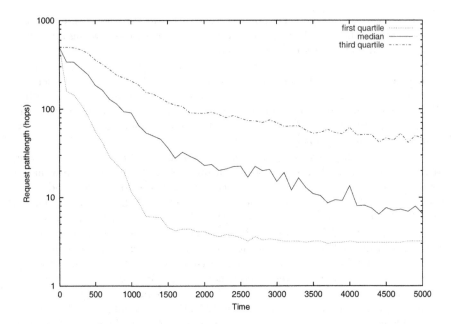

Fig. 2. Time evolution of the request pathlength.

are both random and consistent (that is, all references to a given node will use the same key).

Inserts of random keys were sent to random nodes in the network, interspersed randomly with requests for randomly-chosen keys known to have been previously inserted, using a hops-to-live of 20 for both. Every 100 timesteps, a snapshot of the network was taken and its performance measured using a set of probe requests. Each probe consisted of 300 random requests for previously-inserted keys, using a hops-to-live of 500. We recorded the resulting distribution of *request pathlengths*, the number of hops actually taken before finding the data. If the request did not find the data, the pathlength was taken to be 500.

Figure 2 shows the evolution of the first, second, and third quartiles of the request pathlength over time, averaged over ten trials. We can see that the initially high pathlengths decrease rapidly over time. In the beginning, few requests succeed at all, but as the network converges, the median request pathlength drops to just six.

5.2   Scalability

Next, we examined the scalability of a growing network. Starting from a small network of 20 nodes initialized in the same manner as the previous section, we added new nodes over time and measured the change in the request pathlength.

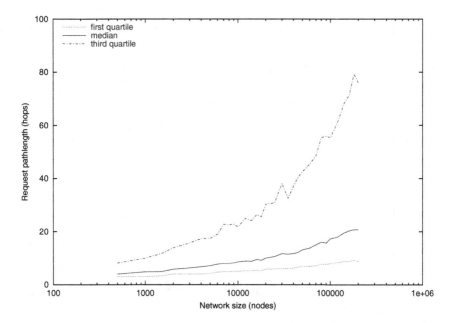

Fig. 3. Request pathlength versus network size.

Inserts and requests were simulated randomly as before. Every five timesteps, a new node was created and added to the network by simulating a node announcement message with hops-to-live of 10 sent from it to a randomly-chosen existing node. The key assigned by this announcement was taken to be the hash of the new node's address. Note that this procedure does not necessarily imply a linear rate of network growth, but rather a linear relationship between the request rate and the growth rate. Since it seems likely that both rates will be proportional to network size (yielding an exponential growth rate in real, as opposed to simulated, time), we believe that this model is justifiable.

Figure 3 shows the evolution of the first, second, and third quartiles of the request pathlength versus network size, averaged over ten trials. We can see that the pathlength scales approximately logarithmically, with a change of slope near 40,000 nodes. We posit that the slope change is a result of routing tables becoming filled and could be improved by adding a small number of nodes with larger routing tables. Section 5.4 discusses this issue in more depth. Where our routing tables were limited to 250 entries by the memory requirements of the simulation, real Freenet nodes should easily be able to hold thousands of entries. Nonetheless, even this limited network appears capable of scaling to one million nodes with a median pathlength of just 30. Note also that the network was grown continuously, without any steady-state convergence period.

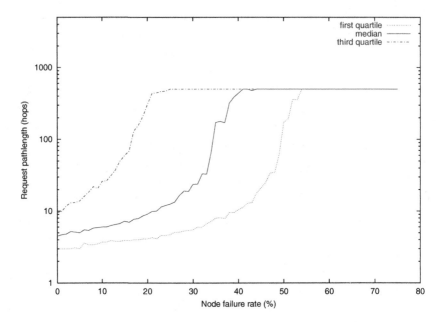

Fig. 4. Change in request pathlength under network failure.

5.3   Fault-Tolerance

Finally, we considered the fault-tolerance of the network. Starting with a network grown to 1000 nodes by the previous method, we progressively removed randomly-chosen nodes from the network to simulate node failures. Figure 4 shows the resulting evolution of the request pathlength, averaged over ten trials. The network is surprisingly robust against quite large failures. The median pathlength remains below 20 even when up to 30% of nodes fail.

5.4   Small-World Model

The scalability and fault-tolerance characteristics of Freenet can be explained in terms of a *small-world* network model[23,31,22,3]. In a small-world network, the majority of nodes have only relatively few, local, connections to other nodes, while a small number of nodes have large, wide-ranging sets of connections. Small-world networks permit efficient short paths between arbitrary points because of the shortcuts provided by the well-connected nodes, as evidenced by examination of Milgram's letter-passing experiment[23] and the Erdös number game cited by Watts and Strogatz[31].

Is Freenet a small world? A key factor in the identification of a small-world network is the existence of a scale-free power-law distribution of links within the network, as the tail of such distributions provides the highly-connected nodes

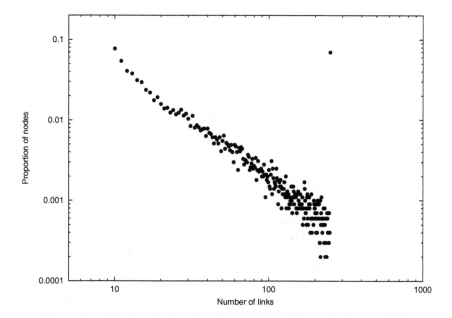

Fig. 5. Distribution of link number among Freenet nodes.

needed to create short paths. Figure 5 shows the average distribution of links (i.e. routing table entries) in the 1000-node Freenet networks used in the previous section. We see that the distribution closely approximates a power law, except for the anomalous point representing nodes with filled 250-entry routing tables. When we used differently-sized routing tables, this cutoff point moved but the power-law character of the distribution remained the same.

In addition to providing short paths, the power-law distribution also gives small-world networks a high degree of fault-tolerance. Random failures are most likely to knock out nodes from the majority that possess only a small number of connections. The loss of poorly-connected nodes will not greatly affect routing in the network. It is only when the number of random failures becomes high enough to knock out a significant number of well-connected nodes that routing performance will be noticeably affected.

6   Security

The primary goal for Freenet security is protecting the anonymity of requestors and inserters of files. It is also important to protect the identity of storers of files. Although trivially anyone can turn a node into a storer by requesting a file through it, thus "identifying" it as a storer, what is important is that there remain other, unidentified, holders of the file so that an adversary cannot remove

Table 1. Anonymity properties of Freenet.

System	Attacker	Sender anonymity	Key anonymity
Basic Freenet	local eavesdropper	exposed	exposed
	collaborating nodes	beyond suspicion	exposed
Freenet + pre-routing	local eavesdropper	exposed	beyond suspicion
	collaborating nodes	beyond suspicion	exposed

a file by attacking all of the nodes that hold it. Files must be protected against malicious modification, and finally, the system must be resistant to denial-of-service attacks.

Reiter and Rubin[25] present a useful taxonomy of anonymous communication properties on three axes. The first axis is the type of anonymity: sender anonymity or receiver anonymity, which mean respectively that an adversary cannot determine either who originated a message, or to whom it was sent. The second axis is the adversary in question: a local eavesdropper, a malicious node or collaboration of malicious nodes, or a web server (not applicable to Freenet). The third axis is the degree of anonymity, which ranges from absolute privacy (the presence of communication cannot be perceived) to beyond suspicion (the sender appears no more likely to have originated the message than any other potential sender), probable innocence (the sender is no more likely to be the originator than not), possible innocence, exposed, and provably exposed (the adversary can prove to others who the sender was).

As Freenet communication is not directed towards specific receivers, receiver anonymity is more accurately viewed as key anonymity, that is, hiding the key which is being requested or inserted. Unfortunately, since routing depends on knowledge of the key, key anonymity is not possible in the basic Freenet scheme (but see the discussion of "pre-routing" below). The use of hashes as keys provides a measure of obscurity against casual eavesdropping, but is of course vulnerable to a dictionary attack since their unhashed versions must be widely known in order to be useful.

Freenet's anonymity properties under this taxonomy are shown in Table 1. Against a collaboration of malicious nodes, sender anonymity is preserved beyond suspicion since a node in a request path cannot tell whether its predecessor in the path initiated the request or is merely forwarding it. [25] describes a probabilistic attack which might compromise sender anonymity, using a statistical analysis of the probability that a request arriving at a node a is forwarded on or handled directly, and the probability that a chooses a particular node b to forward to. This analysis is not immediately applicable to Freenet, however, since request paths are not constructed probabilistically. Forwarding depends on whether or not a has the requested data in its datastore, rather than chance. If a request is forwarded, the routing tables determine where it is sent to, and could be such that a forwards every request to b, or never forwards any requests to b, or anywhere in between. Nevertheless, the depth value may provide some indication as to how many hops away the originator was, although this is obscured by the random selection of an initial depth and the probabilistic means of incrementing it (see section 4). Similar considerations apply to hops-to-live. Further investigation is required to clarify these issues.

Against a local eavesdropper there is no protection on messages between the user and the first node contacted. Since the first node contacted can act as a local eavesdropper, it is recommended that the user only use a node on her own machine as the first point of entry into the Freenet network. Messages between nodes are encrypted against local eavesdropping, although traffic analysis may still be performed (e.g. an eavesdropper may observe a message going out without a previous message coming in and conclude that the target originated it).

Key anonymity and stronger sender anonymity can be achieved by adding mix-style "pre-routing" of messages. In this scheme, basic Freenet messages are encrypted by a succession of public keys which determine the route that the encrypted message will follow (overriding the normal routing mechanism). Nodes along this portion of the route are unable to determine either the originator of the message or its contents (including the request key), as per the mix-net anonymity properties. When the message reaches the endpoint of the pre-routing phase, it will be injected into the normal Freenet network and behave as though the endpoint were the originator of the message.

Protection for data sources is provided by the occasional resetting of the data source field in replies. The fact that a node is listed as the data source for a particular key does not necessarily imply that it actually supplied that data, or was even contacted in the course of the request. It is not possible to tell whether the downstream node provided the file or was merely forwarding a reply sent by someone else. In fact, the very act of successfully requesting a file places it on the downstream node if it was not already there, so a subsequent examination of that node on suspicion reveals nothing about the prior state of affairs, and provides a plausible legal ground that the data was not there until the act of investigation placed it there. Requesting a particular file with a hops-to-live of 1 does not directly reveal whether or not the node was previously storing the file in question, since nodes continue to forward messages having hops-to-live of 1 with finite probability. The success of a large number of requests for related files, however, may provide grounds for suspicion that those files were being stored there previously.

Modification of requested files by a malicious node in a request chain is an important threat, and not only because of the corruption of the files themselves. Since routing tables are based on replies to requests, a node might attempt to steer traffic towards itself by pretending to have files when it does not and simply returning fictitious data. For data stored under content-hash keys or signed-subspace keys, this is not feasible since inauthentic data can be detected unless a node finds a hash collision or successfully forges a cryptographic signature. Data stored under keyword-signed keys, however, is vulnerable to dictionary attack since signatures can be made by anyone knowing the original descriptive string.

Finally, a number of denial-of-service attacks can be envisioned. The most significant threat is that an attacker will attempt to fill all of the network's storage capacity by inserting a large number of junk files. An interesting possibility for countering this attack is a scheme such as Hash Cash[20]. Essentially, this scheme requires the inserter to perform a lengthy computation as "payment" before an insert is accepted, thus slowing down an attack. Another alternative is to divide the datastore into two sections, one for new inserts and one for "established" files (defined as files having received at least a certain number of requests). New inserts can only displace other new inserts, not established files. In this way a flood of junk inserts might temporarily paralyze insert operations but would not displace existing files. It is difficult for an attacker to artificially legitimize her own junk files by requesting them many times, since her requests will be satisfied by the first node to hold the data and not proceed any further. She cannot send requests directly to the other downstream nodes holding her files since their identities are hidden from her. However, adopting this scheme may make it difficult for genuine new inserts to survive long enough to be requested by others and become established.

Attackers may attempt to displace existing files by inserting alternate versions under the same keys. Such an attack is not possible against a content-hash key or signed-subspace key, since it requires finding a hash collision or successfully forging a cryptographic signature. An attack against a keyword-signed key, on the other hand, may result in both versions coexisting in the network. The way in which nodes react to insert collisions (detailed in section 3.3) is intended to make such attacks more difficult. The success of a replacement attack can be measured by the ratio of corrupt versus genuine versions resulting in the system. However, the more corrupt copies the attacker attempts to circulate (by setting a higher hops-to-live on insert), the greater the chance that an insert collision will be encountered, which would cause an increase in the number of genuine copies.

7   Conclusions

The Freenet network provides an effective means of anonymous information storage and retrieval. By using cooperating nodes spread over many computers in conjunction with an efficient adaptive routing algorithm, it keeps information anonymous and available while remaining highly scalable. Initial deployment of a test version is underway, and is so far proving successful, with tens of thousands of copies downloaded and many interesting files in circulation. Because of the anonymous nature of the system, it is impossible to tell exactly how many users there are or how well the insert and request mechanisms are working, but anecdotal evidence is so far positive. We are working on implementing a simulation and visualization suite which will enable more rigorous tests of the protocol and routing algorithm. More realistic simulation is necessary which models the effects of nodes joining and leaving simultaneously, variation in node capacity and bandwidth, and larger network sizes. We would also like to implement a public-key infrastructure to authenticate nodes and create a searching mechanism.

Acknowledgements. This material is partly based upon work supported under a National Science Foundation Graduate Research Fellowship.

References

1. S. Adler, "The Slashdot effect: an analysis of three Internet publications," *Linux Gazette* issue 38, March 1999.
2. Akamai, http://www.akamai.com/ (2000).
3. R. Albert, H. Jeong, and A. Barabási, "Error and attack tolerance of complex networks," *Nature* **406**, 378-382 (2000).
4. American National Standards Institute, American National Standard X9.30.2-1997: *Public Key Cryptography for the Financial Services Industry - Part 2: The Secure Hash Algorithm (SHA-1)* (1997).
5. R.J. Anderson, "The Eternity service," in *Proceedings of the 1st International Conference on the Theory and Applications of Cryptology (PRAGOCRYPT '96)*, Prague, Czech Republic (1996).
6. Anonymizer, http://www.anonymizer.com/ (2000).
7. O. Berthold, H. Federrath, and S. Köpsell, "Web MIXes: a system for anonymous and unobservable Internet access," in *Proceedings of the Workshop on Design Issues in Anonymity and Unobservability*, Berkeley, CA, USA. Springer: New York (2001).
8. D.L. Chaum, "Untraceable electronic mail, return addresses, and digital pseudonyms," *Communications of the ACM* **24**(2), 84-88 (1981).
9. Y. Chen, J. Edler, A. Goldberg, A. Gottlieb, S. Sobti, and P. Yianilos, "A prototype implementation of archival intermemory," in *Proceedings of the Fourth ACM Conference on Digital Libraries (DL '99)*, Berkeley, CA, USA. ACM Press: New York (1999).
10. B. Chor, O. Goldreich, E. Kushilevitz, and M. Sudan, "Private information retrieval," *Journal of the ACM* **45**(6), 965-982 (1998).
11. Church of Spiritual Technology (Scientology) v. Dataweb *et al.*, Cause No. 96/1048, District Court of the Hague, The Netherlands (1999).
12. I. Clarke, "A distributed decentralised information storage and retrieval system," unpublished report, Division of Informatics, University of Edinburgh (1999). Available at http://www.freenetproject.org/ (2000).
13. L. Cottrell, "Frequently asked questions about Mixmaster remailers," http://www.obscura.com/~loki/remailer/mixmaster-faq.html (2000).
14. R. Dingledine, M.J. Freedman, and D. Molnar, "The Free Haven project: distributed anonymous storage service," in *Proceedings of the Workshop on Design Issues in Anonymity and Unobservability*, Berkeley, CA, USA. Springer: New York (2001).
15. Distributed.net, http://www.distributed.net/ (2000).
16. D.J. Ellard, J.M. Megquier, and L. Park, "The INDIA protocol," http://www.eecs.harvard.edu/~ellard/India-WWW/ (2000).
17. Gnutella, http://gnutella.wego.com/ (2000).
18. I. Goldberg and D. Wagner, "TAZ servers and the rewebber network: enabling anonymous publishing on the world wide web," *First Monday* **3**(4) (1998).
19. D. Goldschlag, M. Reed, and P. Syverson, "Onion routing for anonymous and private Internet connections," *Communications of the ACM* **42**(2), 39-41 (1999).
20. Hash Cash, http://www.cypherspace.org/~adam/hashcash/ (2000).
21. T. Hong, "Performance," in *Peer-to-Peer*, ed. by A. Oram. O'Reilly: Sebastopol, CA, USA (2001).

22. B.A. Huberman and L.A. Adamic, "Internet: growth dynamics of the world-wide web," *Nature* **401**, 131 (1999).
23. S. Milgram, "The small world problem," *Psychology Today* **1**(1), 60-67 (1967).
24. Napster, http://www.napster.com/ (2000).
25. M.K. Reiter and A.D. Rubin, "Anonymous web transactions with Crowds," *Communications of the ACM* **42**(2), 32-38 (1999).
26. The Rewebber, http://www.rewebber.de/ (2000).
27. M. Richtel and S. Robinson, "Several web sites are attacked on day after assault shut Yahoo," *The New York Times*, February 9, 2000.
28. J. Rosen, "The eroded self," *The New York Times*, April 30, 2000.
29. A.S. Tanenbaum, *Modern Operating Systems*. Prentice-Hall: Upper Saddle River, NJ, USA (1992).
30. M. Waldman, A.D. Rubin, and L.F. Cranor, "Publius: a robust, tamper-evident, censorship-resistant, web publishing system," in *Proceedings of the Ninth USENIX Security Symposium*, Denver, CO, USA (2000).
31. D. Watts and S. Strogatz, "Collective dynamics of 'small-world' networks," *Nature* **393**, 440-442 (1998).
32. Zero-Knowledge Systems, http://www.zks.net/ (2000).

The Free Haven Project: Distributed Anonymous Storage Service

Roger Dingledine[1], Michael J. Freedman[1], and David Molnar[2]

[1] MIT
{arma, mfreed}@mit.edu
[2] Harvard University
dmolnar@fas.harvard.edu

Abstract. We present a design for a system of anonymous storage which resists the attempts of powerful adversaries to find or destroy any stored data. We enumerate distinct notions of anonymity for each party in the system, and suggest a way to classify anonymous systems based on the kinds of anonymity provided. Our design ensures the availability of each document for a publisher-specified lifetime. A reputation system provides server accountability by limiting the damage caused from misbehaving servers. We identify attacks and defenses against anonymous storage services, and close with a list of problems which are currently unsolved.

1 Introduction

Anonymous publication and storage services allow individuals to speak freely without fear of persecution, yet such systems remain poorly understood. Political dissidents must publish in order to reach enough people for their criticisms of a regime to be effective, yet they and their readers require anonymity. Less extreme examples involve cases in which a large and powerful private organization attempts to silence its critics by attacking either the critics themselves or those who make the criticism publically available. Additionally, the recent controversy over Napster and Gnutella has highlighted both a widespread demand for anonymous publication services for non-political purposes, and the consequences of such services failing to provide the anonymity expected.

Systems meeting these needs are just starting to be deployed, and the exact requirements and design choices are not yet clear. Events in 1999 and 2000 have highlighted some shortcomings of already deployed systems; the identification and removal of Napster users who downloaded Metallica songs[30] and the Gnutella Wall of Shame[12] are two examples. These shortcomings led to the development of a new generation of anonymous publication services, such as Freenet[11], which focus specifically on providing anonymity.

It is in this spirit that the Free Haven Project aims to design, implement, and deploy a functioning distributed anonymous *storage* service. We distinguish storage from publication in that storage services focus less on accessibility and

H. Federrath (Ed.): Anonymity 2000, LNCS 2009, pp. 67–95, 2001.

more on persistence of data. In the process, we hope to clarify some of the requirements for such systems and highlight design choices.

It is not enough simply to talk about "anonymous" storage and publication. In section 2, we enumerate the many different *kinds* of anonymity which cover different aspects of the system, all important for the realization of a truly anonymous system.

Free Haven meets these requirements with a design based on a community of servers called the *servnet*. Each server, or *servnet node*, holds pieces of some documents. These pieces are called *shares*. In addition, each servnet node has a persistent identification or *pseudonym* which allows it to be identified by other servnet nodes or potential Free Haven users. Section 3 describes the design of the Free Haven system and the operations that it supports, including inserting and retrieving documents.

We chose to use a network of pseudonymous servers in order to give each server a *reputation*. This reputation allows servers to be 'paid' without needing the robust digital cash scheme required for systems such as Anderson's Eternity Service[2]. Servers form contracts to store given shares for a certain period of time; successfully fulfilling the contract increases the server's reputation and consequently its ability to store some of its own data on other servnet nodes. This gives an incentive for each server to behave well as long as cheating servers can be identified. We show a technique for identifying cheating servers in section 3.7.

The overall idea is similar to the "give up space now, get space forever" scheme used in Intermemory[10], but allows servers to lose reputation if they start behaving badly. In section 3.9 we discuss the *reputation system*, which is the system that keeps track of trust in each server.

Some of the contracts between servers are formed when a user inserts data into the servnet. Most of them, however, will be formed when two servers swap shares by *trading*. Trading allows the servnet to be *dynamic* in the sense that servnet nodes can join and leave easily and without special treatment. To join, a servnet node starts building up a reputation by storing shares for others. To leave, a server trades away all of its shares for short-lived shares, and then waits for them to expire. The benefits and mechanisms of trading are described in section 3.5.

Such a system has powerful adversaries which can launch a range of attacks. We describe some attacks on the Free Haven design in section 4 and show how well the design does (or does not) resist each attack. We then compare our design with other systems aimed at anonymous storage and publication using the kinds of anonymity described in section 6, allowing us to distinguish systems which at first glance look very similar. We conclude with a list of challenges for anonymous publication and storage systems, each of which reflects a limitation in the current Free Haven design.

2   Anonymity for Anonymous Storage

The word "anonymous" can mean many different things. Some systems claim "anonymity" without specifying a precise definition. While the anonymity requirements of communication channels have been considered previously in depth [6, 19], we are not aware of a similar investigation into the requirements for publication and storage systems.

Information is stored in units called *documents*. The *author* of a document is the entity which initially created the document. The *publisher* of a document is the entity which places the document into the system. Documents may have *readers*, which are entities who retrieve the document from the system. An anonymous storage system may have *servers*, which are participants who provide special services required to keep the system running, such as dedicated disk space or bandwidth.

We do not give formal anonymity definitions here. Instead, we attempt to lay the groundwork for future definitions by enumerating different aspects of anonymity relevant to anonymous storage. This enumeration will allow us to compare Free Haven with related work.

In all of these notions of anonymity, there are at least three distinct subnotions based on what the adversary is assumed to already know. A document may be picked first, and then the adversary wishes to learn who authored, read, published, and so on. A user may be picked first, and the adversary wishes to know which documents the user authored, read, published, and so on. Finally, an adversary may know a document *and* a user, and then attempt to confirm its suspicion that the two are linked.

Author Anonymity: A system is author anonymous if an adversary cannot link an author to a document.

Publisher Anonymity: A system is publisher anonymous if it prevents an adversary from linking a publisher to a document.

Reader Anonymity: To say that a system has reader anonymity means that a document cannot be linked with its readers. Reader anonymity protects the privacy of a system's users.

Server Anonymity: Server anonymity means no server can be linked to a document. Here, the adversary always picks the document first. That is, given a document's name or other identifier, an adversary is no closer to knowing which server or servers on the network currently possess this document.

Document Anonymity: Document anonymity means that a server does not know which documents it is storing. Document anonymity is crucial if mere possession of some file is cause for action against the server, because it provides protection to a server operator even after his or her machine has been seized by an adversary. This notion is sometimes also known as 'plausible deniability', but see below under query anonymity.

Passive-server document anonymity means that if the server is allowed to look only at the data that it is storing, it is unable to figure out the contents of the document. This can be achieved via some sort of secret sharing mechanism. That is, multiple servers split up either the document or an encryption key that recreates the document (or both). An alternative approach is to encrypt the document before publishing, using some key which is external to the server.

Active-server document anonymity refers to the situation in which the server is allowed to communicate and compare data with all other servers. Since an active server may act as a reader and do document requests itself, active-server document anonymity seems difficult to achieve without some trusted party that can distinguish server requests from "ordinary" reader requests.

Query-Anonymity: Query anonymity means that the server cannot determine which document it is serving when satisfying a reader's request. For an overview of private information retrieval (PIR), see [31]. A weaker form of query anonymity is *server deniability* – the server knows the identity of the requested document, but no third party can be sure of its identity. Query anonymity can provide another aspect of 'plausible deniability'. This concept is related to deniable encryption[7].

It seems that some of these notions of anonymity may imply each other. We leave this investigation as future work.

2.1   Anonymity and Pseudonymity

So far, we have restricted ourselves to describing anonymity. We extend these notions to allow for the use of *pseudonyms*: if two transactions in the system can be linked, then the attributes which allow them to be linked make up a pseudonym. For example, in an *author-pseudonymous* system, the documents digitally signed by "Publius" could all be verified as "belonging to Publius" without anyone coming to know who "Publius" is in 'real life.'

Both anonymity and pseudonymity protect the privacy of the user's *location* and *true name*. Location refers to the actual physical connection to the system. The term "true name" was introduced by Vinge[48] and popularized by May[33] to refer to the legal identity of an individual. Knowing someone's true name or location allows you to hurt him or her.

Many different actions can be linked to the same pseudonym, while an anonymous system allows no linking at all. This allows the pseudonym to acquire a *reputation*. Free Haven uses pseudonyms to give each server a reputation; the reputation influences how much data a server can store and provides an incentive to act correctly.

2.2   Partial Anonymity

Often an adversary can gain some partial information about the users of a system, such as the fact that they have high-bandwidth connections or all live in California. Preventing an adversary from obtaining *any* such information may be impossible. Instead of asking "is the system anonymous?" the question shifts to "is it anonymous enough?"

We might say that a system is *partially anonymous* if an adversary can only narrow down a search for a user to one of a "set of suspects." If the set is large enough, it is impractical for an adversary to act as if any single suspect were guilty. On the other hand, when the set of suspects is small, mere suspicion may cause an adversary to take action against all of them.

An alternate approach to classifying levels of anonymity is presented by [41], where anonymity levels for users range from "exposed" to "beyond suspicion". These levels are in terms of an idealized adversary's reasonable belief that a user or set of users has performed some particular action.

Independently, Syverson and Stubblebine have developed a logic for talking about the adversary's view of a set of suspects[46]. The logic gives a formal meaning to a "set of suspects" and the notion of an adversary's belief.

2.3   Reasoning about Anonymity

Suppose an author signs his true name to a document before placing it into an anonymous publication system. Is the system still anonymous? This situation raises a crucial question: where does the responsibility of an anonymous publication system begin, and where does it end? What can such a system reasonably be expected to protect? We can give an answer to these questions by explicitly specifying a model for anonymous publication.

We model anonymous publication systems as a single entity (call it Ted) which coordinates communication between other entities in the network. In our model we have a set of senders $\{Alice_i\}$, and a set of recipients $\{Bob_j\}$. When an Alice sends a message to a Bob, Ted receives the message and delivers it to the appropriate Bob. The privacy characteristics of Ted as a communication channel define the level of anonymity that Ted provides.

These privacy characteristics include linkability; ability to reply, persistence of this ability, privacy of this reply; content leaks; channel leaks; persistence of speech; and authorized readers. We emphasize that Ted is not simply a "trusted third party" (despite the name), but provides a specific set of characteristics and does not provide others. For a more complete look at privacy characteristics, look at the first author's thesis [13].

In addition, we will need to complicate this notion with other characteristics, such as reliability of delivery, cost of using a given path, and availability and fragility of the network.

Thus if we can convince ourselves that a given anonymous publishing design is in some sense 'equivalent' to a Ted with certain privacy characteristics, then we can more easily reason about the level of protection provided by that design – by reasoning instead about Ted. In particular, we can ask the question "what is the responsibility of the system" with respect to Ted.

More formally, for each message M_i which $Alice_i$ sends, there is some probability distribution D_i which describes the chance of each Bob being the recipient of the message. If we can replace Ted with a decentralized system which provides an indistinguishable probability distribution for all messages, then we have shown that the decentralized system is equivalent to this Ted. This may give us an easier way to differentiate between the level of anonymity provided by various projects, because comparing Teds is easier and more intuitive than trying to reason about the effects of trading or caching issues directly.

This description requires significant work before it can become a formal model. For instance, we need to define exactly what we mean by privacy characteristics and enumerate them all; we need to figure out what it means for a probability distribution to be equivalent in this context; and we need to determine exactly how to describe a probability distribution over a complex system like Freenet or Mojo Nation.

3   The Free Haven Design

The overall system consists of the publication system, which is responsible for storing and serving documents, and the communications channel, which is responsible for providing confidential and anonymous communications between parties. This section focuses on the design of the publication system as a backend for the communications channel.

The agents in our publication system are the **publisher**, the **server**, and the **reader**. These agents are layered over the communications channel; currently they communicate with one another via addresses which are implemented as remailer reply blocks[34]. Remailer reply blocks are a collection of encrypted routing instructions which serve as an address for a pseudonym on the Cypherpunks remailer network.

Publishers are agents that wish to store documents in the service; servers are computers which store data for publishers; and readers are people who retrieve documents from the service.

Free Haven is based on a community of servers called the *servnet*. In this community, each server hosts data from the other servers in exchange for the opportunity to store its own data in the network. The servnet is dynamic: data moves from one server to another every so often, based on each server's trust of the others. Servers transfer data by trading. That is, the only way to introduce a new file into the system is for a server to use (and thus provide) more space on its local system. This new file will migrate to other servers by the process of trading.

Each server has a public key and one (or more) reply blocks, which together can be used to provide secure, authenticated, pseudonymous communication with that server. Every machine in the servnet has a database which contains the public keys and reply blocks of the other servers on the network.

Documents are split into shares and stored on different servers. Publishers assign an expiration date to documents when they are published; servers make a promise to keep their shares of a given document until its expiration date is reached. To encourage honest behavior, some servers check whether other servers "drop" data early, and decrease their trust of such servers. This trust is monitored and updated by use of a *reputation system*. Each server maintains a database containing its perceived reputation of the other servers.

3.1   Publication

When an author (call her Alice) wishes to store a new document in Free Haven, she must first identify a Free Haven server which is willing to store the document for her. Alice might do this by running a server herself. Alternatively, some servers might have public interfaces or have publically available reply blocks and be willing to publish data for others.

To introduce a file F into the servnet, the publishing server first uses Rabin's information dispersal algorithm (IDA) [40] to break the file into shares $f_1, \ldots, f_n$ where any k shares are sufficient to recreate F. The server then generates a key pair (PK_{doc}, SK_{doc}), constructs and signs a data segment for each share f_i, and inserts those segments as new data into its local server space. Attributes in each share include a timestamp, expiration information, the public key which was used to sign it (for integrity verification), information about share numbering, and the signature itself.

The robustness parameter k should be chosen based on some compromise between the importance of the file and the size and available space. A large value of k relative to n makes the file more brittle, because it will be unrecoverable after a few shares are lost. On the other hand, a smaller value of k implies a larger share size, since more data is stored in each share.

We maintain a content-neutral policy towards documents in the Free Haven system. That is, each server agrees to store data for the other servers without regard for the legal or moral issues for that data in any given jurisdiction. For more discussion of the significant moral and legal issues that anonymous systems raise, we refer to the first author's thesis[13].

3.2   Retrieval

Documents in Free Haven are indexed by $H(PK_{doc})$, the hash of the public key from the keypair which was used to sign the shares of the document. Readers must locate (or be running) a server that performs the document request. The reader generates a key pair $(PK_{client}, SK_{client})$ for this transaction, as well as a one-time remailer reply block. The server broadcasts a request $H(PK_{doc})$, along with the client's public key, PK_{client}, and the reply block. This request goes to all the other servers that the initial server knows about. These broadcasts can be queued and then sent out in bulk to conserve bandwidth.

Each server that receives the query checks to see if it has any shares with the requested hash of PK_{doc}. If it does, it encrypts each share using the public key PK_{client} enclosed in the request, and then sends the encrypted share through the remailer to the enclosed address. These shares will magically arrive out of the ether at their destination; once enough shares arrive (k or more), the client recreates the file and is done.

3.3   Share Expiration

Each share includes an expiration date chosen at share creation time. This is an absolute (as opposed to relative) timestamp indicating the time after which the hosting server may delete the share with no ill consequences. Expiration dates should be chosen based on how long the publisher wants the data to last; the publisher has to consider the file size and likelihood of finding a server willing to make the trade.

By allowing the publisher of the document to set its expiration time, Free Haven distinguishes itself from related works such as Freenet and Mojo Nation that favor frequently requested documents. We think this is the most useful approach to a persistent, anonymous data storage service. For example, Yugoslav phone books are currently being collected "to document residency for the close to one million people forced to evacuate Kosovo"[37]; those phone books might not have survived a popularity contest. The Free Haven system is designed to provide privacy for its users. Rather than being a publication system aimed at convenience like Freenet, it is designed to be a private low-profile storage system.

3.4 Document Revocation

Some publishing systems, notably Publius, allow for documents to be "unpublished" or *revoked*. Revocation has some benefits. It would allow the implementation of a read-write filesystem, and published documents could be updated as newer versions became available.

Revocation could be implemented by allowing the author to come up with a random private value x, and then publishing some hash $H(x)$ inside each share. To revoke the document, the author could broadcast his original value x to all servers as a signal to delete the document.

On the other hand, revocation allows new attacks on the system. Firstly, it complicates accountability. Revocation requests may not reach all shares of a file, due either to a poor communication channel or to a malicious adversary who sends unpublishing requests only to some members of the servnet. Secondly, authors might use the same hash for new shares, and thus "link" documents. Adversaries might do the same to make it appear that the same author published two unrelated documents. Thirdly, the presence of the hash in a share assigns "ownership" to a share that is not present otherwise. An author who remembers his x has evidence that he was associated with that share, thus leaving open the possibility that such evidence could be discovered and used against him later (that is, breaking forward author anonymity).

One of the most serious arguments against revocation was raised by Ross Anderson [2]. If the capability to revoke exists, an adversary has incentive to find who controls this capability, and threaten or torture him until he revokes the document.

We could address this problem by making revocation optional: the share itself could make it clear whether that share can be unpublished. If no unpublishing tag is present, there would be no reason to track down the author. (This solution is used in Publius.) But this too is subject to attack: if an adversary wishes to create a pretext to hunt down the publisher of a document, he can republish the document *with* a revocation tag, and use that as "reasonable cause" to target the suspected publisher.

Because the ability to revoke shares may put the original publisher in increased physical danger, as well as allow new attacks on the system, we chose to leave revocation out of the current design.

3.5   Trading

In the Free Haven design, servers periodically trade shares with each other. There are a number of reasons why servers trade:

To provide a cover for publishing: If trades are common, there is no reason to assume that somebody offering a trade is the publisher of a share. Publisher anonymity is enhanced.

To let servers join and leave: Trading allows servers to exit the servnet gracefully by trading for short-lived shares and then waiting for them to expire. This support for a dynamic network is crucial, since many of the participants in Free Haven will be well-behaved but transient relative to the duration of the longer-lived shares.

To permit longer expiration dates: Long-lasting shares would be rare if trading them involved finding a server that promised to be available for the next several years.

To accomodate ethical concerns of server operators: Frequent trading makes it easy and unsuspicious for server operators to trade away a particular piece of data with which they do not wish to be associated. If the Catholic Church distributes a list of discouraged documents, server operators can use the hash of the public key in each share to determine if that document is in the list, then trade away the share without compromising their reputation as a server or the availability of the document. In a nondynamic environment, the server would suffer a reputation hit if it chose not to keep the document. While we do not currently offer this functionality, trading allows this flexibility if we need it down the road. In particular, the idea of servers getting 'ISP exemption' for documents they hold currently seems very dubious.

To provide a moving target: Encouraging shares to move from server to server through the servnet means that there is never any specific, static target to attack.

The frequency of trading should be a parameter set by the server operator. When a server Alice wants to make a trade, she chooses another server Bob from her list of known servers (based on reputation), and offers a share x and a request for size and/or duration of a return share. If Bob is interested, he responds with a share y of his own.

Trades are considered "fair" based on the two-dimensional currency of $size \times duration$. That is, the bigger the size and the longer the document is to be held, the more expensive the trade becomes. The price is adjusted based on the preferences of the servers involved in the trade.

The negotiation is finalized by each server sending an acknowledgement of the trade (including a receipt, as described in section 3.6) to the other. In addition, each server sends a receipt to both the buddy of the share it is sending and the buddy of the share it is receiving; buddies and the accountability they provide are described in section 3.7. Thus, the entire trading handshake takes four rounds: the first two to exchange the shares themselves, and the next two to exchange receipts while at the same time sending receipts to the buddies.

By providing the receipt on the third round of the trading handshake, Alice makes a commitment to store the share y. Similarly, the receipt that Bob generates on the fourth round represents a commitment to store the share x. Bob could cheat Alice by failing to continue the protocol after the third step: in this case, Alice has committed to keeping the share from Bob, but Bob has not committed to anything. At this point, Alice's only recourse is to broadcast a complaint against Bob and hope that the reputation system causes others to recognize that Bob has misbehaved. The alternative is to use a fair exchange protocol[35,20], which is unreasonably communications-intensive without a trusted third party.

When Alice trades a share to a server Bob, Alice should keep a copy of the share around for a while, just in case Bob proves untrustworthy. This will increase the amount of overhead in the system by a factor of two or so (depending on duration), but provide greatly increased robustness. In this case, when a query is done for a share, the system responding should include a flag for whether it believes itself to be the "primary provider" of the data, or just happens to have a copy still lying around. The optimum amount of time requires further study.

3.6 Receipts

A receipt contains a hash of the public keys for the source server and the destination server, information about the share traded away, information about the share received, and a timestamp. For each share, it includes a hash of that document's key, which share number it was, its expiration date, and its size.

This entire set of information about the transaction is signed by server Alice. If Bob (or any other server) has to broadcast a complaint about the way Alice handled the transaction, furnishing this receipt along with the complaint will provide some rudimentary level of "proof" that Bob is not fabricating his complaint. Note that the expiration date of both shares is included within the receipt, and the signature makes this value immutable. Thus, other servers observing a receipt can easily tell whether the receipt is still "valid"—that is, they can check to see whether the share is still supposed to be kept on A. The size of each share is also included, so other servers can make an informed decision about how influential this transaction should be on their perceived reputation of the two servers involved in the trade.

We really aren't treating the receipt as proof of a transaction, but rather as proof of *half* of a transaction – an indication of a commitment to keep a given share safe. This is because the trading protocol is not bulletproof: the fact that Alice has a receipt from Bob could mean that they performed a transaction, or it could mean that they performed 3 out of the 4 steps of the transaction, and then Alice cheated Bob and never gave him a receipt. Thus, the most a given server can do when it detects a misbehaving server is broadcast a complaint and hope the reputation system handles it correctly.

3.7   Accountability

Malicious servers can accept document shares and then fail to store them. If enough shares are lost, the document is unrecoverable. Malicious servers can continue their malicious behavior unless there are mechanisms in place for identifying and excising them.

We propose a "buddy system" that creates an association between pairs of shares from a given document. Each share is responsible for maintaining information about the location of the other share, or *buddy*. When a share moves, it notifies its buddy.[1]

Periodically, a server holding a given share should query for its buddy, to make sure its buddy is still alive. If the server that is supposed to contain its buddy stops responding, the server with the share making the query is responsible for reporting an anomaly. This server announces which server had responsibility for the missing share when it disappeared. The results of this announcement are described below under section 3.9.

We considered allowing abandoned shares to optionally spawn a new share if their buddy disappears, but discarded this notion. Buddy spawning would make the service much more robust, since lost shares can be regenerated. However, such spawning could cause an exponential population explosion of shares for the wrong reasons. If two servers are out of touch for a little while but are not misbehaving or dead, both shares will end up spawning new copies of themselves. This is a strong argument for not letting shares replicate.

When a share x moves to a new machine, there are two *buddy notifications* sent to its buddy x'. But since the communications channel we have chosen currently has significant latency, a notification to x' might arrive after x' has already been traded to a new server. The old server is then responsible for forwarding these buddy notifications to the new server which it believes currently holds x'. Since the old server keeps a receipt as a record of the transaction, it can use this information to remember the new location of x'. The receipt, and thus the forwarding address, is kept by the old server until the share's expiration date has passed.

When a buddy notification arrives at a server which has traded away the share, the forwarder is checked and the notification is forwarded as appropriate. This forwarding is *not* done in the case of a document request, since this document request has presumably been broadcast to all servers in the servnet.

We have attempted to distinguish between the design goals of robustness and accountability. The system is quite robust because a document cannot be lost until a high percentage of its shares has been lost. Accountability, in turn, is provided by the buddy checking and notification system among shares, which protects against malicious or otherwise ill-behaving servers. Designers can choose the desired levels of robustness and accountability independently.

---

[1] More precisely, both the server it's moving from and the server it's moving to notify the buddy, as described in section 3.5.

3.8   Communications Channel

The Free Haven design requires a means of anonymously passing information between agents. One such means is the remailer network, including the Mixmaster remailers first designed by Lance Cottrell [17]. Other examples of anonymous communication channels are Onion Routing[47] and Zero Knowledge Systems' Freedom[18]. We refer to David Martin's thesis for a comprehensive overview of anonymous channels in theory and practice[32].

The design and implementation of an anonymous communication channel is an ongoing research topic [1,6,8,9,22,24,25,28,38,41]. The first implementation of the Free Haven design will use the Cypherpunk and Mixmaster remailers as its anonymous channel. For design details, see [16].

3.9   Reputation System

The reputation system in Free Haven is responsible for creating accountability. Accountability in a system so committed to anonymity is a difficult task. There are many opportunities to try to take advantage of other servers, such as merely neglecting to send a receipt after a trade, or wrongly accusing another server of losing a share. Some of the attacks are quite insidious and complex. Some history and issues to consider when developing a reputation system can be found in much more detail in [14].

Other systems exist which use reputations to ensure correct or "better" operation. The most directly relevant is the PGP Web of Trust model for public keys[39]. Other systems include the Advogato[29] and Slashdot message moderation systems, AOL's Instant Messenger[3], and much of real world commerce and law. In another vein, MANET[27] is a DARPA project to produce "a compromise-tolerant structure for information gathering."

Careful trust management should enable each server to keep track of which servers it trusts. Given the large number of shares into which documents are divided—and the relatively few shares required to reconstitute a document—no document should be irretrievably lost unless a large number of the servers prove evil.

Each server needs to keep two values that describe each other server it knows about: reputation and credibility. Reputation signifies a belief that the server in question will obey the Free Haven Protocol. Credibility represents a belief that the utterances of that server are valuable information. For each of these two values, each server also needs to maintain a confidence rating. This serves to represent the "stiffness" of the reputation and credibility values.

Servers should broadcast *referrals* in several circumstances, such as when they log the honest completion of a trade, when they suspect that a buddy of a share they hold has been lost, and when the reputation or credibility values for a server change substantially.

3.10 Introducers

Document request operations are done via broadcast. Each server wants to store its documents on a lot of servers, and if it finds a misbehaving server it wants to complain to as many as possible. But how do Free Haven servers discover each other?

The reputation system provides an easy method of adding new servers and removing inactive ones. Servers that have already established a good reputation act as "introducers." New servers can contact these introducers via the anonymous communication channel; the introducers will then broadcast referrals of this new server. This broadcast by itself does not imply an endorsement of the new server's honesty or performance; it is simply an indication that the new server is interested in performing some trades to increase its reputation. Likewise, a server may mark another as "dormant" given some threshold of unanswered requests. Dormant servers are not included in broadcasts or trade requests. If a dormant server starts initiating requests again, we conclude it is not actually dormant and resume sending broadcasts and offering trades to this server.

3.11 Implementation Status

The Free Haven system is still in its design stages. Although we have a basic proof-of-concept implementation, we still wish to firm up our design, primarily in the areas of accountability and bandwidth overhead. Before deploying any implementation, we want to convince ourselves that the Free Haven system offers better anonymity than current systems. Still, the design is sufficiently simple and modular to allow both a straightforward basic implementation and easy extensibility.

4 Attacks on Free Haven

Anonymous publishing and storage systems will have adversaries. The attacks and pressures that these adversaries may employ might be technical, legal, political, or social in nature. The system's design and the nature of anonymity it provides also affect the success of non-technical attacks.

We now consider possible attacks on the Free Haven system based on their respective targets: on the availability of documents and servnet operation; on the accountability offered by the reputation system; and on the various aspects of anonymity relevant to anonymous storage and publication, as described in section 2. For a more in-depth consideration of attacks, we refer to [13].

This list of attacks is not complete. In particular, we do not have a systematic discussion of what *kinds* of adversaries we expect. Such a discussion would begin with the most powerful adversaries possible, asking questions like "what if the adversary controls all but one of the servers in the servnet?" and scaling back from there. In analyzing systems like Free Haven, it is not enough to look at the everyday, plausible scenarios – every effort must be made to provide security against adversaries more powerful than any the designers ever expect. Indeed, adversaries have a way of being more powerful than anyone ever expects.

4.1   Attacks on Documents or the Servnet

Physical attack: Destroy a server.

Prevention: Because we are breaking documents into shares and only k of n shares are required to reconstruct the document, an adversary must find and destroy many servers before availability is compromised.

Legal action: Find a physical server, and prosecute the owner based on its contents.

Prevention: Because of the passive-server document anonymity property that the Free Haven design provides, the servnet operator may be able to plausibly deny knowledge of the data stored on his computer. This depends on the laws of the country in question.

Social pressure: Bring various forms of social pressure against server administrators. Claim that the design is patented or otherwise illegal. Sue the Free Haven Project and any known server administrators. Conspire to make a cause "unpopular", convincing administrators that they should manually prune their data. Allege that they "aid child pornographers" and other socially-unacceptable activities.

Prevention: We rely on the notion of jurisdictional arbitrage. Information illegal in one place is frequently legal in others. Free Haven's content-neutral policies mean that there is no reason to expect that the server operator has looked at the data he holds, which might make it more difficult to prosecute. We further rely on having enough servers in enough different jurisdictions that organizations cannot conspire to intimidate a sufficient fraction of servers to make Free Haven unusable.

Denial of service: Attack the servnet by continued flooding of queries for data or requests to join the servnet. These queries may use up all available bandwidth and processing power for a server.

Prevention: We must assume that our communications channel has adequate protection and buffering against this attack, such as the use of client puzzles [26]. Most communications channels we are likely to choose will not protect against this attack. This is a real problem.

Data flooding: Attempt to flood the servnet with shares, to use up available resources.

Prevention: The trading protocol implicitly protects against this type of denial of service attack against storage resources. The ability to insert shares, whether "false" or valid, is restricted to trading: that server must find another which trusts its ability to provide space for the share it would receive in return.

Similarly, the design provides protection against the corrupting of shares. Altering (or "spoofing") a share cannot be done, because the share contains a particular public key, and its integrity is verifiable by that key. Without knowledge of the original key which was used to create a set of shares, an adversary cannot forge new shares for a given document.

Share hoarding: Trade until a sufficient fraction of an objectionable document is controlled by a group of collaborating servers, and then destroy this document. Likewise, a sufficiently wealthy adversary could purchase a series of servers with very large drives and join the servnet, trading away garbage for "valuable data." He can trade away enough garbage to have a significant portion of all the data in the servnet on his drives.

Prevention: We rely on the overall size of the servnet to make it unlikely or prohibitively expensive for any given server or group of collaborating servers to obtain a sufficient fraction of the shares of any given document. The failure of this assumption would leave us with no real defense.

4.2   Attacks on the Reputation System

While attacks against the reputation system[2] are related to attacks directly against servers, their goal is not to directly affect document availability or servnet operation. Rather, these attacks seek to compromise the means by which we provide accountability for malicious or otherwise misbehaving servers.

Some of these attacks, such as temporary denials of service, have negative repercussions on the reputation of a server. These repercussions might be qualified as "unfair", but are best considered in the following light: if a server is vulnerable to these attacks, it may not be capable of meeting the specifications of the Free Haven protocol. Such a server is not worthy of trust to meet those specifications. The reputation system does not judge intent, merely actions.

Simple Betrayal: An adversary may become part of the servnet, act correctly long enough to gain a good reputation, then betray this trust by deleting files before their expiration dates.

Prevention: The reputation economy is designed to make this unprofitable. In order to obtain enough "currency" to store data, a server must reliably store data for others. Because a corrupt server must store at least as much data for others as the amount of data it deletes, such an adversary at worst does no overall harm to the system and may even help. This "50% useful work" ratio is a rather loose lower bound — it requires tricking a great number of high-credibility servers into recommending you. A server which engages in this behavior should be caught by the buddy system when it deletes each share.

Buddy Coopting: If a corrupt server (or group of colluding servers) can gain control of both a share and its buddy, it can delete both of them without repercussions.

Prevention: We assume a large quantity of shares in the servnet, making buddy capture more difficult. Servers also can modify their perceived reputation of a server if narrow trading parameters, or constant trading, suggests an attempt to capture buddies. More concretely, a possible work-around involves separating the reply-block addresses for trading and for buddy checking, preventing corrupt servers from acquiring the buddies of the shares they already have. Such an approach adds complexity, and possibly opens other avenues for attack.

---

[2] Parts of this section were originally written by Brian Sniffen in [43].

False Referrals: An adversary can broadcast false referrals, or even send them only to selected servers.
Prevention: The confidence rating of credibility can provide a guard against false referrals, combined with a single-reporting policy (i.e., at most one referral per target per source is used for reputation calculations).

Trading Receipt Games: While we believe that the signed timestamps attest to who did what and when, receipt-based accountability may be vulnerable to some attacks. Most likely, these will involve multi-server adversaries engaging in coordinated bait-and-switch games with target nodes.

Entrapment: There are several ways in which an adversary can appear to violate the protocols. When another server points them out, the adversary can present receipts which show her wrong and can accuse her of sending false referrals. A more thorough system of attestations and protests is necessary to defend against and account for this type of attack.

4.3   Attacks on Anonymity

There are a number of attacks which might be used to determine more information about the identity of some entity in the system.

Attacks on reader anonymity: An adversary might develop and publish on Free Haven a customized virus which automatically contacts a given host upon execution. A special case of this attack would be to include mime-encoded URLs in a document to exploit reader software which automatically loads URLs. Another approach might be to become a server on both the servnet and the mixnet, and attempt an end-to-end attack, such as correlating message timing with document requests. Indeed, servers could claim to have a document and see who requests it, or simply monitor queries and record the source of each query. Sophisticated servers might attempt to correlate readers based on the material they download, and then try to build statistical profiles and match them to people (outside Free Haven) based on activity and preferences; we prevent this attack by using each reply block for only one transaction.

Attacks on server anonymity: Adversaries might create unusually large shares, and try to reduce the set of known servers who might have the capacity to store such shares. This attacks the partial anonymity of these servers. An adversary could become a server, and then collect routine status and participation information (such as server lists) from other servers. This information might be extended with extensive knowledge of the bandwidth characteristics and limitations of the Internet to map servnet topology. By joining the mixnet, an adversary might correlate message timing with trade requests or reputation broadcasts. An alternate approach is simply to spread a Trojan Horse or worm which looks for Free Haven servers and reports which shares they are currently storing.

Attacks on publisher anonymity: An adversary could become a server and log publishing acts, and then attempt to correlate source or timing. Alternatively, he might look at servers who might recently have published a document, and try to determine who has been communicating with them recently.

There are entirely social attacks which can be very successful, such as offering a large sum of money for information leading to the current location of a given document, server, reader, etc.

We avoid or reduce the threat of many of these attacks by using an anonymous channel which supports pseudonyms for our communications. This prevents most or all adversaries from being able to determine the source or destination of a given message, or establish linkability between each endpoint of a set of messages. Even if server administrators are subpoenaed or otherwise pressured to release information about these entities, they can openly disclaim any knowledge.

5 Related Work

There are a number of projects and papers which discuss anonymous publication services. We start this section by providing an overview of some of the related projects and papers. After this section, we continue by examining the amount of anonymity that each project offers.

5.1 The Eternity Service

This work was inspired by Anderson's seminal paper on The Eternity Service[2]. As Anderson wrote, "[t]he basic idea is to use redundancy and scattering techniques to replicate data across a large set of machines (such as the Internet), and add anonymity mechanisms to drive up the cost of selective service denial attacks."

A publisher uploads a document and some digital cash, along with a requested file duration (cost would be based on document size and desired duration). In the simple design, a publisher would upload the document to 100 servers, and remember ten of these servers for the purposes of auditing their performance. Because he does not record most of the servers to whom he submitted the file, there is no way to identify which of the participating eternity servers are storing his file. Document queries are done via broadcast, and document delivery is achieved through one-way anonymous remailers.

There are issues which are not addressed in his brief paper: for instance, if documents are submitted anonymously but publishers are expected to remember a random sample of servers so they can audit them, what do they do when they find that some server is cheating? Anderson passes this responsibility on to the digital cash itself, so servers do not receive payment if they stop providing the associated service. He does not elaborate on the possible implications of this increased accountability to the anonymity of the publishers.

Eternity has several problems that hinder real-world deployment. Most importantly, Eternity relies on a stable digital cash scheme, which is not available today. There is no consideration to maintaining a dynamic list of available servers and allowing servers to smoothly join and leave. Anderson further proposes that a directory of files in the system should itself be a file in the system. However, without a mechanism for updating or revising files, this would appear very difficult to achieve.

5.2 Napster

The Napster service[36] is a company based around connecting people who are offering MP3 files to people who want to download them. While they provide no real anonymity and disclaim all legal liability, an important thing to note about the Napster service is that it is highly successful. Thousands of people use Napster daily to exchange music; if there were greater security (and comparable ease of use), we believe that many thousands more would participate. The existence of Napster shows that demand exists for a distributed storage and retrieval service.

5.3 Gnutella

Gnutella[15] is a peer-to-peer Napster clone. Developed originally by Nullsoft, it is currently maintained as an open source project. The Gnutella developers claim that querying the network is "anonymous." Analysis of the Gnutella protocol reveals features which make this statement problematic.

The header of a Gnutella packet includes two fields: *TTL* (time to live: the number of additional hops after which the packet should be dropped) and *Hops taken* (the number of hops this packet has made since its creation). The TTL is started at some default value based on the expected size of the network, and the Hops value is effectively an inverse of the TTL during the travel of the packet. Because the Hops value is 1 when the packet is initially sent, it is clear when a server is generating a query.

In addition, while the protocol is designed for a user to set up connections with his "friends", there is no infrastructure in place for finding new friends. Instead, the Gnutella site offers a default set of friends with which users can start. Most users will never change this file if the service is functional. This means that the actual network is a hierarchical system, as shown in pictures of the Gnutella network topology[45]. There are a small number of central nodes which would be ideal targets for collecting information about users and queries.

Moreover, only queries are protected. The actual downloads are done by point-to-point connections, meaning that the IP addresses of server and reader are both revealed to each other. This is done for reasons of efficiency, but it is far from anonymous.

Sites such as the Gnutella Wall of Shame [12], which attempts to entrap child pornographers using the Gnutella service, demonstrate that the direct file-transfer portion of the Gnutella service does not adequately protect the anonymity of servers or readers.

5.4 Eternity USENET

Adam Back proposed[4] a simpler implementation of the Eternity Service, using the existing Usenet infrastructure to distribute the posted files all around the world.

To achieve anonymity in publishing, Eternity Usenet employs cypherpunks type I and type II (mixmaster) remailers as gateways from email to newsgroups. Publishers PGP-sign documents which they wish to publish into the system: these documents are formatted in html, and readers make http search or query requests to 'Eternity Servers' which map these requests into NNTP commands either to a remote news server or a local news spool. With the initial implementation, the default list of newsgroups to read consists only of `alt.anonymous.messages`. The Eternity Server effectively provides an interface to a virtual web filesystem which posters populate via Usenet posts. Eternity Usenet uses normal Usenet mechanisms for retrieval, posting, and expiring, so publishers may not have control over the expiration time or propagation rate of their document.

Reader anonymity for Eternity USENET is provided when the system is used in "local proxy" mode, in which the user downloads the entire eternity newsgroup from a remote server. The server can still link the reader to that day's contents of an eternity newsgroup, so the reader anonymity is not as strong as we might like.

Back treats Usenet as an append-only file system. His system provides support for replacing files (virtual addresses) because newer posts signed with the same PGP key are assumed to be from the same publisher. Addresses are claimed on a first-come first-served basis, and PGP signatures provide linkability between an initial file at a given address and a revision of that file. It is not clear what happens when two addresses are claimed at once – since Usenet posts may arrive out of order, it would seem that there might be some subtle attacks against file coherency if two different Eternity Servers have a different notion of who owns a file.

While the system is not directly 'censorable' as we usually consider it, the term 'eternity' is misleading. Usenet posts expire based on age and size. Back does not provide an analysis of how long a given document will survive in the network. The task of making a feasible distributed store of Eternity documents is left as a future work.

5.5 Freenet

Like Gnutella, Freenet[11] is a peer to peer network of servers. When a user wishes to request a document, she hashes the name of that document (where she gets this name is outside the scope of Freenet) and then queries her own server about the location. If her server does not have it, it passes the query on to a nearby server which is "more likely" to have it. Freenet clusters documents with similar hashes nearby each other, and uses a routing protocol to route queries "downhill" until they arrive at the desired document.

Freenet bases document lifetime on the popularity of the document: frequently requested files get duplicated around the system, whereas infrequently requested files live in only a few places or die out completely. While this is a valid choice for a system that emphasizes availability and efficiency, it precludes certain uses of the system, e.g., the Yugoslav phone book collection project described earlier.

Freenet explicitly sets out to provide anonymity. Their goals include both sender and reader anonymity, as well as plausible deniability for servers – the notion that a server does not know the contents of documents it is storing. They provide this last, which we call passive-server document anonymity, by referencing files by $H(name)$ and having users encrypt the documents themselves with *name* before inserting them. This means that anybody who knows the original *name* string can decrypt the document, but the server storing the document is unable to invert $H(name)$ to determine *name*.

Freenet has a similar potential flaw with publisher and reader anonymity to Gnutella, due to the presence of the TTL and Depth (comparable to Hops) fields in the Freenet message headers. Freenet takes steps to avoid the problems of Gnutella's Depth and TTL headers by randomly assigning values to both fields, so that a depth of 1 does not necessarily mean that a request originated with a given node. Packets with TTL 1 are randomly either expired or forwarded onward.

Document requests are also sent through the caching-enabled network (rather than peer-to-peer as they are in Gnutella). Because of these measures, Freenet seems to provide 'more' anonymity than Gnutella.

Further, statistical attacks similar to those described in the Crowds [41] paper might work to pinpoint the location of a given reader or publisher; caching provides protection against this since the network topology for a given document changes after each request. These attacks need to be analyzed further.

Freenet makes files highly accessible and offers some level of anonymity. But since the choice to drop a file is a purely local decision, and since files that aren't requested for some time tend to disappear automatically, it can't guarantee a specified lifetime for a document. We expect that Freenet will provide a very convenient service for porn and popular audio files, but anything less popular will be driven off the system.

5.6   Mojo Nation

Mojo Nation[23] is another peer-to-peer design for robustly distributing resources. The basic operations it supports are publishing and retrieving, but it differs from other works because it employs a digital cash system to help protect against abuse of the system.

In Mojo Nation, a user who wishes to publish a document (call her Alice) uses error correction techniques to split the document into eight pieces, any four of which are sufficient to reconstruct. She then combines hashes of these eight pieces into a second document called a *sharemap*, and proceeds to do the eight-way splitting on this sharemap as well. She sends descriptions of the eight pieces of the sharemap to a separate agent called a *content tracker*, which is responsible for keeping track of how to reconstruct each document.

Other participants in the system serve as *block servers*. They offer storage on their machine to the system. Each block server has a bitmask which describes the subset of 'hash space' (hashes of a piece of a document, that is) that it will store. For each piece of her document, Alice pays the appropriate block server to store that piece. Alice learns about the set of block servers available and interested in her pieces through yet another agent called a *metatracker*. Multiple block servers overlapping on which bitmasks they cover allow for greater redundancy. Alice informs the *publication tracker* when she has published a document, and then other block servers might go to the block servers to which she published and purchase those document pieces.

To retrieve a document, Bob queries the content tracker and receives information about the eight pieces that will reconstruct the sharemap for that document. He asks the metatracker which block servers serve the address space for those pieces, and then purchases them from the appropriate block servers. He then reconstructs the sharemap, and from there repeats the process with the eight pieces of the document he is retrieving. Because of the error correction codes, Bob actually only needs to purchase any four of the pieces for each reconstruction phase.

As in Freenet, document pieces expire based entirely on choices local to the block server. That is, in most cases the most popular files will stay in the system, and the unpopular files will be dropped.

The entire system works based on currency called *mojo*. Participants in the system 'pay' mojo to other participants when they ask for a service that uses resources. In this way, Mojo Nation reduces the potential for damage from resource flooding attacks. A credit and reputation system allows the interactions to be streamlined based on trust built up from past experience.

Mojo Nation employs a centralized bank server to handle Mojo transactions and accounting. It's also not clear that the job of the metatracker can be done in a decentralized way (that is, without producing a bottleneck either because loss of the metatracker implies loss of that service, or because there's no way to smoothly inform participants of metatrackers joining and leaving the system). A good distributed (truly decentralized) anonymous electronic cash system would be much more useful, but as far as we know there still isn't one available.

The goals of Mojo Nation are not anonymity. Rather, they want to be a ubiquitous efficient distributed file distribution system which focuses on document accessibility. It is not yet clear how robust the overall system will be, but the design certainly appears to scale well.

5.7 Publius

Publius[49] attacks the problem of anonymous publishing from a different angle, employing a one-way anonymous channel to transfer documents from publishers to servers. The Publius protocol is designed to maintain availability of documents on these servers.

In this system, a publisher generates a key K for her document, and encrypts the document with this key. She performs Shamir's secret-sharing algorithm to build a set of n key shares, any k of which is sufficient to reconstruct K. From there, she chooses some n of the Publius servers and anonymously delivers the encrypted message plus one share to each of these n servers.

In this way, the document is replicated over each server, but the key is split over the n servers. Document reading is implemented by running a local web proxy on the reader's machine; the n addresses chosen as servers are concatenated into a URL which is presumably published or otherwise remembered. The local proxy fetches each share independently, reconstructs the original key K, and then decrypts the document.

The Publius system provides publisher anonymity by means of a one-way anonymous channel between authors and servers. In addition, because Shamir's secret-sharing protocol is used and each server only receives one share, Publius provides both computational and information-theoretic passive-server document anonymity: a single server is not able to determine anything about a document it stores.

A minor flaw is that readers cannot determine if a share is corrupt simply by examining it: the reader must request all of the shares and attempt to reconstruct in order to determine the integrity of a share. A verifiable secret sharing scheme [44] might make the system more efficient.

Publius provides no smooth decentralized support for adding new servers and excising dead or malicious servers. More importantly, Publius provides no accountability – there is no way to prevent publishers from entirely filling the system with garbage data.

6   An Analysis of Anonymity

We describe the protections offered for each of the broad categories of anonymity. In Table 1, we provide an overview view of Free Haven and the different publishing systems which we examined. We consider the level of privacy provided – computational (C) and perfect-forward (P-F) anonymity – by the various systems.

Computational anonymity means that an adversary modelled as a polynomial-time Turing Machine has no better than a $\frac{1}{2} + neg(k)$ chance of breaking anonymity, for some reasonable security parameter k and negligible function $neg(k)$. Perfect forward anonymity is analogous to perfect forward secrecy: a system is perfect forward anonymous if no information remains after a transaction is complete which could later identify the participants if one side or the other is compromised. This notion is a little bit trickier – think of it from the perspective of an adversary watching the user over a long period of time. Is there anything that the adversary can discover from watching several transactions that he can't discover from watching a single transaction?

Free Haven provides computational and perfect forward author anonymity, because authors communicate to publishers via an anonymous channel. Servers

Table 1. Anonymity Properties of Publishing Systems

Project	Publisher C	P-F	Reader C	P-F	Server C	P-F	Document C	Query C
Gnutella								
Eternity Usenet	+	+	?				+	
Freenet	+	+	?				+	
Mojo Nation	?	?					+	
Publius	+	+					+	
Free Haven	+	+	+	+	+		+	

trade to other servers via pseudonyms, providing computational but not perfect forward anonymity, as the pseudonyms can be broken later. Because trading is constant, however, Free Haven achieves publisher anonymity for publishers trying to trade away all shares of the same document. The use of IDA to split documents provides passive-server document anonymity, but the public key embedded in each share (which we require for integrity checking) makes it trivial for active servers to discover what they are storing. Because requests are broadcast via an anonymous channel, Free Haven provides computational reader anonymity, and different reply blocks used and then destroyed after each request provide perfect forward reader anonymity.

Gnutella fails to provide publisher anonymity, reader anonymity, or server anonymity because of the peer-to-peer connections for actual file transfer. Because Gnutella servers start out knowing the intended contents of the document they are offering, they also fail to provide document anonymity.

Eternity Usenet provides publisher anonymity via the use of one-way anonymous remailers. Server anonymity is not provided, because every Usenet server which carries the eternity newsgroup is a server. Adam Back has pointed out that passive-server document anonymity can be provided by encrypting files with a key derived from the URL; active servers might find the key and attempt to decrypt stored documents. Reader anonymity is not provided by open public proxies unless the reader uses an anonymous channel because the proxy can see the content and timing of a user's queries and downloads. For local proxies, which connect to a separate news server, however, the situation is better because the news server knows only what the user downloads. Even so, this is not quite satisfactory, because the user can be tied by the server to the contents of the eternity newsgroup at a certain time.

Freenet achieves passive-server document anonymity because servers are unable to reverse the hash of the document name to determine the key with which to decrypt the document. For active-server document anonymity, the servers can check whether they are carrying a particular key, but cannot easily match a stored document to a key due to the hash function. Server anonymity is not provided because given a document key, it is very easy to locate a server that is carrying that document – querying any server at all will result in that server carrying the document! Because of the TTL and Hops fields for both reading and publishing, it is also not clear that Freenet achieves publisher or reader anonymity, although they are much better in these regards than Gnutella. We note that the most recent Freenet design introduces randomized TTL and Hops fields in each request, and plans are in the works to allow a publish or retrieve operation to traverse a mixnet chain before entering the Freenet system. These protections will make attacks based on tracking queries much more difficult.

Mojo Nation achieves passive-server document anonymity, because the server holding a share doesn't know how to reconstruct that document. The Mojo Nation design is amenable to integrating publisher anonymity down the road – a publisher can increase his anonymity by paying more Mojo and chaining requests through participants that act as 'relays'. The specifics of prepaying the path through the relays are not currently being designed. It seems possible that this technique could be used to ensure reader anonymity as well, but the payment issues are even more complex. Indeed, the supplied digital cash model is not even anonymous currently; users need to uncomment a few lines in the source, and this action breaks Chaum's patents.

Publius achieves document anonymity because the key is split between the n servers, and without sufficient shares of the key a server is unable to decrypt the document that it stores. The secret sharing algorithm provides a stronger form of this anonymity (albeit in a storage-intensive manner), since a passive server really can learn nothing at all about the contents of a document that it is helping to store. Because documents are published to Publius through a one-way anonymous remailer, it provides publisher anonymity. Publius provides no support for protecting readers by itself, however, and the servers containing a given file are clearly marked in the URL used for retrieving that file. Readers can use a system such as ZKS Freedom or Onion Routing to protect themselves, but servers may still be liable for storing "bad" data.

We see that systems can often provide publisher anonymity via one-way communication channels, effectively removing any linkability; removing the need for a reply block on the anonymous channel means that there is "nothing to crack". The idea of employing a common mixnet as a communications channel for each of these publication systems is very appealing. This would mean that we could leave most of the anonymity concerns to the communication channel itself, and provide a simple back-end file system or equivalent service to transfer documents between agents. Thus the design of the back-end system could be based primarily on addressing other issues such as availability of documents, protections against flooding and denial of service attacks, and accountability in the face of this anonymity.

7   Future Work

Our experience designing Free Haven revealed several problems which have no simple solutions; further research is required. We state some of these problems here and refer to the first author's thesis[13] for in-depth consideration.

Deployed Free Low-Latency Pseudonymous Channel: Free Haven requires pseudonyms in order to create server reputations. The only current widely deployed channels which support pseudonyms seem to be the Cypherpunk remailer network[34] and ZKS Freedom mail. The Cypherpunk and ZKS version 1 networks run over SMTP and consequently have high latency. This high latency complicates protocol design. The recently announced version 2 of ZKS Freedom mail runs over POP and may offer more opportunity for the kind of channel we desire.

Accountability and Reputation: We found it extremely difficult to reason about the accountability in Free Haven, especially when considering the "buddy system." At the same time, accountability is critical to ensuring that documents remain available in the system. Future work in this area might develop an "anonymous system reputation algebra" for formally reasoning about a server's reliability based on various circumstances – this would allow us to verify trust protocols. We sketch this problem in more detail in [14].

Modelling and Metrics: When desiging Free Haven, we made some choices, such as the choice to include trading, based only on our intuition of what would make a robust, anonymous system. A mathematical model of anonymous storage would allow us to test this intuition and run simulations. We also need *metrics*: specific quantities which can be measured and compared to determine which designs are "better." For example, we might ask "how many servers must be compromised by an adversary for how long before any document's availability is compromised? before a specific targeted document's availability is compromised?" or "how many servers must be compromised by an adversary for how long before the adversary can link a document and a publisher?" This modelling might follow from the work of Gulcu and Tsudik[22], Kesdogan, Egner, and Bschkes[28], and Berthold, Federrath, and Kohntopp[6] which apply statistical modelling to mix-nets.

Formal Definition of Anonymity: Closely related to the last point is the need to formalize the "kinds of anonymity" presented in section 2. By formally defining anonymity, we can move closer to providing meaningful *proofs* that a particular system provides the anonymity we desire. We might leverage our experience with cryptographic definitions of semantic security and non-malleability to produce similar definitions and proofs[21]. A first step in this direction might be to carefully explore the connection remarked by Rackoff and Simon between secure multiparty computation and anonymous protocols[42].

Usability Requirements and Interface: We stated in the introduction that we began the Free Haven Project out of concern for the rights of political dissidents. Unfortunately, at this stage of the project, we have contacted few political dissidents, and as a consequence do not have a clear idea of the usability and interface requirements for an anonymous storage system. Our concern is heightened by a recent paper which points out serious deficiencies in PGP's user interface [50].

Efficiency: It seems like nearly everyone is doing a peer-to-peer system or WWW replacement these days. Which one will win? Adam Back pointed out[5] that in many cases, the efficiency and perceived benefit of the system is more important to an end user than its anonymity properties. This is a major problem with the current Free Haven design: we emphasize a quality relatively few potential users care about at the expense of something nearly everyone cares about. Is there a way to create an anonymous system with a tolerable loss of perceived efficiency compared to its non-anonymous counterpart? And what does "tolerable" mean, exactly?

We consider the above to be challenge problems for anonymous publication and storage systems.

8   Conclusion

Free Haven is a decentralized storage service which provides anonymity to publishers, readers, and servers, provides a dynamic network, and ensures the availability of each document for a publisher-specified lifetime. None of these requirements is new by itself, but Free Haven addresses all of them at once.

The current Free Haven design is unsuitable for wide deployment, because of several remaining problems. The primary problem is efficiency. An inefficient design will lead to a system with few users. A system with few users will not provide the anonymity we desire.

Free Haven uses inefficient broadcasts for communication. One way to address this problem is by coupling Free Haven with a widely-deployed efficient file sharing service such as Freenet or Mojo Nation. Popular files will be highly accessible from within the faster service; Free Haven answers queries for less popular documents which have expired in this service.

Filling this role requires facing problems particular to a long-term persistent storage service. Without the requirement of long-term persistent storage, strong accountability measures are less necessary. Without these measures, computational overhead can be greatly lowered, making unnecessary many communications that are used to manage reputation metrics. And without the requirement for such anonymity and the resulting latency from the communications channel, readers could enjoy much faster document retrieval. Solving each of these problems is important: even if Free Haven is not the utility of first resort, it must respond to requests in a timely and reliable manner.

These problems are far from being solved. Until the risks involved in using such systems can be better evaluated, they cannot be used in good conscience for situations where failure is not an option. Much more work remains.

Acknowledgements. Professor Ronald Rivest provided invaluable assistance as Roger's Masters and Michael's Bachelors thesis advisor and caused us to think hard about our design decisions. Professor Michael Mitzenmacher made possible David's involvement in this project and provided insightful comments on information dispersal and trading. Beyond many suggestions for overall design details, Brian Sniffen provided the background for the reputation system, and

Joseph Sokol-Margolis was useful for considering attacks on the system. Andy Oram was instrumental in helping to restructure the paper to improve flow and clarity. Adam Back and Theodore Hong commented on our assessment of their systems and made our related work section much better. Wei Dai caught a very embarrassing error in our description of signature schemes, for which we thank him. Furthermore, we thank Susan Born, Nathan Mahn, Jean-François Raymond, Anna Lysyanskaya, Adam Smith, and Brett Woolsridge, for further insight and feedback.

References

1. Masayuki Abe. Universally verifiable mix-net with verification work independent of the number of servers. In Advances in Cryptology – EUROCRYPT '98, pages 437–447.
2. Ross Anderson. The Eternity Service.
   http://www.cl.cam.ac.uk/users/rja14/eternity/eternity.html.
3. Aol instant messenger. http://www.aol.com/aim.
4. Adam Back. The Eternity Service.
   http://phrack.infonexus.com/search.phtml?view&article=p51-12.
5. Adam Back. Re: another distributed project.
   http://freehaven.net/archives/freehaven/dev/Aug-2000/msg00027.html.
6. Oliver Berthold, Hannes Federrath, and Marit Kohntopp. Anonymity and unobservability on the Internet. In Workshop on Freedom and Privacy by Design: CFP 2000, 2000.
7. Ran Canetti, Cynthia Dwork, Moni Naor, and Rafail Ostrovsky. Deniable encryption. In Advances in Cryptology – CRYPTO '97.
8. David Chaum. Untraceable electronic mail, return addresses, and digital pseudonyms. Communications of the ACM, 4(2), February 1982.
9. David Chaum. The dining cryptographers problem: Unconditional sender and recipient untraceability. Journal of Cryptology, 1:65–75, 1988.
10. Yuan Chen, Jan Edler, Andrew Goldberg, Allan Gottlieb, Sumeet Sobti, and Peter Yianilos. A prototype implementation of archival intermemory. In Proceedings of the fourth ACM Conference on Digital libraries (DL '99), 1999.
11. Ian Clarke. The Free Network Project. http://freenet.sourceforge.net/.
12. The Cleaner. Gnutella wall of shame. http://www.zeropaid.com/busted/.
13. Roger Dingledine. The Free Haven Project. Master's thesis, MIT, 2000.
14. Roger Dingledine, Michael J. Freedman, and David Molnar. Accountability. In Peer-to-peer. O'Reilly and Associates, 2001.
15. Ian Hall-Beyer et. al. Gnutella. http://gnutella.wego.com/.
16. Michael J. Freedman. Design and Analysis of an Anonymous Communication Channel for the Free Haven Project.
   http://theory.lcs.mit.edu/~cis/cis-theses.html, May 2000.
17. Electronic Frontiers Georgia (EFGA). Anonymous remailer information.
   http://anon.efga.org/Remailers/.
18. Ian Goldberg and Adam Shostack. Freedom network 1.0 architecture, November 1999.
19. Ian Goldberg, David Wagner, and Eric Brewer. Privacy-enhancing technologies for the internet. In Proceedings of IEEE COMPCON '97.

20. O. Goldreich, S. Even, and Lempel. A randomized protocol for signing contracts. In Advances in Cryptology – CRYPTO '82.
21. Oded Goldreich. Modern Cryptography, Probabilistic Proofs, and Pseudo-Randomness. Springer-Verlag, 1999.
22. C. Gulcu and G. Tsudik. Mixing e-mail with Babel. In Proceedings of the ISOC Symposium on Network and Distributed System Security, pages 2–16, 1996.
23. Autonomous Zone Industries. Mojonation. http://www.mojonation.com/.
24. M. Jakobsson. Flash mixing. In Principles of Distributed Computing PODC '99.
25. M. Jakobsson. A practical mix. In Advances in Cryptology – EUROCRYPT '98.
26. Ari Juels and John Brainard. Client puzzles: A cryptographic defense against connection depletion attacks. In Proceedings of the 1999 Network and Distributed System Security Symposium, February 1999.
27. Clifford Kahn, David Black, and Paul Dale. MANET: Mobile agents for network trust. http://www.darpa.mil/ito/psum1998/F255-0.html, 1998.
28. Dogan Kesdogan, Jan Egner, and Roland Buschkes. Stop and go mixes: Providing probabilistic anonymity in an open system. In 1998 Information Hiding Workshop, pages 83–98.
29. Raph Levien. Advogato's trust metric. http://www.advogato.org/trust-metric.html.
30. Mark Lewis. Metallica sues Napster, universities, citing copyright infringement and RICO violations. http://www.livedaily.com/archive/2000/2k04/wk2/MetallicaSuesNapster, Univ.html.
31. Tal Malkin. Private Information Retrieval. PhD thesis, MIT. see http://theory.lcs.mit.edu/ cis/cis-theses.html.
32. David Michael Martin. PhD thesis, Boston University, 2000. http://www.cs.du.edu/~dm/anon.html.
33. Tim May. Cyphernomicon. http://www2.pro-ns.net/ crypto/cyphernomicon.html.
34. David Mazieres and M. Frans Kaashoek. The design and operation of an e-mail pseudonym server. In 5th ACM Conference on Computer and Communications Security, 1998.
35. S. Micali. Certified e-mail with invisible post-offices. In Talk at RSA '97.
36. Napster. http://www.napster.com/.
37. University of Michigan News and Information Services. Yugoslav phone books: perhaps the last record of a people. http://www.umich.edu/~newsinfo/Releases/2000/Jan00/r012000e.html.
38. A. Pfitzmann, B. Pfitzmann, and M. Waidner. ISDN-Mixes : Untraceable communication with small bandwidth overhead. In GI/ITG Conference: Communication in Distributed Systems, pages 451–463. Springer-Verlag, 1991.
39. PGP FAQ. http://www.faqs.org/faqs/pgp-faq/.
40. Michael O. Rabin. Efficient dispersal of information for security, load balancing, and fault tolerance, April 1989.
41. Michael K. Reiter and Aviel D. Rubin. Crowds: Anonymity for web transactions. DIMACS Technical Report, 97(15), April 1997.
42. Simon and Rackoff. Cryptographic defense against traffic analysis. In STOC 1993, pages 672–681, 1993.
43. Brian T. Sniffen. Trust Economies in the Free Haven Project. http://theory.lcs.mit.edu/~cis/cis-theses.html, May 2000.
44. Markus Stadler. Publicly verifiable secret sharing. In EUROCRYPT '96, 1996. http://citeseer.nj.nec.com/stadler96publicly.html.

45. Steve Steinberg.   Gnutellanet maps.   http://gnutella.wego.com/file_depot/0-10000000/110000-120000/116705/folder/151713/network3.jpg.
46. Paul Syverson and Stuart Stubblebine. Group principals and the formalization of anonymity. In World Congress on Formal Methods 1999, 1999.
47. P.F. Syverson, D.M. Goldschlag, and M.G. Reed. Anonymous connections and onion routing. In Proceedings of the 1997 IEEE Symposium on Security and Privacy, May 1997.
48. Vernor Vinge. True Names. Short story.
49. Marc Waldman, Aviel Rubin, and Lorrie Cranor. Publius: A robust, tamper-evident, censorship-resistant and source-anonymous web publishing system.
50. Alma Whitten and J.D. Tygar. Why johnny can't encrypt. In USENIX Security 1999, 1999.
    http://www.usenix.org/publications/library/proceedings/sec99/whitten.html.

Towards an Analysis of Onion Routing Security

Paul Syverson[1], Gene Tsudik[2], Michael Reed[1], and Carl Landwehr[3]*

[1] Center for High Assurance Computer Systems, Code 5540, Naval Research
Laboratory, Washington DC 20375, USA.
{lastname}@itd.nrl.navy.mil
[2] Information and Computer Science Dept., University of California, Irvine CA
92697-3425, USA.
gts@ics.uci.edu
[3] Mitretek Systems, Inc., 7525 Colshire Drive, McLean VA 22102, USA.
Carl.Landwehr@mitretek.org

Abstract. This paper presents a security analysis of Onion Routing, an
application independent infrastructure for traffic-analysis-resistant and
anonymous Internet connections. It also includes an overview of the current system design, definitions of security goals and new adversary models.

Keywords: Security, privacy, anonymity, traffic analysis.

1 Introduction

This paper presents a security analysis of Onion Routing, an application independent infrastructure for traffic-analysis-resistant and anonymous Internet
connections. It also includes an overview of the new system, definitions of security goals and new adversary models. Although the conceptual development and
informal arguments about the security of Onion Routing have been presented
elsewhere [9,15,16,10], we have not previously attempted to analyze or quantify the security provided against specific attacks in detail. That is the primary
contribution of this paper.

The primary goal of Onion Routing is to provide strongly private communications in real time over a public network at reasonable cost and efficiency.
Communications are intended to be private in the sense that an eavesdropper
on the public network cannot determine either the contents of messages flowing
from Alice and Bob or even whether Alice and Bob are communicating with
each other. A secondary goal is to provide anonymity to the sender and receiver,
so that Alice may receive messages but be unable to identify the sender, even
though she may be able to reply to those messages.

An initial design has been implemented and fielded to demonstrate the feasibility of the approach. This prototype, which uses computers operating at the
Naval Research Laboratory in Washington, D.C., to simulate a network of five

---

* Work by Carl Landwehr was primarily performed while employed at the Naval Research Laboratory.

H. Federrath (Ed.): Anonymity 2000, LNCS 2009, pp. 96–114, 2001.

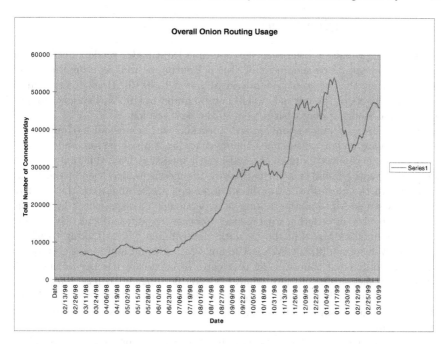

Fig. 1. 30 Day Rolling Average of Onion Routing Usage: 3/1/98 – 3/1/99

Onion Routing nodes, attracted increasing use over the two years it was available. While in operation, users in more than sixty countries and all seven major US top level domains initiated up to 1.5 million connections per month through the prototype system; cf. also Figure 1, which shows connections per day averaged over the preceding 30 days. This demand demonstrates both an interest in the service and the feasibility of the approach. However, the initial prototype lacked a number of features needed to make the system robust and scalable, and to resist insider attacks or more extensive eavesdropping. A design for a second generation system that addresses these issues is complete, and the processes required to release the source code for public distribution have been initiated. Several companies have contacted NRL to with intent to commercially license Onion Routing.

This paper analyzes the protection provided by the second generation design. We start by describing, briefly, the architecture and features of the second generation system relevant to our analysis. In section 3 we define security goals for anonymity and/or traffic-analysis-resistance. In section 4 we give some assumptions about the configuration of our network. In section 5, we set out our adversary model. In section 6, we present a security assessment based on the definitions and assumptions made in earlier sections. Finally, we compare Onion Routing to systems with similar goals, most specifically with Crowds [17].

2   Onion Routing Overview

This section provides a brief overview of Onion Routing for readers not familiar
with it. Conceptual development of Onion Routing as well as a description of
the design for the previous system can be found in [9,16]. Brief description of
different aspects of the current design can be found in [10,20]. Readers familiar
with Onion Routing may wish to skip to the next section.

Onion Routing builds anonymous connections within a network of onion routers, which are, roughly, real-time Chaum Mixes [3]. A Mix is a store-and-forward
device that accepts a number of fixed-length messages from different sources,
performs cryptographic transformations on the messages, and then forwards the
messages to the next destination in an order not predictable from the order of
inputs. A single Mix makes tracking of a particular message either by specific
bit-pattern, size, or ordering with respect to other messages difficult. By routing
through numerous Mixes in the network, determining who is talking to whom
is made even more difficult. While Chaum's Mixes could store messages for an
indefinite amount of time waiting to receive an adequate number of messages
to mix together, a Core Onion Router (COR) is designed to pass information
in real time, which limits mixing and potentially weakens the protection. Large
volumes of traffic (some of it perhaps synthetic) can improve the protection of
real time mixes.

Onion Routing can be used with applications that are proxy-aware, as well as
several non-proxy-aware applications, without modification to the applications.
Supported protocols include HTTP, FTP, SMTP, rlogin, telnet, NNTP, finger,
whois, and raw sockets. Proxies have been designed but not development for
Socks5, DNS, NFS, IRC, HTTPS, SSH, and Virtual Private Networks (VPNs).

The proxy incorporates three logical layers: an optional application specific
privacy filter, an application specific translator that converts data streams into
an application independent format of fixed length cells accepted by the Onion
Routing (OR) network, and an onion management layer (the onion proxy) that
builds and handles the anonymous connections. The onion proxy is the most trusted component in the system, because it knows the true source and destination
of the connections that it builds and manages. To build onions and hence define
routes the onion proxy must know the topology and link state of the network,
the public certificates of nodes in the network, and the exit policies of nodes in
the network.

Onion Routing's anonymous connections are protocol independent and exist
in three phases: connection setup, data movement, and connection termination.
Setup begins when the initiator creates an onion, which defines the path of
the connection through the network. An onion is a (recursively) layered data
structure that specifies properties of the connection at each point along the
route, e.g., cryptographic control information such as the different symmetric
cryptographic algorithms and keys used during the data movement phase. Each
onion router along the route uses its private key to decrypt the entire onion that
it receives. This operation exposes the cryptographic control information for this
onion router, the identity of the next onion router in the path for this connection,

and the embedded onion. The onion router pads the embedded onion to maintain a fixed size and sends it onward. The final onion router in the path connects to a responder proxy, which will forward data to the remote application.

After the connection is established, data can be sent in both directions. The initiator's onion proxy receives data from an application, breaks it into fixed size cells (128 bytes long, at present), and encrypts each cell multiple times – once for each onion router the connection traverses – using the algorithms and keys that were specified in the onion. As a cell of data moves through the anonymous connection, each onion router removes one layer of encryption, so the data emerges as plaintext from the final onion router in the path. The responder proxy regroups the plaintext cells into the data stream originally submitted by the application and forwards it to the destination. For data moving backward, from the recipient to the initiator, this process occurs in the reverse order, with the responder proxy breaking the traffic into cells, and successive onion routers encrypting it using (potentially) different algorithms and keys than the forward path. In this case the initiator's onion proxy decrypts the data multiple times, regroups the plaintext cells, and forwards them to the application.

Normally, either the application that initiates a connection or the destination server will terminate it. Since onion routers may fail, however, any onion router involved in a connection can cause that connection to be terminated. To an application (either at the initiating site or at the destination), such a failure looks the same as if the remote site had simply closed its TCP connection.

Longstanding TCP connections (called 'links' or 'thick pipes') between CORs define the topology of an OR network. Links are negotiated pairwise by CORs in the course of becoming neighbors. All traffic passing over a link is encrypted using stream ciphers negotiated by the pair of onion routers on that link. This cipher is added on top of the onion layers by the COR sending a cell across a link and stripped off again by the receiving COR. Since TCP guarantees sequential delivery, synchronization of the stream ciphers is not an issue. To support a new anonymous connection, an onion proxy creates a random route within the current OR network topology. The (fixed) size of an onion would limit a route to a maximum of 11 nodes in the current implementation. Because connections can be tunneled, however, arbitrarily long routes are possible, even though they will become impractical at some point because of the resulting network latencies.

An eavesdropper or a compromised onion router might try to trace packets based on their content or on the timing of their arrival and departure at a node. All data (onions, content, and network control) is sent through the Onion Routing network in uniform-sized cells (128 bytes). Because it is encrypted (or decrypted) as it traverses each node, a cell changes its appearance (but not its size) completely from input to output. This prevents an eavesdropper or a compromised onion router from following a packet based on its bit pattern as it moves across the Onion Routing network. In addition, all cells arriving at an onion router within a fixed time interval are collected and reordered randomly (i.e., "mixed") before they are sent to their next destinations, in order to prevent an eavesdropper from relating an outbound packet from a router with an earlier inbound one based on timing or sequence of arrival.

If traffic levels are low and requirements for real-time transmission are high, waiting for enough traffic to arrive so that mixing provides good hiding might cause unacceptable transmission delays. In this case, padding (synthetic traffic) can be added to the thick pipes. Conversely, an attacker might try to use a pulse of traffic to track cells flowing through the system. This attack can be made more difficult by imposing limits on the traffic flow over particular links, though this strategy can increase latency.

If a link between two CORs goes down or comes up, that information is propagated among the active CORs and proxies (again using the fixed cell size, and with the same protections as other OR traffic). This information permits proxies to build onions with feasible routes. Since routes are permitted to have loops of length greater than one hop, the number of active nodes does not limit the route length, as long as at least two nodes are active.

An onion router cannot tell the ultimate destination of traffic it forwards to another onion router. The Responder Proxy running on the last onion router in a path, however, can determine where traffic leaving the OR network is bound. Some operators of onion routers may wish to restrict the set of destinations (non onion-router destinations) to which their machines will forward traffic. For example, a commercial onion router might decide that it would forward traffic only to .com sites, or a government onion router might decide only to permit outgoing traffic destined for .gov sites. We call this an "exit policy," and have implemented software so that sites can define and enforce such policies. The onion proxy creating a path through the OR network needs information about exit policies, so that it doesn't create an infeasible route, and the second generation system provides this information. The use of this mechanism could of course warp the traffic flows through the network and might therefore permit some inferences about traffic flow. To counteract the ability of compromised CORs to lie about network topography, public keys, or exit policies, an external audit and verification system for this information has been built into every component. Without both mechanisms, however, we believe far fewer institutions would be willing to operate ORs, and the decreased level of participation could also reduce the effectiveness of our scheme.

The initial OR prototype, since it was not intended for wide deployment, took a number of short cuts. It enforced a fixed length (five hops) for all routes. It did not provide a method for maintaining topology information or communicating topology information among nodes. It did not provide padding or bandwidth limiting facilities. All of these mechanisms are included in the second generation system. To ease its widespread distribution, the second generation system does not include actual cryptographic software. Cryptographic functions are invoked via calls to Crypto APIs, and the operator must provide cryptographic libraries to implement those APIs.

3   Security Goals

Protection of communications against traffic analysis does not require support for anonymous communication. By encrypting data sent over a traffic-analysis-resistant connection, for example, endpoints may identify themselves to one another without revealing the existence of their communication to the rest of the network. However, traffic analysis is a potent tool for revealing parties in conversation, thereby compromising a communication that was intended to be anonymous. Thus, we consider goals for anonymous, as well as private, communication. In fact, the goals for these two cases differ very little; the distinction comes in the specification of the adversary.

There are various basic properties relating initiators, responders, and connections that we wish to protect. Pfitzmann and Waidner[22] have described sender and receiver anonymity as respectively hiding the identity of the sender or receiver of a particular message from an attacker, and unlinkability as a somewhat weaker property, preventing an attacker from linking the physical message sent by the sender with the physical message received by the recipient. In a similar vein, we define:

Sender activity: the mere fact that a sender is sending something.
Receiver activity: the mere fact that a receiver is receiving something.[1]
Sender content: that the sender sent a particular content.
Receiver content: that the receiver received a particular content.

These are the basic protections with which we will be concerned. We will also be concerned with more abstract anonymity protection. For example, it may be far more revealing if these are compromised in combination. As one example, consider 50 people sending the message "I love you" to 50 other people, one each. We thus have sender and receiver activity as well as sender and receiver content revealed for all of these messages. However, without source and destination for each of these, we don't know who loves whom.

One of the combined properties that concerns us is:

Source-destination linking that a particular source is sending to a particular destination.[2]

---

[1] It may be useful to distinguish principals that actually receive messages from those that are the target (intended receiver) of a message. For example, if a message is public-key encrypted for a principal and broadcast to this principal and 99 others, then barring transmission problems, all 100 received the message. However, only one was the intended destination of the message. In this paper, it is with the intended receiver that we are concerned.

[2] In [17], 'unlinkability' is limited to the case where a sender and receiver are both explicitly known to be active and targeted by an adversary; nonetheless they cannot be shown to be communicating with each other. Onion Routing does provide such unlinkability in some configurations, and depending on the adversary, but this is not a general goal for all connections.

This may or may not involve a particular message or transmission. Building on our previous example, suppose 50 people send 50 messages each to 50 other people (2500 messages total). Then, for any sender and receiver, we can say with certainty that they were linked on exactly one message; although we may not be able to say which one. For purposes of this paper we will be concerned with *connections*, specifically, the anonymity properties of the initiator and responder for a given connection.

4   Network Model

For purposes of this analysis, an Onion Routing network consists of onion proxies (or simply proxies), Core Onion Routers (CORs), links, over which CORs pass fixed length cells, and responder proxies, which reconstruct cells into the application layer data stream.

An attempt to analyze the traffic on a real onion routing network might try to take advantage of topological features, exit policies, outside information about communicants, and other details that we cannot hope to incorporate in a mathematical assessment of onion outing networks generally. We make a number of general and specific assumptions to permit us to proceed with the analysis. We also comment on the validity of these assumptions below.

Assumption 1. The network of onion routers is a clique (fully connected graph).
Since links are simply TCP/IP connections traversing the Internet, a COR can maintain many such connections with relatively little overhead, and the second generation implementation allows a COR to have on the order of fifty thick pipe links to other CORs. Beyond that size, one is likely to find regions of highly connected nodes with multiple bridges between them. Assumption 1 thus seems reasonable for OR networks of up to 50 CORs.

Assumption 2. Links are all padded or bandwidth-limited to a constant rate.
This simplification allows us to ignore passive eavesdroppers, since all an eavesdropper will see on any link is a constant flow of fixed length, encrypted cells. In fact, we expect that padding and limiting will be used to smooth rapid (and therefore potentially trackable) changes in link traffic rather than to maintain absolutely fixed traffic flows. Even if fluctuations could be observed, no principal remote from a link can identify his own traffic as it passes across that link, since each link is covered by the stream cipher under a key that the remote principal does not possess.

Assumption 3. The exit policy of any node is unrestricted.
As noted in section 2, we expect that many CORs will conform to this assumption, but some may not. Restrictive exit policies, to the extent that they vary among CORs, could affect the validity of Assumption 4, since the exit policy will limit the choice of the final node in a path. However, since in our adversary model the last COR may always be compromised, it makes no

difference to the security of a connection given our other assumptions. Also note that this assumption is independent of whether or not the connection of some destinations to the final COR is hidden, e.g., by a firewall.

Assumption 4. For each route through the OR network each hop is chosen at random.

This assumption depends primarily on the route selection algorithm implemented by the onion proxy, and secondarily on conflicts between exit policies and connection requests. In practice, we expect this assumption to be quite good.

Assumption 5. The number of nodes in a route, n, is chosen from $2 \leq n < \infty$ based on repeated flips of a weighted coin.

Note that the expected route length is completely determined by the weighting of the coin. The length is extended by one for each flip until the coin-flip comes up on the terminate-route side—typically the more lightly weighted side. Thus, for example, if the coin is weighted so that the probability of extending the route is .8, then the expected route length is 5. Choosing route length by this means, as opposed to choosing randomly within some range was largely motivated by the Crowds design and the security analysis in [17], of which we will say more below.

Many configurations of Onion Routing components are possible, all yielding different kinds and degrees of assurance. [20] We will limit our analysis to the two configurations that we expect to be both the most common and the most widely used.

In the **remote-COR configuration**, the onion proxy is the only OR system component that runs on a machine trusted by the user. The first COR (and any infunnels) are running on a remote untrusted machine.

In the **local-COR configuration**, all components up to the first COR are running on locally trusted machines. This corresponds to a situation where a COR is running on an enclave firewall, and onions might be built at individual workstations or at the firewall depending on efficiencies, enclave policy, etc. It also corresponds to a situation where an individual with good connections to the Internet is running his own onion router to reduce the amount of information available to untrusted components. The important aspect of this connection is that the system from end application to the first COR is essentially a black box. Perhaps contrary to initial appearance, a PC using dial-up connection to a (trustworthy) ISP might naturally be considered to be in this configuration. This view is appropriate with respect to any attacker residing entirely on the Internet because it is excluded from the telephone dial-up connections running between the customer and the ISP, and the ISP is assumed to be trusted.

We must also make assumptions about the entrance policy of sites. Since entrance policy is controlled by the proxy, it is natural to assume that anyone may connect using any protocol in the remote-COR configuration. In practice, CORs might only accept connections from specific principals (subscribers?); although the COR will be unable to determine, hence control, the application being run.

In the local-COR configuration, the entrance policy is effectively to exclude all connections from outside the black box. (However, it still will forward connections from any other COR, and it is assumed to have an open exit policy.) These assumptions are then:

Assumption 6. Every COR is connected to the OR network and the outside via either the remote-COR configuration or the local-COR configuration, but not both.

Assumption 7. The entrance policy for entering the OR network via the remote-COR configuration is unrestricted.

Assumption 8. The entrance policy for entering the OR network via the local-COR configuration is to exclude all but internal connections.

Notice that these policy assumptions also determine the initiator being protected by use of the OR network. For the remote-COR configuration, it is the end application (via its proxy) that is being protected. For the local-COR configuration, it is the local COR that is effectively the initiator being protected. This conforms well with the possibility that a corporate or other enclave may wish to protect not just the activity of individual users of the network but that of the enclave as a whole. Likewise, an individual who is running his own COR would clearly want to protect connections emanating from that COR since he is the only possible initiator of those connections.

5 Adversary Model

One of the main challenges in designing anonymous communications protocols is defining the capabilities of the adversary. Given the tools at our disposal today, the adversary model essentially determines which salient characteristics the system should deploy in order to defeat her.

The basic adversaries we consider are:

Observer: can observe a connection (e.g., a sniffer on an Internet router), but cannot initiate connections.

Disrupter: can delay (indefinitely) or corrupt traffic on a link.

Hostile user: can initiate (destroy) connections with specific routes as well as varying the traffic on the connections it creates.

Compromised COR: can arbitrarily manipulate the connections under its control, as well as creating new connections (that pass through itself).

All feasible adversaries can be composed out of these basic adversaries. This includes combinations such as one or more compromised CORs cooperating with disrupters of links on which those CORs are not adjacent, or such as combinations of hostile outsiders and observers. However, we are able to restrict our analysis of adversaries to just one class, the compromised COR. We now justify this claim.

Especially in light of our assumption that the network forms a clique, a hostile outsider can perform a subset of the actions that a compromised COR can do. Also, while a compromised COR cannot disrupt or observe a link unless it is adjacent to it, any adversary that replaces some or all observers and/or disrupters with a compromised COR adjacent to the relevant link is more powerful than the adversary it replaces. And, in the presence of adequate link padding or bandwidth limiting even collaborating observers can gain no useful information about connections within the network. They may be able to gain information by observing connections to the network (in the remote-COR configuration), but again this is less than what the COR to which such connection is made can learn. Thus, by considering adversaries consisting of collections of compromised CORs we cover the worst case of all combinations of basic adversaries. Our analysis focuses on this most capable adversary, one or more compromised CORs.

The possible distributions of adversaries are

- **single adversary**
- **multiple adversary:** A fixed, randomly distributed subset of CORs is compromised.
- **roving adversary:** A fixed-bound size subset of CORs is compromised at any one time. At specific intervals, other CORs can become compromised or uncompromised.
- **global adversary:** All CORs are compromised.

Onion Routing provides no protection against a global adversary. If all the CORs are compromised, they can know exactly who is talking to whom. The content of what was sent will be revealed as it emerges from the OR network, unless it has been end-to-end encrypted outside the OR network. Even a firewall-to-firewall connection is exposed if, as assumed above, our goal is to hide which local-COR is talking to which local-COR.

6   Security Assessment

As discussed above, there are several possible adversary models. Having specifically ruled out the case of a global adversary, we now focus on the roving adversary model. (The remaining models are subsumed by it.) We begin the security assessment by defining some variables and features of the environment.

Recall that routes are of indeterminate length and that each route is a random walk from the route origin through the network.

We assume a closed system composed of a multitude of users and a set $\mathcal{S}$ of CORs. Let r be the total number of active CORs in the system, and— as mentioned in Section 4—let n be the (variable) length of a specific route $\mathcal{R} = \{R_1, ..., R_n\}$, where each R_j is a COR in the route $\mathcal{R}$. Routes are selected randomly (each route is a random walk from the Route origin through the network) and hops within a route are selected independently (except cycles of length one are forbidden).

Our roving adversary is characterized by c, the maximum number of CORs the adversary is able to corrupt within a fixed time interval (a round). At the end of each round, the adversary can choose to remain in place or shift some of its power to corrupt other CORs. In the latter case, previously-corrupted CORs are assumed to be instantly "healed", i.e., they resume normal, secure operation. $\mathcal{C}_i$ represents the set of CORs controlled by the adversary at round i ($\mathcal{C}_i \subset \mathcal{S}$). We note that this roving adversary model closely follows that found in the literature on proactive cryptography, e.g., [2,13]. This is a standardly accepted model based on the view that system locations can be compromised periodically, but periodic security checks will detect compromises. Resulting responses as well as periodic system updates, etc. will return compromised components to normal.

At present, most connections through an Onion Routing network are likely to be for Web browsing or email. Given the short duration of typical Web and email connections, a static attack is all that can realistically be mounted; by the time a roving attacker has moved, the typical connection will have closed, leaving no trace amongst honest CORs. (This is in contrast to Crowds, cf. below.) Roving attacks are more likely to be effective against longer telnet or ftp connections.

We first analyze connections initiated from the remote-COR configuration and then connections initiated from the local-COR configuration. Within each case we consider short-lived and long-lived connections.

6.1   Assessment for Remote-COR Configuration

Given a route $\mathcal{R}$ as above, suppose that some but not all of the CORs in the route are compromised. There are three significant cases:

1. $R_1 \in \mathcal{C}_i$
   The first node is compromised. In this case sender activity is established by the adversary. Sender content is not lost since senders always pre-encrypt traffic. The probability of this event, assuming a random route and random node compromises, is $P_1 = c/r$.
2. $R_n \in \mathcal{C}_i$ The last node in the route is compromised. In this case receiver content as well as receiver activity are compromised. Sender content, sender activity, and source-destination linking remain protected. The probability of this event is $P_2 = c/r$.
3. R_1 and $R_n \in \mathcal{C}_i$ Both the first and last node in the path are compromised, so sender/receiver activity and receiver content are compromised. Moreover, the COR end-points are now able to correlate cell totals and compromise source-destination linking. Consequently, sender content can be simply inferred. The probability of this event is $P_3 = c^2/r^2$ (unless $n = 2$, in which case $P_3 = c(c-1)/r^2$ since self-looping is not allowed).

The adversary's goal must be to compromise the endpoints, since he gains little by controlling all intermediate (R_i for $1 < i < n$) CORs of a given route $\mathcal{R} = \{R_1, ..., R_n\}$. In the case of short-lived connections, the roving adversary

Table 1. Properties of Attack Scenarios.

	$R_1 \in C_i$	$R_n \in C_i$	R_1 and $R_n \in C_i$
sender activity	Yes	No	Yes
receiver activity	No	Yes	Yes
sender content	No	No	Yes (inferred)
receiver content	No	Yes	Yes
source-destination linking	No	No	Yes
probability	c/r	c/r	c^2/r^2

has, in effect, only one round in which to compromise the connection, and succeeds in compromising all properties of a connection with probability c^2/r^2 (or $c(c-1)/r^2$).

We now consider the roving adversary against a long-lived connection.

At route setup time, the probability that at least one COR on the route of length n is in C_1 is given by:

$$1 - P(\mathcal{R} \cap C_1 = \emptyset) = 1 - \frac{(r-c)^n}{r^n}$$

We now make (a perhaps optimistic) assumption that, if none of the CORs on the route are compromised at route setup time, then the adversary will not attempt the attack. In any case, for such an adversary the expected number of rounds must be at least one more than for an adversary that starts with at least one compromised COR on the route. Given at least one compromised COR on the route, how many rounds does it take for the adversary to achieve source-destination linking?

In general, the attack starts when one of the subverted CORs receives a route setup request. She then proceeds to attempt the discovery of the route's true endpoints.

In either case, at round 1, the adversary can establish:

$$R_s \text{ where } s = min(j \in [1..n] \text{ and } R_j \in \mathcal{R} \cap C_1)$$

as well as:

$$R_e \text{ where } e = max(j \in [1..n] \text{ and } R_j \in \mathcal{R} \cap C_1)$$

While the actual indices e and s are not known to the adversary, she can identify R_s and R_e by timing the propagation of route setup. Moreover, the adversary can trivially test if $R_e = R_1$ or $R_s = R_n$.

The adversary's subsequent optimal strategy is illustrated in Figure 2. As shown in the pseudocode, the game played by the adversary is two-pronged:

1. In each round she moves one hop closer towards route endpoints (moving to the preceding hop of R_s and next hop of R_e.)
2. She also randomly picks a set of (at least $c-2$) routers to subvert from among the uncorrupted set (which is constantly updated). When one of the endpoints is reached, the adversary can concentrate on the other, thus having $c-1$ routers to corrupt (at random) at each round.

In the worst case, it takes a $(c \geq 2)$-adversary $MAX(s, n - e)$ rounds to reach both endpoints. More generally, the greatest value of $MAX(s, n - e)$ is n. (Also, a single roving adversary always takes exactly n rounds to compromise source and destination.)

An interesting open issue is the expected number of rounds a $(c \geq 2)$-adversary needs in order to reach the route endpoints provided that she starts out with at least one compromised COR on the route. In lieu of an analytic solution, it might be interesting to run this for sample sets of test configurations of nodes and adversary nodes for various possible (sets) of connections. We leave this for future work.

6.2   Assessment for Local-COR Configuration

The local-COR configuration is distinguished from the remote-COR configuration by the fact that the first COR in the connection is assumed to be immune from compromise. In the remote-COR configuration, compromising the first COR is the only way to compromise sender properties or source-destination linking. In the local-COR configuration, the only way that source-destination linking or any sender properties can be compromised is if the adversary can somehow infer that the first COR is in fact first. There is no way for this to happen within our threat model unless all other CORs are compromised. (If all CORs connected to the local-COR were compromised they could infer that this was the first COR, but since we have assumed a clique of CORs, this would imply that the local-COR is the only uncompromised COR in the onion routing network.)

There is a way that the first COR could be identified as such that is outside of our described threat model: if the second COR is compromised, and *if* it is possible to predict that some data cells will produce an immediate response from the initiator, then the second COR may be able to infer that the first COR is first by the response time. This possibility is less remote if the last COR is also compromised and we assume that the data sent over it is not end-to-end encrypted for the responder. We will return to this discussion below.

7   Related Work

Basic comparison of Onion Routing to broadly related anonymity mechanisms, such as remailers [11,5] and ISDN-Mixes [14] can be found in [16]. Also mentioned there are such complementary connection-based mechanisms as LPWA [7] and the Anonymizer [1]. These are both very effective at anonymizing the data stream in different ways, but they both pass all traffic directly from the initiator via a single filtering point to the responder. There is thus minimal protection for the anonymity of the connection itself, which is our primary focus. We therefore restrict our comments to related work that is directed to wide-spread Internet communication either below the application layer or specifically for some form of

```
/* assume at least one router initially compromised */
/* assume t>=2 */
/* HEALTHY_ROUTERS is the set of hereto uncorrupted routers */
/* remove_from_set() returns set minus element to be removed; */
/*    if an element not in set, return set unchanged */
/* compute_max_span() returns R_s and R_e, the compromised routers */
/*    farthest apart on the route; */
R_1_found = R_n_found = false;
available_random = c-2;
HEALTHY_ROUTERS = ALL_ROUTERS;
while ( (! R_1_found) && (! R_n_found))
{
    /* identify first, last subverted routers */
    compute_max_span(R_s,R_e);
    /* note that it's possible that R_s=R_e */
    if ( R_s==R_1 )
    {   R_1_found = true;
        available_random ++;
    }
    if ( R_e==R_n )
    {   R_n_found = true;
        available_random ++;
    }
    R_s = prev_hop (R_s);
    R_e = next_hop (R_e);
    subvert (R_s);
    remove_from_set(HEALTHY_ROUTERS, R_s);
    subvert (R_e);
    remove_from_set(HEALTHY_ROUTERS, R_e);
    /* subvert a set of random routers */
    for (i=0; i<available_random; i++)
    {   j = random_router_index(HEALTHY_ROUTERS);
        subvert (R_j);
        remove_from_set(HEALTHY_ROUTERS, R_j);
    }
}
```

Fig. 2. Pseudo-code for the adversary's game.

connection based traffic. For this reason, direct comparisons to local anonymity systems such as TG and SS [12] are omitted due to their small deployable size and tight timing constraints.

We know of only one other published proposal for application-independent, traffic-analysis-resistant Internet communication, viz: that of [6], wherein a system is described that effectively builds an onion for every IP packet. There is thus no connection, either in the sense of a TCP/IP socket, or more significantly, in the sense of a path of nodes that can perform fast (symmetric) encryption on passing traffic. In Onion Routing, computationally expensive public-key cryptography is used only during connection setup. Using an onion for every IP packet makes for real-time capabilities significantly slower than those of Onion Routing and thus less applicable to such things as telnet connections or even Web traffic—if loading pages is expected to be anywhere close to current speeds. On the other hand, for applications that do not have these requirements, such a design may offer better security since there is no recurrent path for packets in an (application) connection.

A commercial system that appears to be quite similar to Onion Routing is being built by Zero Knowledge Systems (www.freedom.net). Like Onion Routing, it establishes a connection in the form of a path of routers that have been keyed for subsequent data passing; however, its underlying transmission is based on UDP rather than TCP/IP. While the system provides other services, such as pseudonym management, it appears to be limited to the configuration comparable to a customer building onions and connecting to an onion router at an ISP. Unless the ISP is trusted, this constitutes the remote-COR configuration. Also, routes appear to be limited to a fixed length of three hops. This means that the middle hop knows the entire route. Besides being more vulnerable to a roving attacker, these observations show that the system is not suited to enclave level protection without some modification and extension. This is not surprising since the design appears focused on the protection of individual users.

Given the above, our remaining comparative comments will be with respect to Crowds. We begin with a brief comparative description. The first thing to note is that Crowds is designed exclusively for Web traffic. Interestingly, though Crowds is only to be used for (short-lived) Web connections, it make use of longstanding cryptographic paths. Once a path is established from an initiator through a Crowd, all subsequent HTTP connections are passed through that path. (The tail of a path is randomly regenerated only beyond a break point and only when broken. Whole paths are regenerated only when new members are brought into the Crowd.) This means that a path initiator is less likely to be identified than would be the case if a new path were built for each connection [17]. This is especially important because, unlike in Onion Routing, a compromised node knows content and destination of all connections passing through it (see below). This means that adversaries have a better means to build likely profiles of repeated connections by the same initiator. The static paths of Crowds makes such profile information less useful by making it harder to know which Crowds member is profiled. If a new path were built for each connection, compromised nodes would have a better chance of intersecting predecessors with the same profile and thus identifying the initiator. On the other hand, known (rather than inferred) path profiles in that case would be much less complete, i.e., forward anonymity (in the sense of [21]) is worse for static paths. Put another way, in the remote-COR configuration, assuming a fixed distributed adversary, the likelihood that some connection one makes will have a compromised first and last node increases over the number of connections made (if the first COR is chosen different each time). However, the compromise pertains only to the current connection. If paths are static, compromise is ongoing.

Encrypted traffic looks the same as it passes along a path through a Crowd. And, the decryption key is available to all path participants. Thus, any compromised node on the path compromises both receiver activity and receiver content. Also, link padding is not a system option. As a result, a local eavesdropper (observing links from the initiator) and any one compromised member of a path completely compromise all properties mentioned in section 3. A local eavesdropper in the remote-COR configuration of Onion Routing compromises sender activity; however, unless the last COR in the connection is also compromised, nothing else is revealed. On the other hand, in this configuration, the first untrusted component of the system is able to compromise sender activity. And, a local eavesdropper together with a compromised last COR compromise all properties in section 3. For Crowds without a local eavesdropper, the first untrusted component of the system (i.e., the next node on the path) cannot identify the initiator with certainty, in fact with any more likelihood than that dictated by the probability of forwarding (i.e., the probability of extending the path vs. connecting to the responder).

In the local-COR configuration Onion Routing provides similar protections to Crowds of sender activity, source-destination linking, and sender content, and much better protection against receiver activity or receiver content, with the adversary model we have set out above and without a local eavesdropper. If we add to the adversary model, things get more complicated.

As noted in section 6.2, if an adversary that has compromised the second COR in a route can predict which data will prompt an immediate response from the initiator (e.g., if the final COR is also compromised), then she may be able to time responses to determine that there can be at most one COR prior in the route. This sort of problem was recognized early on in the design of Crowds. It is a more serious problem for Crowds because the second node alone can read requests and responses, making it easy to find the timing-relevant data. In Crowd, if URLs are included in data coming from a responder that will prompt a subsequent request from the initiator, nodes later on the path will themselves parse the HTML and make these requests back in the direction of the responder, thus eliminating the timing distinction between the first node and any others.

Timing information is thus obscured by having the nodes on the path actively processing and filtering data as well as managing the connection. This is important because it means that all nodes must be able to read all traffic so that the data stream must be anonymous. Therefore, unlike Onion Routing, Crowds inherently cannot be used in circumstances where one would like to identify (and possibly authenticate) oneself to the far end but would like to hide from others with whom one is communicating. Perhaps more importantly, as ever more functionality is added to Web browsers, and since nodes on a Crowds route must be able to read and alter all traffic on a connection, a single compromised node can embed requests, either for identifying information or to open connections directly back to it—bypassing the crowd and identifying the originator. Obvious means of attack such as by use of cookies, or by Java, Javascript, etc. are easily shut off or filtered (along with their provided functionality). However, other more subtle mechanisms are also available (cf. www.onion-router.net/Tests.html for a list of test sites, in particular www.onion-router.net/dynamic/snoop), and more are becoming available all the time. The upshot of all this is that, for Crowds, the anonymity of the connection is always at best as good as the latest installed filtering code for anonymity of the data stream. For Onion Routing, these two functions—anonymity of the connection and anonymity of the data stream—are separate, and a new means to identify the initiator via the data stream only affects the anonymity of the data stream. Even then, it is only employable at the far end of a connection, rather than by any node on an anonymized connection.

The last point of comparison we discuss is performance. Direct comparison in practice is nearly impossible. Each onion routing connection requires several public-key decryptions. So, with respect to cryptographic overhead Crowds has much better performance potential. On the other hand, within an onion routing network, connections are expected to be longstanding high-capacity channels between dedicated machines, possibly with cryptographic coprocessors. The major performance limitation is often likely to be the end user's Internet connection. But, for Crowds the end users are the network. Thus, Crowds members with slow or intermittent connections will affect the performance of everyone in their crowd. One can limit Crowds participation to those with longstanding, high-speed (say T1 or better) Internet connections. But, this will seriously limit the population for whom it is feasible. Depending on the user population, network configuration, and the components that make up the network, one is likely to find very different performance numbers in each of the systems.

8   Conclusions and Future Work

We have presented some of the features of the current Onion Routing design and analyzed its resistance to worst-case adversaries. This design generally resists traffic analysis more effectively than any other published and deployed mechanisms for Internet communication.

We note some ways that the design might be changed to improve security: Adding a time delay to traffic at the proxy could complicate timing attacks against the local-COR configuration to determine the first COR. (Similarly, if the last COR is local to the responder, in the sense of this paper, then it would be possible to add a time delay at the responder proxy.) Of course, this is only necessary when the goal is actually to protect the local COR, for example to protect the activity of an enclave or if the COR is run by one or a few individuals who are the only ones accessing/exiting the onion routing network through that COR. Suppose a typical customer-ISP configuration, in which the initiator is someone connecting through dial-up to an ISP running an onion router. As noted above in Section 4, this could be viewed as a local-COR configuration. But, in this case, it is the anonymity of the individual source rather than the COR that matters. Thus, no delay is necessary. (One could address a semi-trusted local-

COR by building onions at the workstation for a COR, e.g., at an ISP or an enclave firewall. Such options are discussed in [20].)

Finally, if partial-route padding is used on individual connections, besides link padding, then compromise by even internal attackers is complicated. For example, a local eavesdropper or compromised first COR (in the remote-COR configuration) would not be able to easily cooperate with a compromised last COR to break source-destination linking. In fact, the second generation design has been made consistent with the possibility that onion proxies can choose to do this via in-channel signaling to intermediate CORs if they so desire. Also, long-lived application connections could be hopped between shorter-lived Onion Routing connections using specialized proxies. This would both frustrate a roving attacker, and make such connections look more like short-lived connections even to network insiders. We have discussed some of the features such proxies might have, but such proxies have not yet been designed.

Acknowledgments. This work supported by ONR and DARPA. Jim Proto and Jeremy Barrett have done much of the coding of the second generation system, and Mark Levin did much of its design specification. Lora Kassab has investigated route selection algorithms, and her work has influenced the above discussion. Thanks to Mike Reiter and Avi Rubin for helpful discussions about the goals of Crowds. Thanks to Ira Moskowitz, Cathy Meadows, and LiWu Chang for other helpful discussions.

References

1. The Anonymizer. http://www.anonymizer.com
2. R. Canetti and A. Herzberg. "Maintaining Security in the Presence of Transient Faults", Advances in Cryptology—CRYPTO'94, LNCS vol. 839, Springer-Verlag, 1994, pp. 425–438.
3. D. Chaum. "Untraceable Electronic Mail, Return Addresses, and Digital Pseudonyms", Communications of the ACM, vol. 24, no. 2, Feb. 1981, pages 84-88.
4. D. Chaum. "The Dining Cryptographers Problem: Unconditional Sender and Recipient Untraceability", Journal of Cryptology, vol. 1, no. 1, 1988, pages 65-75.
5. L. Cottrell. Mixmaster and Remailer Attacks, http://obscura.obscura.com/~loki/remailer/remailer-essay.html
6. A. Fasbender, D. Kesdogan, O. Kubitz. "Variable and Scalable Security: Protection of Location Information in Mobile IP", 46th IEEE Vehicular Technology Society Conference, Atlanta, March 1996.
7. E. Gabber, P. Gibbons, Y. Matias, and A. Mayer. "How to Make Personalized Web Browsing Simple, Secure, and Anonymous", in Financial Cryptography: FC '97, Proceedings, R. Hirschfeld (ed.), Springer-Verlag, LNCS vol. 1318, pp. 17–31, 1998.
8. I. Goldberg and D. Wagner. "TAZ Servers and the Rewebber Network: Enabling Anonymous Publishing on the World Wide Web", First Monday, vol. 3 no. 4, April 1998.
9. D. Goldschlag, M. Reed, P. Syverson. "Hiding Routing Information", in Information Hiding, R. Anderson, ed., LNCS vol. 1174, Springer-Verlag, 1996, pp. 137–150.

10. D. Goldschlag, M. Reed, P. Syverson. "Onion Routing for Anonymous and Private Internet Connections," Communications of the ACM, vol. 42, num. 2, February 1999.
11. C. Gülcü and G. Tsudik. "Mixing Email with Babel", in 1996 Symposium on Network and Distributed System Security, San Diego, February 1996.
12. D. Martin Jr., "Local Anonymity in the Internet", Ph.D. Dissertation, Boston University, 1999.
13. R. Ostrovsky and M. Yung. "How to Withstand Mobile Virus Attacks", in Proceedings of the Tenth ACM Symposium on Principles of Distributed Computing (PODC '91), ACM Press, 1991, pp. 51–59.
14. A. Pfitzmann, B. Pfitzmann, and M. Waidner. "ISDN-Mixes: Untraceable Communication with Very Small Bandwidth Overhead", GI/ITG Conference: Communication in Distributed Systems, Mannheim Feb, 1991, Informatik-Fachberichte 267, Springer-Verlag, Heidelberg 1991, pp. 451-463.
15. M. Reed, P. Syverson, and D. Goldschlag. "Protocols using Anonymous Connections: Mobile Applications", in Security Protocols: Fifth International Workshop, B. Christianson, B. Crispo, M. Lomas, and M. Roe, eds., LNCS vol. 1361, Springer-Verlag, 1997, pp. 13–23.
16. M. Reed, P. Syverson, and D. Goldschlag. "Anonymous Connections and Onion Routing", IEEE Journal on Selected Areas in Communications, vol. 16 no. 4, May 1998, pp. 482–494. (A preliminary version of this paper appeared in [19].)
17. M. Reiter and A. Rubin. "Crowds: Anonymity for Web Transactions", ACM Transactions on Information System Security, vol. 1, no. 1, November 1998, pp. 66–92. (A preliminary version of this paper appeared in [18].)
18. M. Reiter and A. Rubin. Crowds: Anonymity for Web Transactions, DIMACS Technical Reports 97-15, April 1997 (Revised August 1997).
19. P. Syverson, D. Goldschlag, and M. Reed. "Anonymous Connections and Onion Routing", in Proceedings of the IEEE Symposium on Security and Privacy, Oakland, CA, IEEE CS Press, May 1997, pp. 44–54.
20. P. Syverson, M. Reed, and D. Goldschlag. "Onion Routing Access Configurations", in DISCEX 2000: Proceedings of the DARPA Information Survivability Conference and Exposition, Hilton Head, SC, IEEE CS Press, January 2000, pp. 34–40.
21. P. Syverson, S. Stubblebine, and D. Goldschlag, "Unlinkable Serial Transactions", in Financial Cryptography: FC '97, Proceedings, R. Hirschfeld (ed.), Springer-Verlag, LNCS vol. 1318, pp. 39–55, 1998.
22. A. Pfitzmann and M. Waidner, "Networks without User Observability", Computers & Security, vol. 6 (1987), pp. 158–166.

Web MIXes: A System for Anonymous and Unobservable Internet Access

Oliver Berthold[1], Hannes Federrath[2], and Stefan Köpsell[1]

[1] Dresden University of Technology, Fakultät Informatik
{ob2, sk13}@inf.tu-dresden.de
[2] International Computer Science Institute, Berkeley
hannes@icsi.berkeley.edu

Abstract. We present the architecture, design issues and functions of a MIX-based system for anonymous and unobservable real-time Internet access. This system prevents traffic analysis as well as flooding attacks. The core technologies include an adaptive, anonymous, time/volume-sliced channel mechanism and a ticket-based authentication mechanism. The system also provides an interface to inform anonymous users about their level of anonymity and unobservability.

1   Introduction

Using Internet services nowadays means leaving digital traces. Anonymity and unobservability on the Internet is a sheer illusion. On the other hand, most people agree that there is a substantial need for anonymous communication as a fundamental building block of the information society. The availability of anonymous communication is considered a constitutional right in many countries, for example for use in voting or counseling.

We are doing research on anonymity and unobservability in the Internet to evaluate the feasibility and costs of such systems and to explore several deployment opportunities within the Internet. Our goal is to explore the foundations and to provide a secure and anonymous technical infrastructure for the Internet.

Systems that provide **unobservability** ensure that nobody, not even the transport network, is able to find out who communicates with whom. However, the communicating parties may know and usually authenticate each other. Example: Paying users browsing a patent data base.

Systems that provide **anonymity** ensure that client or server (or both) can communicate without revealing identity. Example: Users browsing the World Wide Web.

During the last three years we developed several MIX-based and proxy-based anonymity services (for web surfing and similar real-time services). Our academic interest is to show that anonymity and unobservability can be efficiently realized. The special objective is to develop a theoretical background for the efficient implementation of anonymity services in the Internet. We are building an anonymous transport system based on a specific IP format. The goal is to

H. Federrath (Ed.): Anonymity 2000, LNCS 2009, pp. 115–129, 2001.

provide asynchronous (like SMTP) as well as nearly synchronous modes of communication (like HTTP). The system should also be able to handle various kinds of packets.

The web site of our project is http://www.inf.tu-dresden.de/~hf2/anon/.

Anonymity and unobservability are not new security goals. The following systems that provide anonymity services are known both in literature as well as in the Internet: (selection)

- Anonymizer [1],
- Crowds [2],
- Onion Routing [3],
- Freedom [4].

The attacker models for these systems are different, i.e., these systems provide different levels of anonymity. A comparison of these systems is given in [5].

This paper is organized as follows. In section 2 we give an overview of the architecture of our system. Section 3 deals with several attacks and their prevention. In section 4, we explain additional design issues of our practical system and their implementation.

2   Components and Functionality

Basically, we use

- a modified Mix concept with
- an adaptive chop-and-slice algorithm (see below),
- sending of dummy messages whenever an active client has nothing to send,
- a ticket-based authentication system that makes flooding attacks impossible or very expensive and
- a feedback system that gives the user information on his current level of protection.

The MIX concept [6] as well as the adaptive chop-and-slice algorithm will be described in this section. The ticket-based authentication procedure is explained in section 3.1 and the feedback mechanism in section 3.1.

The complete system consists of three logical parts: the JAP (Java Anon Proxy) on the client-side, the MIXes and the cache-proxy on the server-side. These parts are concatenated into a chain, building the anonymous tunnel. All network traffic to be anonymized is sent through this tunnel. In principle, a single user remains aonymous since the tunnel has many entrances (users), but only one exit. Every user can possibly cause the traffic observed at the tunnel-exit.

JAP. JAP is connected to the first MIX via Internet. Ideally, the MIXes should be connected via separate high-speed connections due to performance reasons. However, this would be very complex and expensive, hence our MIXes use only the Internet.

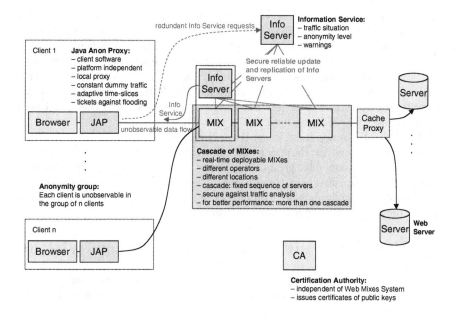

Fig. 1. Architecture of our service

The JAP is a program which is installed locally on each user's computer. All network traffic to be anonymized goes through this software. The JAP transforms the data so that it can be anonymized by the MIXes.

Following functions are provided by JAP:

- Registration of the user to the MIXes,
- Periodical set-up of time-slice-channels (generating and sending of asymmetrically encrypted channel-building messages),
- Sending and receiving data via the channels. Dummy messages (for instance, random bits or encrypted zero bits) are generated if there is nothing to send.
- Listening for requests coming from the browser or other programs of the client that like to communicate in an anonymous way,
- Filtering of content that would be dangerous for the anonymity, e.g., cookies and active contents like JavaScript, ActiveX and other embedded objects,
- Transforming data into the MIX-format and sending through an anonymous channel,
- Receiving data from the active MIX-channel and forwarding it to the originating application,
- Periodical utilization of an info-service, so that the user gets feedback about his current level of anonymity.

MIXes. Our basic concepts are very similar to other systems based on the idea of MIXes [6]. A MIX scrambles the order of data streams and changes their coding using cryptography to make traffic correlation attacks difficult.

The MIXes are simple computers connected via the Internet. They form a logical chain, called "MIX-cascade". The first MIX receives data sent by the JAPs. A MIX makes some cryptographic transformations (strips a layer of encryption, prevents replay attacks, reorders messages and creates a batch that consists of all messages) and sends the data to the next MIX.

The last MIX sends the data to the cache-proxy.

By means of constant dummy traffic, all senders send messages at any time to create the same anonymity group. If necessary, random data is generated which cannot be distinguished from genuine encrypted traffic. Dummy traffic has to be sent between the endpoints of a communication relation. Dummy traffic between MIXes only is not sufficient to prevent traffic analysis.

Our attacker may

- control up to $n - 1$ MIXes if n is the total number of MIXes in the MIX-cascade,
- control the cache-proxy and knows the receiver and content of all messages because all traffic goes (mostly unencrypted) through the cache-proxy to the Internet,
- block every message, generate his own messages and modify all messages. These active attacks will be recognized and consequently prevented by a ticket-based authentication system explained in section 3.1.

Cache-proxy. The cache-proxy sends the data to the Internet and receives the answers from the servers (e.g., web servers). The answers will be sent back to the user via the MIXes (in reverse order). As JAP does, the cache-proxy has to send dummy traffic as well.

Once a time-slice-channel is established, it can transport a certain number of bytes. Thereafter, the channel is released automatically. If more data needs to be transmitted sequential time-slice connections must be established. See section 3.1 for more information.

Another functionality of both JAP and cache-proxy affects the HTTP protocol. As far as security and performance are concerned, it makes sense that the cache-proxy automatically loads every object embedded into a HTML-page, e.g., links to embedded images. The cache-proxy can then send the whole page (including the embedded objects) at the same time through the anonymous channel. This idea was proposed the first time by the Crowds project [2].

In order to realize this idea, both cache-proxy and JAP must provide the following functions:

- Cache-proxy scans the data received from a web server for embedded objects.
- Cache-proxy automatically requests these objects and sends them through the anonymous channel to the user's JAP. In addition, cache-proxy should provide traditional caching functionality in order to reduce the number of requests sent to the Internet.

- JAP replies to the requests for embedded objects by sending data already received from the cache-proxy. The number of requests sent from JAP through the anonymous channel is thereby dramatically reduced.

Info-service. Info-service provides data for maintenance and operation of the anonymous network. It provides

- addresses and public keys of the MIXes,
- information on the traffic situation,
- the availability of MIXes,
- data about the achievable level of anonymity, i.e., the number of active users in the anonymous network.

A screenshot of the graphical user-interface of the info-service is given in section 4.2.

3   Attacks and Solutions

For real-time communication, we additionally developed the following concepts both to make traffic analysis harder and to increase the efficiency.

Traffic analysis means that an attacker who is able to control the cache-proxy, can link a particular request to the same user. Every message was possibly sent by a different group of users, so that the attacker can use this information to intersect the anonymity group.

Several attacks exist against the basic concept of MIXes. The attacker's goal is to observe users or to stop the service (Denial-of-Service attack, DoS-attack).

We describe concepts which prevent these attacks or make them very difficult and eventually identify the attacker.

3.1   Solutions against Observation

There are two sorts of attacks: passive and active attacks.

A passive attacker can only eavesdrop on communication links, but cannot modify any network traffic.

It is impossible to detect passive attacks. The only solution is to prevent them.

Dummy messages. Dummy messages are sent from the starting point (i.e., client) of a communication into the MIX network to make traffic analysis harder.

Sending dummy messages guarantees that all users send the same amount of data during each time slice. Since all traffic (including the dummies) is encrypted, no one, even an attacker, who observes all network cables can know which user sends dummies and which one sends real information.

If the group of users does not change (especially when nobody leaves the group), a passive attacker cannot split the group.

Thus it is necessary that each user operates at least one channel at all times. He has to:

- periodically send channel-building messages,
- send real data or dummy traffic on his channels,
- receive data sent by the cache-proxy.

Each MIX has to send dummy messages back to the user if the user does not receive real data. This ensures that each user receives the same amount of data during each time slice. Since at least the trustworthy (i.e., "unattacked") MIX will send these dummies, it successfully avoids these attacks, supposing that any other MIX (or the cache proxy) does not send dummies.

Adaptive chop-and-slice algorithm. Large messages (and streaming data) are chopped into short pieces of a specific constant length, called "slice". Each "slices" is transmitted through an anonymous MIX channel. In addition, active users without an active communication request send dummy messages. Thus nobody knows the starting time and duration of a communication, because all active users start and end their communication at the same time. Otherwise, an observer could determine where and when the anonymous channel starts and ends and could find out who is communicating with whom. Depending on the traffic situation, we modify the throughput and duration of the anonymous channel. The concept of chopping long communications into slices was introduced the first time in [8].

We use a modified version with an adaptive duration or throughput. Once a time-slice-channel is established, it can transport a certain number of bytes and is afterwards released automatically. If an anonymous connection takes longer than one time-slice, it will be composed of a number of time-slices. In this case, JAP provides ID numbers, which cache-proxy uses to refer to an anonymous connection (Slice number Sl, see Fig. 2).

In comparison to sending each MIX message separately, a MIX channel is more efficient, because it's not necessary to decrypt all these messages using a slow asymmetric algorithm. Since a MIX must collect all messages of the users before sending them to the next one, the delay time in every MIX is proportional to the length of messages.

To establish a new slice, a user sends (together with all other users) a conventional MIX message through the MIXes. This message contains a symmetric key for each MIX. This key will be used to decrypt or encrypt data, which will be sent later through the channel. The time when the channel starts is defined by the state of the whole system. Normally, it starts when the last slice ends. The slice ends when a committed number of bytes have been transferred. In case of an error, especially if an attacker has manipulated some data, the channel is supposed to stop immediately. Otherwise, the attacker can possibly observe which channel is damaged and is thereby able to correlate sender and receiver.

Ticket-based authentication system. A very difficult problem occurs when an active attacker floods the anonymity service with messages in order to uncover a certain message.

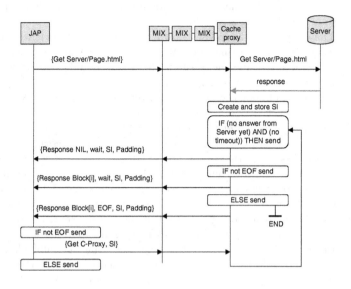

Fig. 2. Time Slice Protocol

We believe that we have found a new concept to suppress flooding of messages both from outsiders (normal users) and insiders (MIXes).

Firstly we limit either the available bandwidth or the number of concurrently used time slices for each user.

Secondly every user has to show that he is allowed to use the system at the respective time "slice" by providing a ticket only valid for a certain "slice". To protect the identity of the user, the ticket is a blinded signature [7] issued by the anonymous communication system. More precisely, each MIX issues a limited number of tickets for each channel and user.

Detailed description of procedure:

Step 1:   The user established a connection to a MIX. This connection guarantees confidentiality and integrity and authenticates both MIX and user (i.e., it is possible to use SSL). The user owns a digital certificate and authenticates himself to the MIX. The MIX checks that he gets this certificate for the first time (so it is impossible to get more than one ticket by reconnecting to the MIX). The certificate authority guarantees that each user gets one and only one certificate or it must be recognizable that different certificates belong to the same user (i.e., by including the user's identity).

Step 2:   Now the user sends a blinded message to the MIX, which the MIX should sign. This message consists of a key for a symmetric cipher and some bits forming a redundancy.

Step 3:   The MIX signs the message using a special key (pair), which is only valid for a certain time slice. We are using RSA and for each new key pair (for each time slice) we use the same modulus n, but we change the public and private exponents.

Step 4:   The user unblinds the message and verifies the signature. Now he owns a valid ticket, which is not linkable to him.

Step 5:   The user repeats steps 1-4 for each MIX.

Step 6:   The user generates the message (channel-building message or data message). Assuming that there are k MIXes. The user concatenates the ticket that he gets from MIX k with the data he wants to send. Then he encrypts the message. He uses the public key of MIX k in order to encrypt the first part of the message. For the rest of the message he uses the symmetric key included in the ticket. Next, he concatenates the ticket issued by MIX $k - 1$ with the generated message for MIX k. He encrypts the message in the same way using the public key of MIX $k - 1$ and so forth until he encrypts the ticket issued by the first MIX.

Step 7:   The user sends the message (generated in step 6) through the MIX-cascade.

If the MIX uses the same prime numbers p and q (and therefore the same modulus n) for the asymmetric encryption/decryption of the message and for signing/checking the tickets, there will be no additional overhead for verifying the tickets.

The ticket exactly fits in the first (asymmetric encrypted) part of the message (step 6). The MIX decrypts the message and verifies the ticket in one step by decrypting the message using the product of it is secret decryption key and it is public signature test key. Furthermore, the MIX extracts the symmetric key, which will be used for the channel and verifies the ticket by checking the redundancy.

As we already explained, a ticket only consists of a symmetric key and a redundancy. For an acceptable level of security, about 200 bits are needed to store a ticket. Since we use RSA, the size of the ticket would increase at least up to 1024 bits.

Each ticket has unused space of about 800 bits. It is possible to store other data in this free space, but it must be known when the ticket is requested. This is actually not a disadvantage, since the ticket is used for the channel-building message. The free space of each ticket could be used to store a part of the message, which is addressed to the next MIX. Thus the channel-building message would become smaller, because we only need 200 bits per Mix instead of 1024 (except for the last MIX).

In order to use this optimization, we have to change the procedure as follows:

Steps 1-4 are modified so that the tickets will be requested sequentially starting at the last MIX. The user generates the next ticket (step 2). He chooses the symmetric key, computes the redundancy and fills the free space with the first bytes of the already generated message.

Since we know the whole remaining message at the time we generate a ticket, we can use a fingerprint of this message as redundancy. The MIX can calculate the fingerprint in step 7 and thus verify the integrity of the whole received message.

Step 1-4 (and perhaps step 6) can be done parallel, so that we can only send one large message (requesting many tickets) instead of many short ones. This will increase the efficiency, especially the authentication (step 1) has to be done only ones.

If the duration of one time slice is long enough, the overhead for the ticket method won't be very high, since we'll need only one ticket per MIX and channel. The most expensive factor is that the user must directly get the tickets from each mix through an encrypted channel.

Using tickets is useful in order to add the dimension of a prepaid payment system for the anonymity system, too.

However, this has not yet been implemented.

Measurement of anonymity level. If the attacker observes all network traffic, he is able to reduce the number of possible senders (i.e., the number of members within the anonymity group) of a message. At the extreme, he may be able to identify the user who sends the message. This is called "intersection attack". The intersection attack can only be prevented if the anonymity group remains constant.

If the group of active users had changed, the linked messages must have been sent by a user, who is member of the intersection of all groups of users.

Dummy traffic makes intersection attacks more difficult, but does not completely prevent them. If all active users permanently send dummy messages, each received message could possibly come from any user.

However, up to now, it is not clear how to prevent such an attack, especially if we consider a global observer.

The anonymity level depends on the number of active users within the system. We need a mechanism or a heuristic that informs the user of his level of protection when he requests contents from the Internet.

In our design we inform each user of his current level of anonymity. The user can decide to recede his communication relation if the anonymity level becomes less than a user-defined threshold, i.e., the number of active users in the system. We believe that it is important for the user to be aware of his degree of privacy. This makes the system more reliable and trustworthy for the user.

Each MIX has to publish periodically

1. the number of active users and
2. the logout time of each user who leaves the group.

The client (JAP) receives this information via the info-service and computes the time when the first linkable message of the current session was sent. JAP computes how many users were active from this time on, using the published logout times. These users represent the anonymity group, because only they are possible senders of all messages.

When a new connection is established, JAP stores the time and number of active users. Every time the MIXes publishes the logout times, JAP decreases the size of the anonymity group for each detected relevant logout. A logout is relevant if the corresponding logout was earlier than the stored starting time. The user will be alerted if the anonymity group becomes too small.

The information about the number of active users and logout times are digitally signed by each MIX. So it is impossible for the attacker to manipulate them in order to fake a bigger anonymity group.

The client should always assume that the lowest published number of active users and the highest number of logouts is true in order to prevent attacks from a MIX itself.

Since it is impossible to prevent the intersection attack, we can only give advice to users on how to mitigate the effect of intersection attacks: The success of an attack can be further reduced by avoiding linkable events such as Cookies, request of personal web pages or usage of pseudonyms in chat services more than once.

If an attacker also uses active attacks, he can increase his chance to identify a sender. In order to do so, he tries to exclude particular users from the group of possible senders by

– blocking some messages or destroying a network cable,
– sending messages, which appear to be sent by other users, and
– manipulating messages.

However, it is possible to detect active attacks.

3.2   Protection against DoS-Attacks

In section 3.1 we described a procedure for detecting active attacks, but we did not discuss what to do if we detected such one. If an attack is ignored or affected message is simply deleted, the attacker has partly reached his goal.

One solution could be to delete all affected messages or to close all open channels. As a consequence, it would be very easy to start a DoS-attack: The attacker only has to send one broken message in order to impair the whole MIX-cascade. If the attacker is unable to break the anonymity, he may simply prevent the usage of the MIX-cascade.

A better solution is to give each honest user or MIX the chance to prove that he/it has sent correct messages only.

If an error occurs, each MIX will have to prove that it has worked correctly. An attacking MIX cannot do so and is consequently identified. If all MIXes worked correctly, the user, who has sent the broken message is the attacker.

In order to prove the correctness of each participant (including the MIXes) and to detect network errors (or attacks), all output should be digitally signed.

Detailed description of procedure:

a. If a MIX cannot verify the signature, it requests the output of the previous MIX again. If it does not get correct data after a certain period of time (timeout), it will signal a signature-error. In this case, it is not clear who the attacker is. Possible candidates are:
   - the MIX itself,
   - the previous MIX,
   - the network between these MIXes.

b. If MIX i detects an error, it publishes the whole decrypted message (including the error). Now everybody is able to encrypt that message by using the public key of the MIX. If the result is identical with the received message, the MIX has proved that it has decrypted the received message correctly, but that message nevertheless contains an error. The error must have occurred at or caused by the previous MIX.

c. All preceeding MIXes $i - x$ ($x = 1 \ldots i - 1$) are obliged to contribute to the following "uncovering-procedure" until the error has been found:
   1. MIX $i - x$ has to provide the input-output correlation of the certain message and everyone can verify that the MIX has decrypted the message correctly (see b.).
   2. If the error is found, the uncovering-procedure has to stop immediately and the results have to be published. That means that MIXes $i - x + 1 \ldots i - 1$ are attackers.
   3. If the check was successful, the MIX has to publish the decrypted message (like MIX i).

d. If all MIXes prove that they have worked correctly, only the sender of the broken message can be the attacker. He is the only one who was able to generate a message, which contains an error that would be detected by MIX i.

Hence faulty MIXes can be excluded unless they have been proven that working correctly. A user, who produces errors can also be excluded from the group of users.

A user can only carry through a DoS-attack for a long time if he periodically changes his identity. This is possible if he works together with a corrupt certificate authority. After a period of time, no one will trust this certificate authority any longer.

Nevertheless, there still remains a disadvantage: The trustworthy MIX has to uncover his decryption. If all other MIXes are attackers and work together, they could determine the sender and receiver of a message. However, the attacker "loses" one MIX each time the uncovering-procedure will be performed.

If at least two MIXes are trustworthy, the uncovering-procedure won't break the anonymity:

1. **A user has cheated:** There is no need to protect this user, because the only reason for his message was to confuse the system.

2. **A MIX has cheated:** The first trustworthy MIX of the cascade, which gets a faulty message, starts the uncovering-procedure. This procedure continues until the attacking MIX is reached. If the second trustworthy MIX is before the attacking MIX, the attacker will not be able to detect the sender of a message, because the trustworthy MIX will not perform an invalid uncovering-procedure.

   If the second trustworthy MIX is behind, the receiver of the message is not detectable. The attacker may get the correct message through the uncovering-procedure, but the second trustworthy MIX protects the correlation between sender an receiver.

The described uncovering-procedure is useful for the asymmetric encrypted MIX messages as well as to verify the transmissions of the channels. On each channel, a redundancy for each mix (i.e., a message digest of the data already sent) is sent.

Additionally, each MIX has to store all transmitted data and the channel-building-messages. If an error occurs, it will be able to prove that it has decrypted the data of the channel correctly by using the symmetric key included in the corresponding channel-building message.

One specific feature of the channel is that the data will reach the receiver in very small pieces. If the verification of the channel is done later, the attack may have already been successful. This is possible, even if all other MIXes are trustworthy. But in this case the attacker will lose at least one attacking MIX every time he attacks a channel. This is not acceptable even for a very strong attacker, so that the anonymity of a normal user will not be reduced, if the uncovering-procedure is performed.

4 Other Design Issues

4.1 General

The main focus of our development process is the usability of the whole system. This includes two aspects. Firstly we try to make the handling of the Client (JAP) as easy as possible, so that many people are able to use it. This includes the installation and configuration as well as the design of the user interface.

The second aspect of usability covers the performance, especially the throughput and the delay time of the anonymous network access.

4.2 The Client (JAP)

The development is based on the following requirements:

- The client must be executable on different hardware/operating systems, including at least Windows (95, 98, NT, 2000), Linux, Apple Macintosh.
- The client (JAP) must be easy to install by the user. It should be possible to do this via the Internet or CD-ROM without special knowledge.

- The configuration must be as easy as possible. Even users without extensive knowledge in security and cryptography should be able to configure the system.
- Users must be protected from thinking to be anonymous if they use a misconfigured client.
- A anonymous network access should be possible, even if the user is behind a firewall or proxy.
- The user interface must show and explain the user's current level of anonymity.
- It must be easy to switch between anonymous or non-anonymous network access.

At the moment, JAVA is used as the programming language. That's because of the JAVA-capability: "Write once, run anywhere". Later it should be possible to develop special versions for each operating system. These versions will provide a better performance and lesser resources will be needed. A suitable integration into the look & feel of the target operating system will increase the user-friendliness.

For the execution of the JAP it is necessary to have Java Runtime Environment Version 1.1.8 or equivalent, the GUI-library "Swing" (Version 1.1.1), and a cryptographic library, presently "logi-crypt", installed. These libraries are completely written in JAVA so that we can easily distribute them with our client. All other files needed for the JAP (the JAVA byte code, pictures, help files and so on) are included in one single archive (.jar-file). This file must be copied to the target system and can directly be executed.

In order to make the configuration process easy, it should be possible to download the whole configuration data via Internet. Of course, we have to develop a secure infrastructure for this.

Furthermore, many users gain access to the Internet via an ISP. The provider can force the surfer to use a special web-proxy that does not allow direct Internet connections. In order to give such people the chance to surf anonymously, it must be possible to connect to the first MIX via the web-proxy of the ISP. Therefore, all data must be embedded into the HTTP-Protocol.

Fig. 3 shows the "Anonym-O-Meter", our first attempt to give the user feedback about his current level of protection. This is an area of our future research as well.

4.3   The MIX-Servers

A main point concerning the development of the MIXes is the performance, since this has a great influence on the usability of the whole system. Nevertheless, we also focus on easy administration and maintenance. In contrast to the JAP-user, administrators have a deeper knowledge in computers, and possibly in security.

Our MIXes are implemented using C++ as programming language. We do not use JAVA due to performance reasons. C++ has become a standard and

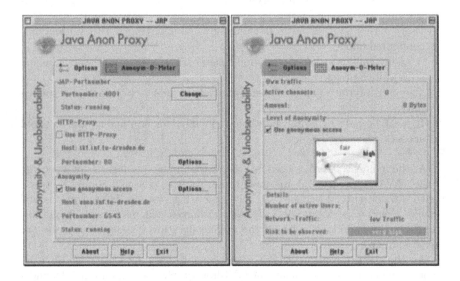

Fig. 3. Screenshot

is available on many operating systems. Differences result from using the system functions like network input/output or from programming the graphical user interface. Since MIXes are console applications without any GUI, this is unproblematic. We only need a few system calls. The main tasks of MIXes are cryptographic and algorithmic operations. In order to port the MIXes to a new target operating system, only a few modules/functions must be adapted. Our goal is to support a few important and capable operating systems (for instance Linux, Solaris, AIX and Windows NT).

The administration is realized via a special network interface implemented by the MIXes. Thus, it is possible to separate the MIXes and the administration tools physically and logically. Presently, we are thinking about a GUI for administration purposes written in JAVA.

Acknowledgements. We would like to thank Prashant Agarwal, Christoph Federrath, Mary Weiss and the anonymous referees for their very useful hints and suggestions.

References

1. The Anonymizer. http://www.anonymizer.com
2. Michael K. Reiter, Aviel D. Rubin: Crowds: Anonymity for Web Transactions. ACM Transactions on Information and System Security 1/1, November 1998, 66-92.
3. Onion Routing. http://www.onion-routing.net
4. The Freedom Network. http://www.freedom.net
5. Oliver Berthold, Hannes Federrath, Marit Köhntopp: Project "Anonymity and Unobservability in the Internet". Workshop on Freedom and Privacy by Design / Conference on Freedom and Privacy 2000, Toronto/Canada, April 4-7, 2000, 57-65.
6. David Chaum: Untraceable Electronic Mail, Return Addresses, and Digital Pseudonyms. Communication of the ACM 24/2 (1981) 84-88.
7. David Chaum: Blind Signature System. Crypto '83, Plenum Press, New York 1984, 153.
8. Andreas Pfitzmann, Birgit Pfitzmann, Michael Waidner: ISDN-MIXes – Untraceable Communication with Very Small Bandwidth Overhead. 7th IFIP International Conference on Information Security (IFIP/Sec '91), Elsevier, Amsterdam 1991, 245-258.

Privacy Incorporated Software Agent (PISA): Proposal for Building a Privacy Guardian for the Electronic Age

John J. Borking

Vice-President Dutch Data Protection Authority
jbo@registratiekamer.nl

1   Introduction

In the coming years, electronic commerce (E-commerce) and electronic government (E-government) will become more and more part of citizens' every day life. Many transactions will be performed by means of computers and computer networks. However, several hurdles have to be taken before E-commerce and E-government can develop its full potential.

An essential element of E-commerce and E-government is the collection of information on large computer networks, where either the information itself is the product sought, or information about products and services is being retrieved. Currently the retrieval of information on large computer networks, in particular the Internet, is getting more and more complicated. The volume of the stored information is overwhelming, and time and capacity needed for retrieval of information is growing strongly. Congestion in computer networks is a serious problem.

Numerous services are currently available to ease these problems, ranging from simple push technologies such as "PointCast" which brings information to your doorstep by "narrow-casting" or filtering information based on an individual's specified interests; to sophisticated systems that allow for the "personalization" of network user sessions and the tracking of user activities. Collaborative filtering of a user's "clickstream" or history of Web-based activity, combined with neural networks, which look for detailed patterns in a user's behavior, are just beginning to emerge as powerful tools used by organizations of all kinds.

While the majority of these technologies are at the moment essentially being in design and utility, they are indicative of the types of products that are being developed. The end result culminates in the creation and development of Intelligent Software Agent Technologies (ISATs). Intelligent Software Agents are software programs, at times coupled with dedicated hardware, which are designed to complete tasks on behalf of their user without any direct input or supervision from the user.[1] Agents for that purpose contain a profile of their users. The data

---

[1] Ted Selker of IBM Almaden Research Center defined an intelligent software agent as a software thing that knows how to do things that you could probably do yourself if you had the time.

H. Federrath (Ed.): Anonymity 2000, LNCS 2009, pp. 130–140, 2001.

in this profile are the basis for the actions an agent performs: searching for information, matching this information with the profile and performing transactions on behalf of its u ser.

2   Specific Technology Objectives

At first glance, intelligent agent technologies (ISAT) appear to hold out great promise for automating routine duties and even conducting high level transactions. However, upon greater reflection, it becomes clear that ISATs could present a significant threat to privacy relating to the wealth of personal information in their possession and under their control. Accordingly, it is highly desirable that their development and use reflect European privacy standards (i.e. European Union Directives 95/46/EC and 97/66/EC) in order to safeguard the personal information of their users.

The functionality and utility of user agents, lies in what they can do for the user. Remember their whole raison-d'Řtre is to act on one's behalf and function as one's trusted personal servant, serving one's needs and managing one's day-to-day activities.

Their powers are constrained by a number of factors: the degree of software sophistication, the number of services with which they can interact, and, most importantly, the amount of personal information that they possess about the user.

3   User Profiling

It is this issue of "user profiling" that is at the core of the privacy risk associated with the use of ISATs. Typically, an ISAT user profile would contain a user's name, contact numbers and e-mail addresses.

Beyond this very basic information, the profile could contain a great deal of additional information about a user's likes and dislikes, habits and personal preferences, frequently called telephone numbers, contact information about friends and colleagues, and even a history of Web sites visited and a list of electronic transactions performed.

Because agents could be requested to perform any number of tasks ranging from downloading the daily newspaper to purchasing concert tickets for a favorite singer, the agent is required to know a great deal of information about the user.

In order to function properly, ISATs must also have the following characteristics[2]:

– Mobility, or a connection to a communications network;
– Deliberative behavior, or an ability to take an action based on a set of criteria;

---

[2]   See J.J.Borking, B.M.A van Eck, P.Siepel -Intelligent Software Agents and Privacy-A&V 13- The Hague 1999, p.12 -14

- The following three abilities – to act autonomously, co-operatively, and to learn.

Depending upon the levels of security associated with the user profile, this information may be saved in a plain text file or encrypted. However, the security of the data residing within the agent is only one part of the concerns regarding privacy. The arguably more significant concern is the dissemination of information during transactions, and in the general conduct of the agent's activities on behalf of the user.

As an agent collects, processes, learns, stores and distributes data about its user and the user's activities, the agent will possess a wide variety of information which should not be divulged unless specifically required for a transaction. In the course of its activities, an agent could be required, or be forced to divulge information about the user that he or she may not wish to be shared. The most important issue here is one of openness and transparency. As long as it is clear to the user exactly what information is being requested, what purpose it is needed for, and how it will be used (and stored), the user will be in a position to freely make decisions based on informed consent. Of even greater concern is the situation where the ISAT may not be owned directly by the user but is made available (rented, leased) to the user by an organization in order to assist in accessing one or more services[3].

4   Privacy Threats of ISATs

Summarizing, there are two main types of privacy threats that are posed by the use of ISATs:

1. Threats caused by agents acting on behalf of a user (through loss of control over the activities that are executed to get the right results, through the unwanted disclosure of the user's personal information and when an agents runs into a more powerful or an agent in disguise),
   And;
2. Threats caused by foreign agents that act on behalf of others (via traffic flow monitoring, data mining and even covert attempts to obtain personal information directly from the user's agent or by entering databases and collecting personal data)[4]. Resuming, the user is required to place a certain degree of trust in the agent – that it will perform its functions correctly as requested. However, this trust could well come with a very high price tag, one that the user may have no knowledge or awareness of – the price to his or her privacy. Failing to ensure such trust may prove to be a mayor hindrance for the development of electronic transactions and commerce.

Most Member States in the European Union have by now implemented the European Directives 95/46/EC and 97/66/EC. The first mentioned Directive

---

[3] See J.J.Borking, op.cit. p. 27
[4] See J.J. Borking, op.cit. p.28 - 31

provides a general legal framework for the protection of personal data. The second one contains specific privacy requirement for telecommunication. The current challenge is to implement the EU based national legislation in such a way that effective consumer and citizen privacy protection is the result.

5 Privacy-Enhancing Technologies (PET)

Conventional information systems generally record a large amount of information. This information is often easily linked to an individual. Sometimes these information systems contain information that is privacy-sensitive to some individuals. To prevent information systems from recording too much information the information systems need to be adjusted.

There are a number of options to prevent the recording of data that can be easily linked to individuals. The first is not to generate or record data at all. The second option is not to record data that is unique to an individual (identifying data). The absence of such data makes it almost impossible to link existing data to a private individual. These two options can be combined into a third one. With this third option, only strictly necessary identifying data will be recorded, together with the non-identifying data. In PISA we will study how this Privacy Enhancing Technology (PET) can be implemented in software agents.

The conventional information system contains the following processes: authorization, identification and authentication access control, auditing and accounting. In the conventional information system, the user's identity is often needed to perform these processes. The identity is used within the authorization process, for instance, to identify and record the user's privileges and duties. The user's identity is thus introduced into the information system. Because in a conventional information system all processes are related, the identity travels through the information system.

The main question is: is identity necessary for each of the processes of the conventional information system? For authentication, in most cases, it is not necessary to know the user's identity in order to grant privileges. However, there are some situations in which the user must reveal his identity to allow verification of certain required characteristics. For identification and authentication, access control and auditing the identity is not necessary. For accounting, the identity could be needed in some cases. It is possible that a user needs to be called to account for the use of certain services, e.g. when the user misuses or improperly uses the information system.

6 Identity Protector (IP)

The introduction of an Identity Protector (IP)[5], as a part of the conventional information system, will structure the information system in order to protect

---

[5] cf. R.Hes and J.J.Borking editors, Privacy Enhancing Technologies: The path to anonymity. revised edition, A&V 10, The Hague 1998

the privacy of the user. The IP can be seen as a part of the system that controls the exchange of the user's identity within the information system.

The Identity Protector offers the following functions:

1. Reports and controls instances when identity is revealed;
2. Generates pseudo-identities;
3. Translates pseudo-identities into identities and vice versa;
4. Converts pseudo-identities into other pseudo-identities;
5. Combats misuse.

An important functionality of the IP is conversion of a user's identity into a pseudo-identity. The pseudo-identity is an alternate (digital) identity that the user may adopt when consulting an information system (see Figure 1).

The user must be able to trust the way his personal data is handled in the domain where his identity is known. The IP (as system element), can be placed anywhere in the system where personal data is exchanged. This offers some solutions for privacy-compliant information systems. Techniques that can be used to implement an IP are: digital signatures, blind digital signatures, digital pseudonyms, and trusted third parties. In PISA the technological objective is to solve the problems of design and implementation of an IP in software agents to be used on the electronic highway for privacy issues.

7   PET-Agent (PISA)

The challenge is to design an PET-agent that independently performs these tasks, while fully preserving the privacy of the persons involved, or at least up to the level specified by the persons themselves. The agent should for that purpose be able to distinguish what information should be exchanged in what circumstances to which party. The challenge here is to implement privacy laws, specifically the European Directive 95/46/EC (being the highest privacy standard at this moment in the world) and other rules into specifications for a product. Next the specifications have to be implemented by software programming. Also there should be appropriate (cryptographic) protection mechanisms to ensure the security of the data and prevent 'leakage' to third parties. PET-agents (PISA) will enable the user in its quality of consumer or citizen in e-commerce and e-government transactions and communications to protect himself against loss of his informational privacy contrary to systems like P3P where an asymmetric situation exists to the benefit of the web site owner. PISA empowers the consumer and citizen to decide at any time and in any circumstance when to reveal his or her identity.

8   Specific Demonstration Objectives

Thus, if the use of agents could lead to so many potential privacy risks, one wonders if it could be possible for anyone to use ISATs safely. I believe this

PISA Model 1: PET wrapped around the agent

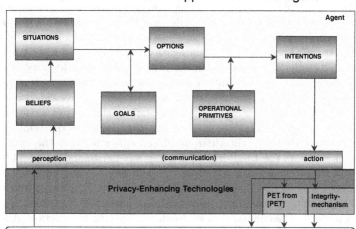

PISA (privacy incorporated software agent)

PISA model 2: PET integrated in the software agent

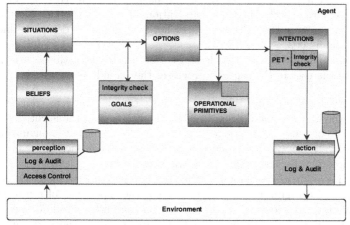

Security services to support the PET and integrity check mechanisms
(e.g. a crypto-mechanism to perform digital signatures)
PET as in [PET] Cf.J.J.Borking et all.: Intelligent software agents and privacy p. 39 The Hague 1999 ISBN 9074087132

Fig. 1. The identity protector separates the identity and pseudo domains

still remains within the realm of possibility, and that the answer lies in the use of so-called privacy-enhancing technologies (PET). The tracking and logging of a person's use of computer networks is a major source of potential privacy violation. Conventional information systems perform the following transactions: authorization, identification and authentication access control, auditing and accounting. At each phase, a user's identification is connected with the transaction. However, by means of a system element (filter) called the "Identity Protector" (IP) the design of a system will go a long way to protecting privacy. The introduction of an IP into an information system can improve the protection of the user's information by structuring the system in such a way as to remove all unnecessary linkages to the user's personally identifying information.

The Identity Protector filter can be placed either between the user and the agent; this prevents the ISAT from collecting any personal data about the user without the knowledge and prior consent of the user. Conversely, the IP can be located between the agent and the external environment, preventing the ISAT from divulging any personal information unless specifically required to do so in order to perform a particular task or conduct a specific transaction. Additional technical means may also be integrated into the ISAT in order to bring even more transparency to the user in the operation of the agent, thus ensuring the user's knowledge, and if necessary, informed consent.

An international team consisting of the Dutch Physics and Electronics Laboratories (TNO), The Dutch Technical University of Delft, Sientient, a Dutch company designing data mining systems, Italsoft from Roma (Italy), CIME-Labs an d Toutela from Paris, the Canadian National Research Council and the Registratiekamer (Dutch Data Protection Authority) will build a demonstrable PISA not later than 2003.

The main objectives of the demonstrator are to show the security of the privacy of the user in the types of processes that could be employed:

- Clearly detailed audit logging and activity tracking of agent transactions so that the user can monitor and review the behavior of the agent;
- The use of programs to render the user and/or the agent anonymous, or alternatively, the use of a "pseudo-identity" unless identification is specifically required for the performance of a transaction;
- The use of identification and authentication mechanisms such as digital signatures and digital certificates to prevent the "spoofing" of a user or their agent by a malicious third party intent on committing fraud or agent theft;
- The use of data encryption technology to prevent unauthorized "sniffing" or accessing of agent transaction details;
- The use of trusted sources: the agent can be instructed to only visit sites that have been independently verified (through a variety of means such as trusted seals, audits, etc.) as having proper privacy provisions in place;
- Placing limitations on an agent's autonomy so they only perform a certain range of activities – limited activities will be permitted to be freely conducted without additional authorization; any requests for unauthorized transactions will be flagged for the user to scrutinize.

The integration of these technologies into the core of the ISAT, combined with a process that places similar technology between the agent and the external environment would result in a demonstration system PISA that shows and enjoyed the maximum protection against threats to the user's privacy enabling users protecting themselves not being dependent systems like P3P or on other privacy seals. The international team hopes to get a subsidy of the European Commission under EU Technology program.

9   Contribution to EU Technology Programme and Key Action Objectives

The PISA-project contributes to EU - IST-programme and key action line II4.1 and II4.2 objectives:

II4.1: "To develop and validate novel, scalable and interoperable technologies, mechanisms and architectures for trust and security in distributed organizations, services and underlying infrastructures".

With the focus on:

"Building technologies to empower users to consciously and effectively manage and negotiate their "personal rights" (i.e. privacy, confidentiality, etc.). This includes technologies that enable anonymous or pseudonymous access to information society applications and services, for example by minimizing the generation of personal data."

II4.2: To scale-up, integrate, validate and demonstrate trust and confidence technologies and Architectures in the context of advanced large-scale scenarios for business and everyday life. This work will largely be carried out through trials, integrated test-beds and combined RTD and demonstrations.

Focus on:

"Generic solutions that emphasize large-scale interoperability and are capable of supporting broad array of transactions (e.g. e-purses and e-money), applications and processes. Development of solutions that reconcile new e-commerce models and processes with security Requirements, paying particular attention to the needs of SMEs and consumers Validation should generally include assessing legal implications of proposed solutions, especially in the context of solutions aimed at empowering users to consciously and effectively manage their personal "rights and assets".

PISA contributes at building a model of a software agent within a network environment, to demonstrate that it is possible to perform complicated actions on behalf of a person, without the personal data of that person being compromised. In the design of the agent an effective selection of the presented privacy enhancing technologies will be implemented. We label this product as a Privacy Incorporated Software Agent (PISA).

The PISA demonstration model is planned to be a novel piece of software that incorporates several advanced technologies in one product:

- Agent technology, for intelligent search and matching;
- Data mining or comparable techniques to construct profiles and make predictions;
- Cryptography for the protection of personal data, as well as the confidentiality of transactions.

Additionally the project involves:

- Legal expertise to implement the European privacy legislation and the needed development of new legal norms in this field;
- System design knowledge in order to turn legal boundary condition into technical specifications;
- Advanced software programming skills to implement the privacy boundary conditions.

In order to prove the capability of the PISA-model, we propose to test it in a model environment in two cases in e-commerce that closely resembles a real-life situation.

Case 1: Matching Supply and Demand on the Labor Market

The demonstrator will be applied to a practical case, which is suitable to test several aspects of privacy protection. Testing of the demonstrator will be done in a local network environment. The proposed test object is the matching of supply and demand on the labor market. In the coming years it is expected that the matching on the labor market will increasingly be performed through such (Internet based) intermediaries. The agent on behalf of the consumer/citizen carries in this process the profile of a person, including sensitive information about his or her history, (dis) abilities, skills, labor history etc. When matching this information with the available functions, a match has to be made between the user profile and the demands of the party requiring personnel. In this process personal data will be exchanged in an anonymous way. After the match has been made successfully and so has been reported by the agent to its user, he or she may decide to reveal his/her identity.

Case 2: Matching Supply and Demand for Vehicle and Real Estate Markets

The second demonstrator will be an extension of an existing Web portal, providing a range of intermediation services oriented towards both individual consumers and business users, addressing areas like buying and selling of vehicles (cars, vans, boats, ...), buying, selling and renting of real estate, etc. Respecting and protecting privacy of the users posting requests on this site is a key aspect of user acceptance of the intermediation services proposed. Testing of the demonstrator will be done in a local network environment. The proposed test object is the matching of supply and demand on the vehicle and real estate markets. In the coming years it is expected that the matching on these markets will increasingly be performed through such (Internet based) intermediaries. In the intermediation process, the agent matches requests and offerings posted by individuals, which may encompass confidential information not to be disclosed to the outside world.

10   Innovation

E-commerce/E-government and other ICT developments introduce a fundamentally new modus of consumer-transactions with new challenges to data protection. A growing awareness exists that, next to a legal framework, effective privacy protection should be supported by technical and organizational measures. This is particularly needed in view of the difficulty to attach global electronic transactions to a particular jurisdiction. In order to increase the visibility of privacy compliance websites involved in E-commerce activities apply so-called "privacy seals" like P3P. These are mere visual statements of compliance, the credibility of which is difficult to judge for consumers.

Rather than relying on legal protection and self-regulation only, the protection of consumers' privacy is probably more effective if transactions are performed by means of technologies that are privacy enhancing. This group of technologies is commonly referred to as Privacy Enhancing Technologies (PET).

In the context of E-commerce on the consumers market, a major current initiative to increase privacy compliance is the so-called P3P, under development by the W3C consortium. Major players in the software industry back the W3C consortium. P3P provides for a standardized language and interface for both consumer and website to provide their personal data and privacy preferences. Transactions can be accomplished according to the specified level of openness given by consumers on their personal data. The P3P, as being developed now, does not foresee any "negotiation" between consumer and market party. It is basically a compliance check between consumer preferences and website policy, therefore relatively static and it needs active user input for each transaction. Given the limited capability of P3P it is also difficult to implement the privacy principles underlying the European Directive into this technology. Although an essential first step, P3P is not sufficient for effective and efficient privacy protection of consumers.

As will be demonstrated later E-commerce and E-government will only lift off if the search for matches of supply and demand and the accompanying negotiation on privacy preferences can be performed in a distributed way. This would both decrease the load on network capacity and on the time spent by a consumer. Intelligent agents are the right types of software for this task. In contrast to current systems like P3P, agents should be able to negotiate intelligently with the consumer, a website or with each other. Skills to negotiate privacy and a common platform for communication will have to develop. This level of sophistication will enable developers to implement more deeply the principles of privacy into the technology itself. Once equipped with these skills a "PET-agent" will become an enabler of secure E-commerce and E-government and will provide a structural feed back and control of the user over his personal or to him identifiable data in cyber space preventing harmful privacy int rusions.

11   Dutch Data Protection Authority

The project results will be of importance to the Dutch Data Protection Authority and other privacy commissioners in several respects.

Firstly the resulting model software will be an element towards an effective and user-friendly implementation of the European Directive 95/46/EC. Parallel to the legal approach, the emergence of new forms of electronic business and interactions urges for a data protection approach that ties in more closely with the dynamic technological environment. On a time scale of a few years, the software agents to be built, will become an important instrument for data protection, additional to the legal instruments used now. The results to be achieved will have a feedback on the legislative process within the EU as well.

For the DDPA participating in the protect helps the office to develop practical ways to make its task effective as well as a way to keep up its renowned high standard of expertise on the connection between ICT and privacy. It is necessary to be within the arena of technology development and to translate the Directive 95/46/EC into design recommendations if the organization should retain its viability as authority, and to serve the consumers within the EU, in matters of data protection.

A fruitful collaboration between the DDPA and the industrial partners, finally, will also help to keep up the competitive advantage of the European software industry in designing tools that provide trust and security as added values.

Identity Management Based on P3P

Oliver Berthold[1] and Marit Köhntopp[2]

[1] Dresden University of Technology, Department of Computer Science, D-01062
Dresden, Germany
`Oliver.Berthold@gmx.de`
[2] Independent Centre for Privacy Protection Schleswig-Holstein, Germany;
Unabhängiges Landeszentrum für Datenschutz Schleswig-Holstein, Postfach 71 21,
D-24171 Kiel, Germany
`marit@koehntopp.de`

Abstract. Identity management is a powerful mechanism to enhance
user-privacy. In this paper we will examine the idea of an identity management system built atop of an anonymous-communication network.
First, we will develop some basic approaches to realize identity management, and we will introduce the Platform for Privacy Preferences Project
(P3P) as a standard for exchanging personal data in the World Wide
Web. After discussing the feasibility of using P3P as a basis, we will
outline some possibilities for designing an identity management system
using P3P. For this purpose, other building blocks, especially considering the representation of different kinds of pseudonyms as the core of
an identity management system, are described. Finally, we will sketch
possible future developments of identity managers.

1 Introduction

Several projects deal with anonymity in the Internet. Assuming the existence of
a network allowing anonymous communication in the lower OSI layers, a mechanism for managing, disclosing, verifying, and negotiating personal data on higher
layers is required to give users the choice between real anonymity, pseudonymity,
optional self-identification, authentication, and mandatory identification where
necessary [6]. Powerful services for identity management should be designed to
enable the user to choose the degree of anonymity and the security level of an
authentication appropriate to a given context. Additionally, she should be able
to negotiate her preferences with the ones of other involved parties. The aim of
our project is to realize an identity management system and exert influence on
both technical and legal standardization processes concerning this topic.

1.1 The Idea of Identity Management

Identity management is something we do in normal conversation everyday when
we decide on what to tell one another about ourselves. As a part of this process,
each person considers the situational context and the role she is currently acting

H. Federrath (Ed.): Anonymity 2000, LNCS 2009, pp. 141–160, 2001.

in as well as the respective relationship to the communication partners. Therefore, it makes a difference whether a person is at home, in the office, with her family, doing sports in her club, going shopping etc. Sometimes this goes as far as a person being known by different names in different contexts, e.g. by using specific names, nicknames or pseudonyms suiting the occasion. This common social behavior is the inspiration for an identity management in a digital world, where all disclosed data can potentially be linked and aggregated to informative user profiles. By managing her identity, roles, and personal data, a user may decide whom to give which data to, when to act anonymously (like when real-life shopping in a city), when to use a pseudonym, when to authenticate herself etc. Ideally, the different pseudonyms which represent her identity or roles can be linked only if the holder so desires.

An identity management system empowers the users to maintain their privacy and control their digital identity. It contains considerable advantages for providers as well. Surveys[1] show that users currently do not trust the Internet and e-commerce mainly because of security and privacy risks. Secondly, most users fill in false personal data in web forms (like "Mickey Mouse") when they see no reason to give authentic data. Identity management and other measures for empowering the users, as well as building in technical privacy baselines, could support e-commerce: Users with no fear of risking their privacy are more willing to use the Internet and its services. The providers not only would get more customers, the quality of the personal data a user explicitly discloses will also increase.

Identity management is useful for realizing an "e-government", too. Even for applications which require authenticity, like user participation processes or voting, a person's real name is not needed in most cases, but the use of certified pseudonyms would be sufficient. Thus, registration offices would issue pseudonymous certificates for some cryptographic keys to be used in specific e-government applications. Attributes like the graduation, the profession, a specific membership or the holding of certain licenses could be certified. Different properties of pseudonyms and certificates have to be supported, concerning for instance the expiration, the non-repudiation, and the possibilities for checking, exposing, revoking, or passing them on to other users.

For an identity management system in relation with commercial applications which cannot be realized totally anonymously, providers would issue certificates for customers and their personal data which is needed for the purchase or shipment and for personalization of their offer. Again the user's real name is not required, but pseudonyms are sufficient, and with integrating third parties the provider can even do without personal address data. Additionally, attributes like "Has bought products at ACME Inc. for $ 1000" can be certified, which could be used as a voucher for discounts on future purchases and act as a financial incentive to strengthen customer loyalty. To prove authenticity, the certificates could be checked online. Others would have an expiration date. Some of the certificates would be transferable, others would not, depending on the application.

---

[1] E.g. http://www.cdt.org/privacy/survey/findings/ and
http://www.privacyexchange.org/iss/surveys/surveys.html.

1.2   Existing Approaches to Identity Management Systems

The basic ideas of identity management systems have already been described by David Chaum since 1985, although the term itself seems to be newer. His fundamental text "Security without Identification: Card Computers to Make Big Brother Obsolete" [4] comprises the vision of a personal "card computer" to handle all payments and other transactions of the user while protecting her security and privacy. Moreover, it sketches the building blocks for such a system. Unfortunately there has been no implementation of the "big picture" given in the article, yet. But now the requirements of an underlying anonymous network and appropriate infrastructures become more and more available.

Since 1995 the concept of an "Identity Protector" has been in discussion [16]. Most existing implementations center around identity protectors in specific applications, but not directly controlled by the user, or at least not in her own space. A good identity management system could be regarded as an universal, generic identity protector on the user side.

The "Personal Reachability and Security Management" for callers and the subscribers being called was developed and prototypically implemented in the context of the Kolleg "Security in Communication Technology" as an example of Multilateral Security [8]. It also contains a concept for user identification and the way users handle identity functions. Users are able to communicate anonymously, or by using a pseudonym – having the freedom of choice and using a negotiation protocol. Furthermore, users may present themselves in different roles by means of different identity cards, being issued as pseudonyms. For the purposes of identification and recognition, each user participating in the communication employs digital identity cards which are stored as data structures in her personal digital assistant (PDA). They may contain several data items including a cryptographic key pair used for digital signatures and the encryption of communication contents. Certificates issued from some certification authorities (CA) confirm the validity of the identity card and its data.

Thinking of business models concerning personal data, Hagel and Singer proposed the concept of "infomediaries" [9]: "In order for customers to strike the best bargain with vendors, they will need a trusted third party – a kind of personal agent, information intermediary, or infomediary – to aggregate their information with that of other consumers and to use the combined market power to negotiate with vendors on their behalf." Some of the existing infomediaries provide the possibility for managing different personae, e.g. digitalme[2] and PrivaSeek[3] [7]. However, from the privacy point of view, a great disadvantage of present-days infomediaries is the lack of user control: The personal data are stored on the server which might log and analyze each access to gain a detailed picture of the user's behavior. Sometimes infomediaries even build psychograms with sensitive personal data about the user's psyche. In many cases the providers will not tell the users about their profile because they regard the process of analyzing the user's behavior as a trade secret.

---

[2] http://www.digitalme.com/.

[3] http://www.privaseek.com/.

1.3   Criteria for Identity Management Systems

The existing approaches towards identity management systems are not sufficient or might even be potentially privacy-invasive in current implementations. Instead, a powerful identity management system, like the one we aim to develop, should meet the following criteria [11]:

− *Privacy protection baseline*
  as much privacy as possible through ...
  - anonymous underlying communication network,[4]
  - trustworthy user device, e.g. trustworthy personal digital assistant,
  - transparency, e.g. through open source and an informative user interface,
  - validation of the data security level by independent experts,
  - data security concerning the communication with other parties,
  - personally restricted access to the identity manager, e.g. through biometrics;
− *empowering the user*
  by the following means:
  - convenient user interface to manage different pseudonyms/roles/identity cards [8], [2],
  - storage of personal data under user control,
  - possibility of recording the communication in order to be able to reconstruct which party possesses which personal data,
  - negotiation tool for the decision which data the user wants to disclose under what conditions,
  - supporting user-controlled privacy facilities like grant of consent, data inspection, desire for change, desire for removal, and revocation of consent,
  - negotiation tool for other aspects like personal reachability or security configuration,
  - possibility of support from privacy protection authorities, e.g. help with configuration;
− *representation of pseudonyms/roles/identity cards with different properties*
  through cryptographic means (blind signatures, credentials, secret-key certificates) and integration of public key infrastructures [14];
− *based on standardized protocols and open data structures*
  with possible extensions so that the identity management system is not restricted to Internet or phone communication or to only few specific applications;
− *possibility for easy monitoring*
  through privacy protection authorities or other auditing facilities;
− *compliance with legal framework.*

---

[4] Additionally, anonymous cash and anonymous delivery services would be useful for aspects of identity management in e-commerce. By use of the cryptographic means needed for an identity management system anyway, at least anonymous "tokens" or vouchers could be created which could serve as money. Moreover, they could help realizing anonymous delivery services as well.

2   The Platform for Privacy Preferences Project

Seeking existing standards for exchange of personal data suitable for putting on an identity management system, the most popular and most universal approach is the Platform for Privacy Preferences Project (P3P)[5], which is being developed by the World Wide Web Consortium (W3C) [15].

2.1   General Functionality of P3P

P3P enables web sites to express their privacy practices in a standard format that can be retrieved automatically and interpreted easily by user agents. P3P user agents will allow users to be informed of web site practices (in both machine- and human-readable formats) and to automate decision-making based on these practices when appropriate.

When a P3P-compliant client requests a resource, a service sends a link to a machine-readable privacy policy in which the organization responsible for the service declares its identity and privacy practices. The privacy policy enumerates the data elements that the service proposes to collect and explains how each will be used, with whom data may be shared, and how long the data will be retained. Policies can be parsed automatically by user agents – such as web browsers, browser plug-ins, or proxy servers – and compared with privacy preferences set by the user. Depending on those preferences, a user agent may then simply display information for the user, generate prompts or take other actions like accepting or rejecting requests. The matching process takes place in a "safe zone", in which a P3P-compliant server should only collect a minimum of information about a client.

2.2   A Closer Look on the Technical Details of P3P 1.0

A basic P3P interaction might proceed as follows:

1. The agent requests a web page from a service.
2. The service responds by sending a reference to a P3P policy in the header of its HTTP response. A policy consists of one or more statements about a service's privacy practices.
3. The agent fetches the policy, evaluates it according to the user's ruleset (which represents her preferences, e.g. expressed in APPEL – A P3P Preference Expression Language [1]), and determines what action to take: e.g. request, limit, or block the required data transfer, optionally prompting the user to inform her or to ask her for a decision.

A typical P3P policy expressed as XML may look as shown in table 1.

P3P defines a Base Data Schema which all P3P-compliant user agent implementations must take into account. It specifies a wide variety of commonly used data elements, but also provides basic data types, which can be conveniently reused by other schemas, e.g. "personname" or "contact" (postal, telecom, online).

---

[5] http://www.w3.org/P3P/.

Table 1. P3P policy expressed as XML

Elements of a P3P policy	Typical example for a privacy policy of a shop
URL of P3P version and the policy	```<POLICY xmlns="http://www.w3.org/2000/P3Pv1" discuri="http://www.catalog.example.com/ PrivacyPracticeBrowsing.html">```
Entity: description of the legal entity making the representation of the privacy practices	```<ENTITY> <DATA-GROUP> <DATA ref="#business.name"> CatalogExample </DATA> <DATA ref="#business.contact-info.postal.street"> [...] </DATA> </DATA-GROUP> </ENTITY>```
Disputes: dispute resolution procedures	```<DISPUTES-GROUP> <DISPUTES resolution-type="independent" service="http://www.PrivacySeal.example.org" [...] </DISPUTES> </DISPUTES-GROUP>```
Access: the ability of the individual to view identifiable information	```<ACCESS><contact_and_other/></ACCESS>```
Statement: data practices that are applied to particular types of data; with purpose, recipient, retention policy, and data groups consisting of some standard data elements, and with the "miscdata" element which in this case stands for some financial data as indicated in the categories field	```<STATEMENT> <PURPOSE><current/></PURPOSE> <RECIPIENT><ours/></RECIPIENT> <RETENTION><stated-purpose/></RETENTION> <DATA-GROUP> <DATA ref="#user.name" /> <DATA ref="#user.home-info.postal" /> <DATA ref="#user.home-info.telecom.telephone" optional="yes" /> <DATA ref="#user.home-info.online.email" optional="yes" /> <DATA ref="#dynamic.miscdata"> <CATEGORIES><financial/><CATEGORIES/> </DATA> </DATA-GROUP> </STATEMENT> [...] </POLICY>```

The P3P Base Data Schema defines the "user" data set as a record comprising the user's name, her birth date, a user's identity certificate, gender, employer, department, jobtitle, home info and business info. It is always optional whether the user fills in the correct information or not, but the server may require a value in a data field.

Additionally, P3P allows the definition of new data elements which have to be assigned to categories like the predefined data elements. Categories are attributes of data elements that provide hints to users and user agents as to the intended uses of the data. They build a group of a set of single data elements. A single data element like "user.name.personname" can belong to multiple categories at the same time. Categories allow users to express more generalized preferences and rules for the exchange of their data. Often, they will be included when defining a new element or when referring to data that the user is prompted to type in (as opposed to data stored in the user data repository). Categories in P3P 1.0 address physical contact information, online contact information, unique identifiers, purchase information, financial information, computer information, navigation and click-stream data, interactive data, demographic and socioeconomic data, content, state management mechanisms, political information, health information, and preference data. To add new categories, the "<other-category>"-tag shall be used in addition to a human-readable explanation.

Furthermore, P3P provides a flexible and powerful mechanism to extend its syntax and semantics using the element "<EXTENSION>". The meaning of the data within the "<EXTENSION>" element is defined by the extension itself. Thus, it is not only possibly to extend the P3P vocabulary, but to lay down rules for the interpretation of such any data attributes.

Because users may wish to use their user agent to help them convey distinct identities to different sites (e.g. establishing single-session anonymous relationships with certain sites, long-term pseudonymous relationships with other sites, and identified relationships with even other sites), the P3P specification provides the optional use of "personae" in the user agent. A persona is defined as a unique identifier for a set of data element values in the user's data repository that the user wants to use during the current browsing session [1]. Implementations could offer to store multiple values for the same data element and allow users to conveniently choose between certain sets of values when giving out information from the repository (e.g. a set of values to be used in the office and a different set to be used on weekends). Thus, different kind of pseudonyms might be used, including automatically-generated pseudonyms. For each persona, the behavior of the user agent when interpreting a site's P3P policy may be different. APPEL provides a mechanism for the user to specify various rules or rulesets depending on the persona.

2.3   Outlook on the Future Functionality of P3P

In P3P 1.0 some significant sections from earlier drafts of the specification were removed in order to facilitate rapid implementation and deployment of a P3P first step. Future releases will include e.g. the possibility of a negotiation[6] between the user and a web site. Moreover, P3P will support future digital certificate and digital signature capabilities as they become available.

2.4   Compliance of P3P with the Criteria for an Identity Management System

Considering the possibility to use the P3P protocol as an underlying technical standard for the data exchange which is necessary for an identity management system, the compliance with the criteria for a powerful identity management system have to be checked. Table 2 shows which requirements are met by P3P in the current version and in future versions.

---

[6] Stefan Brands points out that such an automated negotiation mechanism as it is planned in P3P (and in fact has been proposed in earlier versions of the specification, but was eliminated for getting a sleeker version 1.0) could be uses to implement the negotiation process in the certificate showing protocol of his secret keys [3, page 27].

Table 2. Requirements met by P3P

Criterion	Addressed by P3P?
Privacy protection baseline	P3P can only act as a module in a larger context, thus it does not realize the full privacy protection itself, but may be integrated. Nevertheless, some privacy principles which can be technically achieved or supported, are already realized in P3P: transparency and anonymity to a certain degree (through preferences or safe zone). Besides, it is planned to integrate P3P in small devices under user control later on.
Empowering the user	In P3P 1.0 this is addressed by: <ul><li>informed consent by user choice (including which personal data, recipients, purposes),</li><li>data management with categories,</li><li>storage of personal data under user control,</li><li>possibility of recording the communication,</li><li>possibility of loading configuration files from privacy protection authorities.</li></ul>Negotiation is not addressed in P3P 1.0, but will be realized in further versions. Furthermore, user control possibilities for expressing privacy functions are not addressed, but can be added on the base of P3P, e.g. via projects like DASIT (http://sit.gmd.de/MINT/projects/dasit.pdf).
Representation of pseudonyms / roles / identity cards with different properties	This is addressed by the persona concept (depending on the user agent) and structured data types and fields for managing certificates provided by P3P. It would be necessary to integrate cryptographic means, e.g. by P3P's extension mechanism concerning syntax and semantics.
Based on standardized protocols and open data structures	P3P 1.0 will realize this because it: <ul><li>will be an open standard protocol and coacts with other commonly used standards (like HTTP, XML),</li><li>defines a base data schema,</li><li>allows a flexible expansion of the data schema,</li><li>comprises an extension mechanism concerning syntax and semantics.</li></ul>
Possibility for easy monitoring	P3P 1.0 provides the possibility of online monitoring and comparison of the privacy policies, but cannot guarantee that companies follow them.
Compliance with legal framework	Legal aspects are not directly addressed, because this is mostly independent of P3P; nevertheless the technical standard does not contradict the legal framework.

Important is the fact, that no property of P3P contravenes the given criteria. In contrast, in the specifications both on the server and the client side, the designers of P3P already make arrangements for the possibility of realizing different personae in P3P-compliant user agents. Thus, P3P may help to realize an identity management system, although it can only be one of several building blocks.

3   Building Blocks for an Identity Management System

The criteria for an identity management system lead to a more detailed specification of some building blocks. The need for some of them is quite obvious, e.g. a comfortable user interface, the underlying anonymous network or a suitable legal baseline. The core component is the realization of different kinds of pseudonyms by different cryptographic means. Related to providing some kinds of pseudonyms is the existence of an appropriate infrastructure of third parties (TPs) acting as certification authorities.

3.1   Properties of Pseudonyms

A pseudonym is an identifier of a subject [13]. It could be an other name instead of the real name of a person (as some authors, actors, or pop stars choose). A digital pseudonym is a bit string which is unique as ID and suitable to be used to authenticate the holder, i.e. they can be realized with digital signatures. If different occurrences of a holder's pseudonym can be linked, it is possible to establish a specific reputation. If there is a trusted third party involved in a transaction, it may give the interacting parties some guarantees like ensuring a fair deal by revealing the identity of a party or to cover the claim in the case of abuse. For some applications the number of pseudonyms per person may be limited, e.g. for an election. Additionally, there might be other limitations, e.g. an expiration date. Table 3 illustrates typical examples for pseudonyms and their properties.

There are many further constellations for using different kinds of pseudonyms.[7] In many cases, it is important for other parties who are involved in a transaction where pseudonyms are used, to figure out what kinds of pseudonyms they are. This knowledge is both useful for the holder of the pseudonym and for other partners to estimate under which circumstances which persons might link different occurrences of the pseudonym, reveal the identity, revoke it or block it. Additionally, it is important to know the degree of authenticity and to be aware of guarantees which may be related with the use of the pseudonym.

3.2   Realization of Some Pseudonym Properties

A digital pseudonym can be realized as a public key, i.e. a unique bit string with a corresponding private key to test digital signatures: A CA certifies that a specific

---

[7] E.g. some special pseudonyms may be defined for groups where the identity of a single member may only be revealed by cooperation of a certain number of group members.

Table 3. Typical examples for pseudonyms and their properties (Part 1)

Example	Pseudonym Description	transferable?	linkable?	identity revealable by TP?	limited validity?	Remarks
person uses pseudonym for a wide variety of relationships over a long period of time	person pseudonym: substitute for name	−	+			Should not be transferable to other persons.
person uses pseudonym for e-commerce (i.e. all dealers); club membership	role pseudonym: assigned to the role a person is currently playing	−	+			Should not be transferable to other persons; can be used for many transactions; linkable; possible establishment of a reputation which may be used for other partners.
person uses a different pseudonym for each dealer; club membership	relationship pseudonym: dependent on communication partner	−	+			Should not be transferable to other persons; can be used for many transactions; linkable; possible establishment of a reputation which may be used for one partner.
person uses a different pseudonym for each role and for each dealer; club membership	role-relationship pseudonym: combination of role pseudonym and relationship pseudonym	−	+			Should not be transferable to other persons; can be used for many transactions, but only per role *and* relationship; linkable, but only per role *and* relationship; possible establishment of a reputation which may be used for one partner and in one role.

bit string has been presented from a person who has certain properties or fulfils certain demands. This bit string is the public key of a digital signature system; only the holder of the pseudonym knows the corresponding private key. If she signs a document with her private key, other parties may check it with the public key of the pseudonym to be sure about its authenticity. The CAs which assign properties to pseudonyms may achieve this by means of blind digital signatures.

Convertible credentials provide realizing pseudonymous authentication without one identifiable bit string. There are various concepts: Chaum's Credentials [5], Brands' Secret Keys [3] and Lysyanskaya's Pseudonym Systems [12]. With all these kinds of credentials, it is possible that the user can obtain a credential from one organization using one of her pseudonyms, but demonstrate possession of the credential to another organization without revealing her first pseudonym.

Table 4. Typical examples for pseudonyms and their properties (Part 2)

Example	Pseudonym Description	transferable?	linkable?	identity revealable by TP?	limited validity?	Remarks
person uses a different pseudonym for each transaction	transaction pseudonym: kind of role or relationship pseudonym for only one transaction	−	−	in the case of abuse, where required		Unlinkable (unless by means of context data); in the case of abuse, TP should be able to reveal the identity or to cover the claim.
voucher to spend a specific amount at a company	voucher	+	−		no double-spending; time limit	Transferable; not reusable; unlinkable.
person provides evidence to be of age	attribute pseudonym / certificate	−	−	+, or only valid in combination with other pseudonym	+, or only valid in combination with other pseudonym	From TP; not transferable; unlinkable.
one single vote per adult in an election	is-a-person transaction pseudonym (one unique pseudonym per person and application)	−	−		time limit, or only valid for a specific transaction	Each adult may use only one pseudonym; it is not transferable; not reusable; unlinkable.
(not) transferable annual ticket for public transport	pseudonym with time limit	+ −	+		− time limit	With date of expiration.
driver's license	revocable certificate	−			revocable or blockable	Online check or revocation lists of TP.

For this purpose, a credential can be converted into a credential for the currently used pseudonym. Therefore the use of different credentials is unlinkable. The approaches of Chaum, Brands and Lysyanskaya differ in some properties: Whereas Chaum's credentials do not prevent an unauthorized lending of credentials (i.e. the sharing of identity), the newer approaches motivate the user not to give away her credentials by tying them tightly to her digital identity. Additionally the involvement of CAs is much more reduced compared to Chaum's system.

The following paragraphs illustrates how to achieve certain properties of pseudonyms.

Preventing the transfer of pseudonyms: There are some possibilities to take care that pseudonyms will not be transferred to other persons:

- In the case of abuse, the user's identity may be revealed (as stated below).
- Giving away one's own digital identity could be an inevitable consequence of the transfer of a pseudonym; thus, it would be a high risk for the holder of a pseudonym (like the approaches of pseudonym systems and secret keys).
- All pseudonyms of a person may be stored in a tamper-resistant device (perhaps smartcards); thus, there would be a high risk of giving it to another person.
- Additionally, the use of biometrics for working with the pseudonym on a tamper-resistant device could prevent using other persons' pseudonyms.

If a tamper-resistant device was used, it would have one private key which would be certified by a CA. In order to certify pseudonyms, a CA would receive the pseudonyms which are signed with the private key of the device and/or of the user. After checking the signature, the CA would sign them and send back the certified pseudonyms. To ensure the confidentiality, the certified pseudonyms would be additionally encrypted by the public key of the device.

Preventing the possibility of linking pseudonyms: To prevent linking pseudonyms, blind signatures may be used if a single use of a document is sufficient: To certify specific attributes, the CA or the vendor signs a blinded document of the user. The user may present the unblinded – and therefore unlinkable – document. A multiple use of the document could be recognized because there is only one unblinded representation. With this method, the user may pass on her document to other parties.

Other methods are based on the use of convertible credentials (see above). Chaining various CAs with different tasks is another solution for unlinkable pseudonyms, here illustrated with three CAs: After encrypting the pseudonym first with the public key of CA1 and then the result with the public key of CA2, the user sends the string ca2(ca1(pseudonym)) to CA3 along with the information about her real name. CA3 signs the string and sends it to CA2, which checks the signature of CA3. If it is valid, CA2 decrypts the string, signs it and sends it to CA1. There the new signature is checked again, before the CA decrypts the string. This yields a pseudonym which can only be linked to the real name if all CAs collaborate.

Possibility to reveal the user's identity: It is much easier to propagate the use of pseudonyms in e-commerce if there is the guarantee that no party may trick the other. For that reason, a trustee can be involved whose task is in the case of abuse to cover the claim or to reveal the identity of the fraudulent party for disputing the assignment of damages. Naive implementations consisting of an integration of a single third party, which is involved in each communication process of the user, may be a threat to privacy itself. Therefore, solutions with less involvement should be preferred, e.g. the concept of identity escrow [10]: A party B receives a guarantee that a third party C can determine A's identity without being involved in the day to day operation, but is only called in when anonymity must be revoked. With concepts of chaining or secret sharing schemes, the cooperation of multiple instances for revealing the user's identity could be enforced.

Limited number of uses: The limited number of uses may be important for vouchers and can be realized as follows: Each use of a pseudonym is signed by the user, and the signature is stored in a database. If a multiple use has to be prohibited, a double signature would be rejected so that the pseudonym cannot be used again (or not more times than allowed). A (transferable) voucher could be represented by a private key. It would be issued by a vendor who holds the corresponding public key. In order to redeem the voucher, the customer would sign a document "The voucher XYZ was redeemed." with the private key of the voucher. The vendor would check the digital signature with the public key of the voucher to be sure that it is a voucher he issued. He stores this signed document in a database to be able to prevent multiple uses.

Limited validity: A limited validity, e.g. a time limit or the restriction to a specific application, has to be stated in the certificate of the pseudonym. The issuer of the certificate, e.g. a CA or a vendor, would sign a document which includes the pseudonym, its properties or specific type and the limitations of its validity. A time limit is reasonable for many applications not only because of the erosion of the cryptographic security over time regarding specific keylengths or algorithms. Furthermore, in many cases a permanent online check that a certificate has not been revoked would not be necessary, and the duration for storing users' pseudonyms in databases to prevent multiple use could be reduced.

Possibility of revocation: CAs can revoke certificates or block the access to them, e.g. the certificate representing a driver's license of a person. Several problems, which are already well-known in respect to digital signatures, arise: Does the certificate has to be checked online each time, or are black- or whitelists sufficient? How can the integrity and the availability of the entire public key infrastructure be ensured?

3.3 Infrastructure to Support Pseudonyms

The requirements for an infrastructure supporting pseudonyms differ depending on their desired properties. Nevertheless, the public key infrastructure which is needed for the use of digital signatures could be a good basis for tasks of identity management as well.

The tasks of a CA may comprise the generation and certification of pseud-onyms, the generation of credentials and the generation of (blinded) attribute certificates. There are differences in the requirements whether online checks are necessary, and if so, under which conditions the identity may be revealed or certi-ficates may be revoked or blocked, and whether there is a limitation in assigning pseudonyms (e.g. limited number, only after identification at a registration office). Further tasks of trustees may comprise the involvement in transactions on behalf of one or multiple parties considering the payment, the delivery, or giving guarantees for a fair deal.

3.4   Comfortable User Interface for Managing Pseudonyms

A well-designed human-machine interface is important for an identity manager to enable the user to "change their appearance". Depending on the context, the user may choose different roles or pseudonyms. The user should be warned if other parties may link some information, which has been given explicitly or implicitly (by context information), so that the desired degree of anonymity is not guaranteed anymore. Incorrect usage or accidentally false decisions of the user should be prevented as far as possible.

To visualize the amount of personal data third parties may possess, data-bases for log files of the recorded communication with a powerful and scalable inference mechanism could be provided. This may not be possible in each configuration, especially for small and less powerful devices like PDAs with limited display and storage or when the user changes her computer equipment in different environments. Thus, the user interface and the behavior of the user agent may differ a lot depending on the context.

4   Integration into P3P

As shown before, P3P's standardized data format and data exchange mechanism could be used for an identity management system although it is not specialized on that purpose. Looking into the P3P specification, there are different possibilities:

1. **Persona concept:** The existing data sets could be used in combination with the concept of different personae which is supported by P3P. This means that the user agent would provide multiple data sets and allow the user to select the appropriate values from a list if desired. The user's preference file could distinguish between different roles.
2. **Definition of new data schemas:** P3P-compliant web sites could introduce new data schemas, e.g. for role pseudonyms, relationship pseudonyms, or role-relationship pseudonyms, but for transaction or attribute pseudonyms as well. User agents could build their own data repositories of the defined elements. The semantics, which would be associated with the data elements, could be realized in the application both on the server and client side, but would be somewhat independent of P3P.
3. **Extension:** The P3P functionality, i.e. syntax and semantics, would be extended by its EXTENSION mechanism. By use of extra XML namespaces, methods for digital signatures or credentials could be provided. However, this would require the specification of many formats and methods.

4.1   The Persona Concept

The disadvantage of P3P's current persona concept is the lack of authenticity because of the missing digital signatures which will be provided not until the next version.[8] Nevertheless, it is a starting point for developers to experiment with user agents which provide different repositories for multiple personae, and for users to get accustomed to it.

Here is an example for an APPEL rule which accepts the data transfer for the user's persona "bank customer":

```
<APPEL:RULE behavior="request"
  persona="bank customer"
  description="My bank collects data only for itself and its agents">
  <APPEL:REQUEST-GROUP>
    <APPEL:REQUEST uri="http://www.my-bank.com/*"/>
  </APPEL:REQUEST-GROUP>
  <POLICY APPEL:connective="and">
    <STATEMENT APPEL:connective="and">
      <RECIPIENT APPEL:connective="or-exact">
        <ours/>
      </RECIPIENT>
    </STATEMENT>
  </POLICY>
</APPEL:RULE>
```

4.2   Definition of New Data Schemas

This approach uses P3P only as a shell taking advantage of its mechanism of defining new structured data sets. It could be suitable for some specific applications. For a broader use, both syntax and semantics would have to be standardized, at least between the communicating parties, but, for even more impact, also in official standards. The problem of lacking authenticity can be solved within the applications, but the support of digital signatures, as it is planned for the next version of P3P, would be reasonable.

The following example shows the realization of a voucher, leaving out the additional elements for encapsulating the data by means of a digital signature[9]. The signature of the vendor is needed because in the process of redeeming, he will check that it is in fact one of the vouchers he issued. Moreover, while redeeming the voucher, the vendor would ask for the signature of the used pseudonym.

The new type called ACMEvoucher could be structured this way:

```
ACMEvoucher.amount (of primitive type number)
ACMEvoucher.expire (of basic type date)
ACMEvoucher.nymcert (of basic type certificate)
```

---

[8] The standardization process of W3C's "XML-Signature Syntax and Processing" is in an advanced stage, see working draft version from October 31, 2000, http://www.w3.org/TR/2000/CR-xmldsig-core-20001031/.

[9] The digital signature can be realized as proposed from the XML-Signature Working Group of the W3C, http://www.w3.org/Signature/.

The public key of the pseudonym is represented in the "ACMEvoucher.nym-cert" field. The certificate type is a structured type to specify identity certificates. It consists of the field "key" of primitive type binary and the field "format" of primitive type text, which may be a registered public key or authentication certificate format. Both fields belong to the category "unique identifiers".

For the definition and the introduction of two new data elements called book-voucher and perfume-voucher, both of the above type ACMEvoucher, the follo-wing code could be placed at http://www.ACME.com/voucher-schema:

```
<DATASCHEMA xmlns="http://www.w3.org/2000/P3Pv1">
  <DATA-STRUCT name="ACMEvoucher.amount"
    short-description="Amount" size="63">
    <CATEGORIES><purchase/></CATEGORIES>
  </DATA-STRUCT>
  <DATA-STRUCT name="ACMEvoucher.expire"
    structref="http://www.w3.org/TR/P3P/base#date"
    short-description="Expire Date"
    size="63">
    <CATEGORIES><purchase/></CATEGORIES>
  </DATA-STRUCT>
  <DATA-STRUCT name="ACMEvoucher.nymcert"
    structref="http://www.w3.org/TR/P3P/base#certificate"
    short-description="Pseudonymous Certificate"
    size="0">
    <CATEGORIES><purchase/></CATEGORIES>
  </DATA-STRUCT>
<DATA-DEF name="book-voucher" typeref="#voucher"/>
  <DATA-DEF name="perfume-voucher" typeref="#voucher"/>
</DATASCHEMA>
```

Continuing with the example, in order to reference a book voucher the service could send the following references inside a P3P policy:

```
<DATA-GROUP base="http://www.ACME.com/voucher-schema">
  <DATA ref="#book-voucher.amount"/>
  <DATA ref="#book-voucher.date.ymd"/>
  <DATA ref="#book-voucher.nymcert.key"/>
  <DATA ref="#book-voucher.nymcert.format"/>
</DATA-GROUP>
```

Remember that a realization without any digital signature would not be very useful.

In general, three kinds of data elements are needed:

1. elements of certificates, pseudonyms, or credentials
2. elements for describing the semantics of the elements in 1. (e.g. the informa-tion which test keys should be used for a blind digital signature)
3. elements for the digital signature over the entire data set (to be tested with keys from fields in 1. or 2. which are signed by a CA).

4.3   The Extension Mechanism

This is P3P's most powerful method to realize the needed functionality of an identity management system. The same problem occurs as in the above cases: The work for authenticity and pseudonymity has to be done outside P3P. There could be only defined or standardized interfaces which may support identity management functionality to have the possibility of sharing the data between several applications. In addition, it would be useful to standardize certain kinds of pseudonyms so that all parties are aware of the implications which are associated with the use of those pseudonyms. Then, it may be visualized by the user agent that the other party uses a specific pseudonym type. Moreover, the guarantees which tied to the use of the pseudonym to ensure fair deals may be presented.

4.4   Additional Requirements

Because P3P uses structured data sets for addressing privacy aspects, P3P user agents may provide the possibility to log the transferred information into a database. This would comprise details about the web site's policy including the contact information, the amount of the personal data, the presented purposes for data processing, and other possible recipients. Thus, the user is able to anticipate who will have dossiers about her (or about which of her pseudonyms) and what information they comprise. This functionality is also useful for e-commerce aspects regarding contracts in general, because then the negotiated agreement of all partners could be recorded. Such log files should be stored in a way that a manipulation could not happen or at least would be noticed.

5   Possibilities and Limitations of Identity Management Systems

Identity managers could become a common tool for each member of our information society. They could be integrated as a module in all communication systems, e.g. computers with network access or mobile phones. The use would not be restricted to the Internet world, but in form of a PDA it could manage all other purposes where smartcards are used today or in the future. Thus, it may comprise many of the areas where personal data are exchanged, not only in business-to-consumer application, but also in communicating with other people or in e-government applications. The user could even record information about personal "live" contacts to keep her database up to date. Unfortunately, not all data trails are transparent to the user or her identity manager, e.g. biometric surveillance methods or the data flow through covert channels would not be noticed. However, this growing complexity and intransparency of our world is a serious problem independent from the use of identity managers which could at least help a bit to cope with that situation.

All the same, the power and possible influence of an identity manager would lead to an increasing dependency of such systems. First, confidentiality and integrity are important properties which an identity manager has to guarantee. This is not an easy task from the security point of view. Furthermore, privacy aspects are difficult to visualize, because a potential risk could easily be under- or overestimated. The identity manager's trustworthiness can be increased by means of evaluation and certification of the whole system by independent experts, both from governmental institutions and – like the open source approach – from any interested person in the (Internet) community. Secondly, the availability is a relevant point as well. While the stored information in the identity manager can be regularly archived in backup media, the functionality may be not available in certain situations when one module in the entire process including the communication with the CAs will not work or when the identity manager itself may get lost. Thirdly, an unauthorized use of the identity manager of another person has to be prevented, because it may have the effect that the attacker takes over the very valuable (digital) identity of the victim. Biometric authentication methods could be of help here.

Furthermore, the risk of being forced to disclose personal data may increase, because the identity manager mirrors a great part of the user's life. Due to the desired authenticity, the quality of the data will be high. Thus, an identity manager is an attractive aim for attackers – with all kinds of methods including social engineering or the pressure to accept an adverse compromise. This deals not only with the personal data of the holder herself, but extends additionally to third persons' data, e.g. of the communication partners, which may be stored in the identity manager for a long time. These aspects will have to be discussed in both the social and the legal context.

6   Conclusions and Outlook

The idea of a powerful identity management seems to be a good way to achieve a high degree of self-determined privacy for a user in our information society. The necessary building blocks exist already or are being developed. For a widespread use, standardized data structures and exchange protocols are relevant. P3P 1.0 as a first basic standard for addressing privacy aspects provides some appropriate mechanisms for that goal, although much work is to be done. Digital signatures and negotiation procedures have to be integrated in future P3P versions for this purpose. Furthermore, it is important to standardize different kinds of pseudonyms with their realization by cryptographic means and an integration in an infrastructure of CAs and trustees. P3P-compliant user agents with respect to this additional functionality have to be developed and supported.

P3P essentially provides means for automated, but legally binding contract making between two parties, where one agrees to provide certain information and the other agrees to process this information only within the negotiated limits. To make P3P function, it is not only necessary to provide a technical framework (which is already in place mostly), but also a legal framework to make these automated contracts legally binding and internationally enforceable. This is by far the more complex, but also more important aspect of this technology.

Identity management plays a role in a joint project of the Independent Centre for Privacy Protection Schleswig-Holstein and Dresden University of Technology.

Both privacy points of views and ideas of business models as well as legal aspects are being investigated. Integrating existing standards, ways for realizing different kinds of pseudonymity and possibilities to exchange and negotiate personal data will be proposed. To empower the users to maintain their privacy and control their digital identity in various environments, it is necessary to develop user interfaces to manage personal data on PCs as well as small devices with limited display and storage. Further work is needed to find appropriate ways for visualizing the amount of personal data third parties may possess, e.g. by integrating databases for log files of the recorded communication with a powerful and scalable inference mechanism.

There are many chances for identity management systems, but it is important that the user is aware of the limitations of those tools as well. Otherwise, the use could be even more dangerous to the right of self-determination, because the users might fully rely on the protection through the identity manager without being cautious anymore.

References

1. A P3P Preference Exchange Language (APPEL); Marc Langheinrich (Ed.); W3C Working Draft 20 April 2000; http://www.w3.org/TR/2000/WD-P3P-preferences-20000420 (newer version in the W3C member area: Working Draft 3 October 2000; http://www.w3.org/P3P/Group/Preferences/Drafts/WD-P3P-preferences-20001006.html).
2. Oliver Berthold, Hannes Federrath: Identitätsmanagement; in: Helmut Bäumler (Ed.): E-Privacy; Proceedings Summer School of the Independent Centre for Privacy Protection Schleswig-Holstein, August 28, 2000, Kiel; Vieweg, Wiesbaden 2000, 189-204.
3. Stefan Brands: Rethinking Public Key Infrastructures and Digital Certificates – Building in Privacy; Thesis; Brands Technologies; 1999; http://www.xs4all.nl/~brands/.
4. David Chaum: Security Without Identification: Card Computers to Make Big Brother Obsolete; http://www.chaum.com/articles/Security_Wthout_Identification.htm. Original version: Security Without Identification: Transaction Systems to Make Big Brother Obsolete; Communications of the ACM, Vol. 28 No. 10, October 1985; 1030-1044.
5. David Chaum: Showing Credentials without Identification: Transferring Signatures between Unconditionally Unlinkable Pseudonyms; in: J. Seberry/J. Pieprzyk (Eds.): Advances in Cryptology – AUSCRYPT '90, volume 453 of Lecture Notes in Computer Science, 8-11 January, 1990, Sydney, Australia, Springer; 246-264.
6. Roger Clarke: Identified, Anonymous and Pseudonymous Transactions: The Spectrum of Choice; in: Simone Fischer-Hübner, Gerald Quirchmayr, Louise Yngström (Eds.): User Identification & Privacy Protection: Applications in Public Administration & Electronic Commerce; Kista, Schweden; June 1999; IFIP WG 8.5 and WS 9.6; http://www.anu.edu.au/people/Roger.Clarke/DV/UIPP99.html.
7. Lorrie Faith Cranor: Agents of Choice: Tools that Facilitate Notice and Choice about Web Site Data Practices; Proceedings of the 21st International Conference on Privacy and Personal Data Protection; September 13-15, 1999; Hong Kong SAR, China; 19-25; http://www.research.att.com/~lorrie/pubs/hk.pdf.

8. Herbert Damker, Ulrich Pordesch, Martin Reichenbach: Personal Reachability and Security Management – Negotiation of Multilateral Security; in: Günter Müller, Kai Rannenberg (Eds.): Multilateral Security in Communications – Technology, Infrastructure, Economy; Proceedings Multilateral Security in Communications, July 16-17, 1999, Stuttgart; Addison-Wesley-Longman, Munich 1999; 95-111.

9. John Hagel, Marc Singer: Net Worth: Shaping Markets When Customers Make the Rules; Harvard Business School Press, U.S.; 1999.

10. Joe Kilian, Erez Petrank: Identity Escrow; in: H. Krawczyk (Ed.): Advances in Cryptology – CRYPTO '98; Volume 1642 of Lecture Notes in Computer Science; Springer, Berlin 1998; 169-185; http://www.cs.technion.ac.il/~erez/ident_crypto.ps.

11. Marit Köhntopp: Identitätsmanagement; 2000; http://www.koehntopp.de/marit/publikationen/idmanage/.

12. Anna Lysyanskaya: Pseudonym Systems; Master's Thesis at the Massachusetts Institute of Technology; June 1999; http://theory.lcs.mit.edu/~cis/theses/annasm.ps.gz.

13. Andreas Pfitzmann, Marit Köhntopp: Anonymity, Unobservability, and Pseudonymity – A Proposal for Terminology; in this volume.

14. Birgit Pfitzmann, Michael Waidner, Andreas Pfitzmann: Secure and Anonymous Electronic Commerce: Providing Legal Certainty in Open Digital Systems Without Compromising Anonymity; IBM Research Report RZ 3232 (#93278) 05/22/00, IBM Research Division, Zurich, May 2000; http://www.semper.org/sirene/publ/PWP_00anoEcommerce.ps.gz.

15. The Platform for Privacy Preferences 1.0 (P3P1.0) Specification; Massimo Marchiori (Ed.); W3C Candidate Recommendation 15 December 2000; http://www.w3.org/TR/2000/CR-P3P-20001215/.

16. Henk van Rossum, Huib Gardeniers, John Borking et al.: Privacy-Enhancing Technologies: The Path to Anonymity, Volume I u. II; Achtergrondstudies en Verkenningen 5a/5b; Registratiekamer, The Netherlands & Information and Privacy Commissioner/Ontario, Canada; August 1995; http://www.ipc.on.ca/english/pubpres/sum_pap/papers/anon-e.htm.

On Pseudonymization of Audit Data
for Intrusion Detection*

Joachim Biskup and Ulrich Flegel

University of Dortmund, D-44221 Dortmund, Germany
{Joachim.Biskup, Ulrich.Flegel}@cs.uni-dortmund.de

Abstract. In multilaterally secure intrusion detection systems (IDS) anonymity and accountability are potentially conflicting requirements. Since IDS rely on audit data to detect violations of security policy, we can balance above requirements by pseudonymization of audit data, as a form of reversible anonymization. We discuss previous work in this area and underlying trust models. Instead of relying on mechanisms external to the system, or under the control of potential adversaries, in our proposal we technically bind reidentification to a threshold, representing the legal purpose of accountability in the presence of policy violations. Also, we contrast our notion of threshold-based identity recovery with previous approaches and point out open problems.

1 Introduction

Stimulated by the increasing reliance on information and communication technology, particularly the broadening offer of services on the Internet, potentially conflicting demands emerge, such as accountability and anonymity. To establish accountability, suboptimal preventive security mechanisms and intrusion detection facilities are meant to complement one another. Since intrusion detection is based on audit data, which in part can be associated with real persons, it deals with personal data. Conventional approaches to intrusion detection prioritize the interests of IT-system owners, emphasizing accountability, event reconstruction, deterrence, as well as problem and damage assessment.

Unobservability, anonymity and unlinkability as instruments derived from the concept of informational self-determination, confine the collection and processing of personal data. Basic preconditions of informational self-determination are either the data subject's informed consent on or the legal or contractual necessity of processing the personal data, accompanied by strict purpose binding for collecting, processing and communicating personal data.

Since data in processible form is perfectly reproducible, and since formally verifying, that a conventional IT system as a whole preserves its users' rights wrt. informational self-determination, is impractical, it is insufficient to legally interdict misuse of personal data [1]. Consequently there is an increasing demand for the technical enforcement of privacy principles in multilaterally secure

---

* The work described here is currently partially funded by Deutsche Forschungsgemeinschaft under contract number Bi 311/10-1.

H. Federrath (Ed.): Anonymity 2000, LNCS 2009, pp. 161–180, 2001.

systems, taking into account all, and acceptably balancing contrary security requirements of all involved parties [2]. A multilaterally secure Intrusion Detection System (IDS) that respects the users' desire for privacy, may allow them to act pseudonymously, hiding the association between the data and the real persons, as far as the detection goals can still be achieved. To hold people responsible for violations of the security policy, a multilaterally secure IDS also (re)identifies users upon good cause shown.

In this paper we survey and contrast approaches to employ pseudonyms in intrusion detection, and we propose an approach to pseudonyms with the ability for threshold-based identity recovery, that is, the circumstances accompanying the necessity of reidentification can be described as the transgression of a threshold. By technically binding reidentification to a threshold, we can enforce a strong binding to the purpose of establishing accountability for violations of policy.

The rest of this paper is organized as follows. First we selectively review pertinent European legislation that inspires technical purpose binding (section 2), identify important aspects of pseudonymization (section 3) and survey related approaches (section 4). We then present our approach, specifying the underlying trust and threat model (Sect. 5), exemplifying the targeted audit environment (section 6), and proposing to apply secret sharing to pseudonymization (Sect. 7). A more technically inclined elaboration can be found in [3]. We conclude pointing out open issues for investigation (Sect. 8).

2   European Legislation

According to consideration (2) in the EC directive [4], IT-systems must respect the right to privacy. Since it is one objective of the European Community (EC) to ensure "economic and social progress by common action to eliminate the barriers which divide Europe" (ibid., consideration (1)), within the EC a harmonization of national laws has been initiated to achieve similar levels wrt. protection of personal data (ibid. considerations (3),(5),(7)-(9)). Based on articles 25, 26 and 4, for third countries the directive, as well as resulting national laws, are authoritative regarding to export and processing of personal data from and on EC territory, respectively. The directive [4] amalgamates various traditions in dealing with personal data. We found exemplary statements about fundamental protection principles in German law, specifically a census sentence [5] of the German Constitutional Court, which postulates the informational self-determination (ibid. C II 1a). This sentence clarifies that there exists no insignificant data, since its sensitivity depends not merely on its nature, but rather on its linkability and processibility, as well as the pursued objective (ibid. C II2). To fix data sensitivity, the objectives are fixed beforehand, and consequently the nature and scope of data being collected, as well as the nature of processing results have to be fixed. This fundamental privacy principle is henceforth referred to as *purpose binding*. Further principles require that personal data being collected is *adequate*, *relevant* and *not excessive* with respect to a legal purpose of processing, which is proportional wrt. to the data sensitivity (ibid. C II 1b).

3 Assessing Pseudonymization

Consider multilaterally secure intrusion detection balancing accountability requirements of system owners and anonymity demands of users. In this scenario, both parties are represented by system security officers (SSO) and data protection officials (PPO), respectively. It is part of an individual's right of informational self-determination to separate different spheres of life on demand, for example by acting more or less anonymously. An entity is called anonymous if an attacker cannot link its identity with its role or activities within an anonymity group. Though there are several methods to achieve anonymity, we focus on pseudonymization here. By means of pseudonymization we unlink events from identities.

We consider some criteria determining the strength of anonymity. The strength should be proportionate wrt. the risk posed by data collection and processing, as well as the effort required by an attacker. The *threat model* defines which potentially colluding parties may collect and correlate information. This model influences *when* and *where* data needs to be pseudonymized, since this should happen, before it enters domains monitored by adversaries.

Another role plays an instance with the ability for *reidentification*. The participant(s) required for identity recovery depend on the *method* of pseudonymization and on the pseudonym *introducer*. Generally, for the purpose of accountability, identity recovery should be independent from the pseudonymous entities. On the other hand, the IDS and SSOs are considered adversaries to the entities' privacy, requiring the IDS for identity recovery either to depend on the cooperation of a PPO, or to restrict analysis results exclusively to detected security policy violations. Consequently domains controlled by an IDS and by SSOs should by organizational and technical means be strictly separated from domains where personal data is processed in the clear.

The strength of anonymity depends on the cardinality of the *anonymity group*. The losses of an attacker should be higher than the gains when damage by reidentification is done to all members of the anonymity group instead of just one entity. For scarce anonymity group populations it seems advisable to choose a new pseudonym per transaction.

To what degree inferences can be extracted from audit data depends on the *linkability* of features being pseudonymized. Feature selection for pseudonymization and the class of pseudonyms being employed substantially influence linkability. For a discussion about user identifying features and feature selection refer to [6]. We need to trade the strength of anonymity off against the quality of analysis, which depends on the linkability of certain features.

Assuming an entity has only one identity, it may wish to act under one or more pseudonyms. We consider various classes of pseudonyms achieving increasing degrees of anonymity [1]:

Entity-based pseudonyms are substitutes for the identity of an entity being used for many transactions in differing contexts and relations. Actions of the same entity are linkable via equality of pseudonyms. Frequent use of the pseudonym implies the risk of information cumulation and eventually reidentification. Entity-based pseudonyms can be extended to represent groups of entities, severely limiting the capability to account events to individual entities.

public: Identity assignment is publicly available such as phone numbers, reidentification is feasible for everyone.

non-public: Identity assignment is available to a few selected parties only, such as unpublished phone numbers, which may reidentify the entity.

anonymous: Only the entity itself is acquainted with the assignment of its identity to the pseudonym.

Role-based pseudonyms are assigned to the roles an entity assumes in the context of different relations. Pseudonyms for roles mitigate the risk of reidentification by means of information cumulation.

relation-based: A pseudonym is used for many transactions in the context of a given relation, such as a customer number. Busy relations allow information cumulation and eventually reidentification.

transaction-based: A pseudonym is used in the context of a relation for one transaction only, similar to one-time passwords.

An IDS shouldn't collect and permanently store data not strictly necessary for the purpose of analysis (data avoidance). As soon as data becomes unnecessary for that purpose, it should be discarded (data reduction). An example is found in the IDS ANIDA (see section 4.4), where the anomaly detection component reduces the audit stream by discarding non-anomalous data, before it is handed to the misuse detection component. This approach is based on the following two assumptions: Known attack behavior as defined in misuse detection approaches is always detected as being an anomalous deviation from normal behavior as defined by anomaly detection approaches. Not all detectable anomalies posing a security threat are covered by the attack behavior encoded in misuse detection systems.

Finally, since false positives are affecting a users' privacy due to undesirable reidentifications, detection approaches with low false positive rate are required [7], [8].

4   Related Approaches

First of all we roughly describe the relevant details in work related to pseudonymous intrusion detection. Subsequently we review some more general approaches to anonymous service access.

4.1   IDA

The *Intrusion Detection and Avoidance* system (IDA) and its fundamental privacy concepts are described in [9], [10] and [6]. IDA audits certain system calls concerned with user sessions and clearance levels as well as object creation, deletion, access and respective permission modifications. Apart from protecting personal data by conventional mechanisms, IDA developed the notion of pseudonymous audit analysis. The kernel reference monitor introduces non-public entity-based pseudonyms before audit data is passed to the audit trail and the kernel-integrated analysis component, including anomaly detection as well as misuse detection analysis. The IDA concept incorporates the introduction of pseudonyms wherever subject identifiers are used, particularly for access control. To prevent information cumulation with respect to a pseudonym, relation-based pseudonyms based on combinations of subject and object identifiers are proposed. These role-based pseudonyms are proposed for use in access control only, but not for audit analysis which in IDA requires linkability across subjects. Analysis proceeds on pseudonymized audit data. The close coupling of the analysis and decision components to the reference monitor allows enforcement of decisions without the need for automated reidentification. Obviously, in the IDA approach pseudonymization is deeply entangled with the innards of the operating system, limiting ease of application to todays off-the-shelf platforms.

The IDA concept proposes symmetric encryption of subject identifiers in audit data. To limit the risk of information cumulation and hence reidentification with respect to the entity-based pseudonyms, pseudonym changes by rekeying after certain time intervals are proposed. Since IDA can react without requiring automatic reidentification, enforcement of purpose binding for identity recovery is handled external to the system by sharing the symmetric key between SSO and PPO. Prerequisite to this proceeding is the symmetric key used in monitored systems being safe against attackers, meaning SSOs must not be able to control the responsible subsystems.

To prevent reidentification by correlation of information other than subject identifiers in audit trails or in profiles, it is proposed to pseudonymize all features that uniquely identify subjects. In addition it is proposed to pseudonymize features an attacker may have external knowledge about, such as actions and their time stamps, parameters and required privileges.

4.2   AID

Privacy related aspects concerning the *Adaptive Intrusion Detection* system (AID) are described in [11], [12], [6], [13] and [14]. In case of conflicting descriptions in those publications we base our summary on the latest information available. The AID implementation comprises a central RTworks based misuse detection[1] analysis station and distributed event monitoring agents. The Solaris based analysis station controls and adaptively polls the agents for Solaris BSM and Windows NT audit data respectively. Available publications do not describe the Windows NT matters.

AID uses Solaris BSM to audit system calls and selected applications concerned with user sessions, file creation, deletion, accesses and respective permission modifications as well as processes and administrative activities, some being non-attributable to any user. The fundamental concepts of pseudonymous audit analysis of IDA and AID are fairly similar, but the realizations differ in detail. AID introduces pseudonyms on monitored hosts after audit records have been

---

[1] Further work on a neural network based anomaly detection analysis component has been announced in several publications, but results to date have not been published.

emitted by the Solaris user level process auditd. Owing to the implementation of AID being based on an off-the-shelf platform, there is no holistic concept as in IDA, pseudonymizing occurrences of identifying features outside the BSM audit stream. Monitoring agents pseudonymize audit records, add supplementary information needed for misuse analysis and convert the records into a reduced format. Analysis proceeds on pseudonymous records in the central station.

Reidentifications occur automatically if the expert system generates an alarm, or when alarm reports are generated, and before audit trails are archived in encrypted form. All AID monitoring agents reporting to the same central analysis station use the same key to symmetrically encrypt identifying features in order to pseudonymize them. It follows, that if an adversary monitors the key on any AID host, the adversary is able to reidentify any audit records he monitors. Since AID uses a confidential channel (SecureRPC) for audit data transport, an adversary is limited to AID host access, the central station being the most desirable target. Consequently SSOs must not be able to observe either the pseudonymization keys, or the audit data, as well as the activities of users on any AID host. In the AID Solaris/Unix environment an SSO must therefore neither be able to control any of the AID machines, nor to monitor user activities. These are severe limitations, considering that particularly SSOs would want to control and monitor at least the security of the central analysis station. Reviewing archived audit records requires cooperation of an SSO and a PPO because the archive encryption key is shared between SSOs and PPOs. AID logs automatic reidentifications to an audit, but there are no provisions forcing SSOs to make this audit available to PPOs.

AID symmetrically encrypts identifying features such as real and effective user and group IDs of subjects and object owners, audit, session, terminal and process IDs as well as host names and home directories in paths if they denote the user name. Additionally the AID concept proposes pseudonymization of host platform types, names of originating hosts and home directory names in command execution parameters and the respective environment. To limit the risk of reidentification by information cumulation with respect to the non-public entity-based pseudonyms, as in IDA, pseudonym changes by rekeying after irregular time periods are proposed.

4.3   Chalmers Firewall Audit Pseudonymizer

[7], [8] and [15] describe a yet to be named anomaly detection tool that uses statistical methods to analyze pseudonymous audit data. The tool analyzes login event audit records produced by a proxy-based firewall. Pseudonyms seem to be introduced in large batches[2] of audit records, before exporting the batches and pseudonym mappings for anomaly analysis.

Some identifying features are pseudonymized: user names, server host names, client host names as well as free text fields containing user and host names. Other potentially identifying features not being used as profile discriminators,

---

[2] The pseudonymizer though technically is prepared to pseudonymize audit data on the fly.

but statistically analyzed, such as activities and time stamps, were not pseud-onymized. Audit records are pseudonymized by replacing them bijectively with sequentially numbered place holders denoting the respective feature type (e.g. user0, user1, ...). Host names and each domain name part are mapped separately. The employed kind of non-public entity-based pseudonyms is memory inefficient, and after reidentifications the respective mappings are easily remembered by SSOs. IP addresses are mapped to an address in the same address class, allowing to determine an IP addresse's class from its pseudonym. The mapping of pseudonyms to the substituted data is stored in a separate database. Analysis proceeds on pseudonymized audit records. In [8] it is proposed to use group-based pseudonyms and thereby losing the ability to account events to individual users.

There are no documented precautions taken protecting the confidentiality of the pseudonym mapping neither while in transit nor during analysis. Reidentification is not supported in an automatic way and seems to be established manually by the SSO. The question remains, what technically keeps an SSO from reidentifying all audit records independently from analysis results. Certainly the concept could be extended to avoid such problems.

Both [7] and [8] propose and discuss several improvements. Based on [6], information cumulation regarding pseudonyms could be limited by changing the mapping of pseudonyms. This would also limit the problems generated by easily remembered pseudonyms. To restrict leakage of personal or business related information it is proposed to insert dummy or chaff audit records blurring the genuine patterns and statistics of resource usage. Similar to ANIDA's GRPs (see Sect. 4.4) it is proposed to associate users with groups to support the SSO's intuitive manual anomaly detection capabilities. These associations are not to be mixed up with aforementioned lossy group-based pseudonyms.

4.4 ANIDA

Privacy aspects concerning the Windows NT based *Aachener Network Intrusion Detection Architecture* (ANIDA) are described in [16]. In contrast to the other reviewed systems ANIDA's architecture is focused towards analysis of network-based audit data from client-server applications and underlying protocol stacks. The concept comprises components monitoring all traffic on the network and traffic exchanged with selected networked services. ANIDA fundamentally requires cooperation with a generic distributed authentication and access control mechanism. As a result, the monitored services need to support this mechanism. For the purpose of concealing identifying information related to a connection, Kerberos was chosen and modified concerning the tickets, initial authentication and some protocol steps. An approach to concealing even the fact of a connection taking place is realized by the integration of MIXes [17], [18] with Kerberos.

ANIDA uses a kind of transaction-based pseudonyms introduced by the authentication service after user authentication, or by one (or more) trusted MIX(es). The pseudonyms are supplemented with group identifiers confirming group memberships for the purpose of access control. The anonymity group of a user therefore comprises all members of those groups she itself is member of

[16]. Kerberos tickets were modified to use these augmented pseudonyms, referred to in ANIDA parlance as group reference pseudonyms[3] (GRP), instead of a client principal name. Furthermore the client's host network address is omitted from tickets. GRPs are valid and can be used for several transactions until the bearing ticket expires. Thus, GRPs can be classified somewhere in between relation-based and transaction-based pseudonyms. Choice of appropriate timeouts allows balancing strength of anonymity against the overhead involved in making out tickets.

Reidentification requires cooperation of the GRP introducer (the Kerberos authentication server or the MIX), which must be independent of SSOs and could be administered by PPOs. As there are no monitoring components internal to client hosts and the GRP introducer, SSOs should not be able to observe activities on client hosts and the GRP introducer.

The ANIDA approach implies group-based and thus coarse-grained access control and entity profiling for anomaly detection. While group-based access control is widely in use for authorization of network service accesses, it would be too coarse-grained for system internal authorizations such as file accesses. Group-based profiling for anomaly detection offers several advantages, such as requiring cooperation of the group majority to achieve unnoticed profile drift defining malicious behavior as acceptable. This concept emerged with NIDES [19].

In order to support the principle of data reduction, the anomaly analysis component supplies the misuse analysis component only with audit data known to be free of anomalies. In ANIDA's case the misuse analysis will not miss any anomalous data because the transaction-based anomaly detection technique used in ANIDA claims to isolate all anomalies with respect to well-defined valid transactions. In this scenario misuse detection based analysis should not be solely dependent on the linkability of the group identifiers. Otherwise it could become confused and mistake different entities for a single one, possibly leading to false alarms.

4.5   More General Approaches

Some related work is described in [20], [21] and [22]. They propose modifications to authentication, based on the observation, that traditional access control requires the collection of identifying data before access is granted. The collected data is required to settle extraordinary circumstances. Instead, authentication components can collect information strictly necessary for the purpose of access control and require a guarantee, that identifying data can be recovered with the help of an independent third party.

The approaches in [20] and [21] generate transaction-based pseudonyms during user authentication, comprising a zero-knowledge proof, that identity recovery is possible later on. [22] presents an approach based on [23], basically interpreting electronic cash as certificates of pseudonyms, leading to entity-based

---

[3] Again, this kind of transaction-based pseudonyms including group associations is not to be mixed up with lossy group-based pseudonyms.

pseudonyms, but not transaction-based pseudonyms as in [20] and [21]. Entity-based pseudonyms provide linkability as required for some intrusion detection methods, respectively, but linkable pseudonyms allow cumulation of information related to the user of the pseudonym, which can eventually enable reidentification. After an initial session login entity-based pseudonyms could be used in traditional access control scenarios.

Since in aforementioned approaches pseudonyms are introduced before resources are accessed, the identity of actors is protected against the entire accessed system. In the case of transaction-based pseudonyms this comes at the cost of major efforts required to modify the concerned access control systems traditionally used in off-the-shelf operating systems. On the other hand we were mainly interested in pseudonymous intrusion detection. If we can afford to place trust in a component to correctly introduce pseudonyms on behalf of the actors, and if we can technically separate observability of identifying accesses from pseudonymous event processing, we can easily integrate pseudonymous audit with major operating systems.

Different from related work, our approach allows for transaction-based pseudonyms that guarantee automatic reidentification independently of a third party, if certain conditions bound to a specified purpose are met.

5   Trust and Threat Model of Our Approach

For an IDS observing user activities within a host, seamless integration with an off-the-shelf operating system is important, for it relies on event data, i.e. audit records, collected within the host. Wrt. Unix operating systems this always implies potential integrity loss of event data in case an attacker achieves `root` privileges. If we can afford to rely on event data under these conditions, we can also afford to rely on pseudonyms introduced within the same machine, after user authentication was performed and users are identified in the clear. Stronger approaches would require pseudonym introduction prior to or during user authentication at the console, which comes at the expense of major modifications of the operating system (see Sect. 4.5).

Starting from here, we have to take into account conflicting security requirements of basically two parties. Firstly, users are interested in anonymous use wrt. to IT system owners. Secondly, the IT system owners, specifically their representatives responsible for the system security (SSO), when faced with policy violations, are interested in establishing accountability. Neither party can be allowed to control the event generator as well as the pseudonymizer. Otherwise the respective mutual security requirement were at risk. We thus introduce a third party, the personal data protection official (PPO). The PPOs are trusted by the users to protect their anonymity interests, and they are trusted by the SSOs to protect their accountability requirements. In accordance with their position, PPOs control both, event generators and pseudonymizers (see Fig. 1). Users may verify both components for proper functionality, SSOs may do so during official user inactivity times. As outlined above, corruption of the event generator threatens accountability. Corruption of the pseudonymizers additionally threatens anonymity.

The event generators, either by themselves or by appropriate extensions, forward sensitive audit data to remote analyzers only if that data is required to detect harmful behavior of the involved entities. Pseudonymizers are implanted just behind the standard audit services, or their extensions, respectively. The pseudonymizers inspect audit data, and they substitute identifiers by carefully tailored pseudonyms. Exploiting Shamir's cryptographic approach to secret sharing, these pseudonyms are actually shares, which can be used for reidentification later on, if justified by sufficient suspicion. Sufficient suspicion is defined by a threshold on weighted occurrences of potentially harmful behavior, and accordingly, by a threshold on shares belonging together. Exceeding such a threshold results in the ability to reveal the secret, i.e. to recover the identity behind the pseudonyms. Thus the analyzers, holding the pseudonymized audit data including the shares, can reidentify the data if and only if the purpose of accountability requests to do so.

Since SSOs are considered potential adversaries threatening the anonymity of users, they must be confined to pseudonymous event data for user observation. Consequently, attacks on user anonymity are expected and countered as soon as pseudonymized event data leaves the pseudonymizer (see Fig. 1).

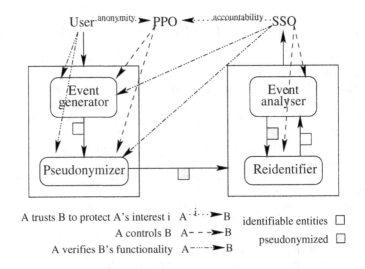

Fig. 1. Model of trust relationships in our approach

6   Envisioned Audit Architecture

Most modern operating systems offer similar audit components, and in the majority of cases is the identity of acting subjects part of the event information being recorded. A comprehensive solution requires pseudonymizing all event data observed by SSOs, but for our first prototype we chose to support the *syslog* event format only. Other possible event generators to be considered include process accounting, network packet event data, TCSEC C2 audit data [24], [25], such as produced by Sun's BSM.

syslogd collects event data from user and kernel level sources, and it can additionally be fed remotely. syslogd can distinguish event sources, henceforth referred to as *facilities*, and event severity levels. Via *syslog* we can can collect host-based data from applications and the kernel. Using additional kernel modules we can also collect event data derived from sources associated with the network. Out-of-band data derived from other sources is covered by corresponding applications using *syslog*. Owing to its uniformity and availability in all significant Unixes, *syslog* is widely utilized by the kernel and by user level applications for auditing. Generally, merely serious user actions appear in syslog events, but many important network services audit via syslog with diverse detail levels.

Pseudonymization can take place somewhere between the event generator and the border of the domain controlled by attackers. Placing the pseudonymizer closer to the event generator reduces opportunities to observe exposed plaintext identities, but scalability and ease of implementation suffer. We decided to pseudonymize the output event stream of syslogd by having the daemon write into pipes connected to the pseudonymizer. This way we can also pseudonymize event data normally written by applications to separate files.

6.1   Required Parsing

A pseudonymizer receives audit records from syslogd containing directly or indirectly identifying features [6]. Since each feature may contribute with a specific priority to an attack scenario A_g, the pseudonymizer shall be able to distinguish different event types and associate each embedded feature type with an attack scenario and the respective priority or weight. The PPO specifies a priori knowledge about the syntax of events and features to be pseudonymized. In cooperation with the SSO, the PPO models suspicions justifying reidentification by specifying associations between features and attack scenarios, defining the weight of each feature's contribution to its associated attack scenario, as well as each scenario's threshold.

To locate and pseudonymize identifying features in *syslog* audit records, we have to parse them. See Fig. 2 for some typical *syslog* records generated by applications on a host named pony.

For brevity we will henceforth omit the *time and date* and *host* fields from audit records. Since the syntax of the records is mainly determined by the originating facility, recognition of different event and feature types is based on the evaluation of syntactical contexts, e.g. by means of regular expressions for pattern matching as defined in POSIX 1003.2 Sect. 2.8.

The *facility* (framed fields 1 and 8 in Fig. 3) of a record indicates an application or a kernel component, optionally followed by its *process ID* (frame 2 in Fig. 3).

An audit record represents an event, whose type is uniquely specified by the *event type context* (frames 3 with 4, and 9 with 12 in Fig. 3) and the facility.

```
Oct 20 20:48:29 pony identd[22509]: token TWpldDmO2sq65FfQ82zX == uid 1000 (deedee)
Dec 19 16:02:45 pony su: BAD SU deedee to root on /dev/ttyp1
Dec 19 16:03:27 pony su: BAD SU deedee to root on /dev/ttyp1
Dec 19 16:03:53 pony su: BAD SU deedee to root on /dev/ttyp1
Dec 19 16:04:11 pony su: BAD SU deedee to root on /dev/ttyp1
Dec 19 16:04:39 pony su: deedee to root on /dev/ttyp1
Dec 20 09:58:46 pony postfix/smtpd[22190]: connect from pony.puf[192.168.1.1]
Dec 20 09:58:48 pony postfix/smtpd[22190]: BFF41AD8D: client=pony.puf[192.168.1.1]
Dec 20 09:58:52 pony postfix/cleanup[29752]: BFF41AD8D: message-id=<385D1476.4FDB096B@manda.rk>
Dec 20 09:58:53 pony postfix/qmgr[1519]: BFF41AD8D: from=<dexter@secret.lab>, size=7910 (queue active)
Dec 20 09:58:53 pony postfix/smtpd[22190]: disconnect from pony.puf[192.168.1.1]
Dec 20 09:58:55 pony postfix/local[4864]: BFF41AD8D: to=<deedee@puf>, relay=local, delay=7, ...
```

Fig. 2. Sample *syslog* audit records from host **pony**

Fig. 3. Syntactical concepts in two sample *syslog* audit records from Fig. 2

Each event type may contain a number of identifying *features* (frames 5, 7, 10, 11 and 13 in Fig. 3) of a type specified by a *feature type context* and the event type. A feature (f.i. frame 5 in Fig. 3) thus is an instance of a feature type determined by context (f.i. frames 4 and 6 in Fig. 3).

To determine a feature's contribution to an attack scenario A_g, we assign its type f to a group I_g and a weight function $w_{fg}()$, representing A_g and the priority of f's contribution to A_g, respectively. The triplets $\langle f, I_g, w_{fg}() \rangle$ expand to quintuples:

$$\langle \text{facility, event type context, feature type context}, I_g, w_{fg}() \rangle$$

Above tuples, understood as a decision tree, such as in Fig. 4, can be used to parse audit records. By sequentially matching facility, event type context and

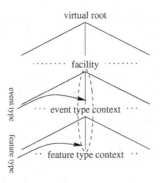

Fig. 4. Representation of the parser knowledge as a tree

feature type contexts, we isolate the event's features, that are to be pseudonymized. For each feature, the corresponding entry in I_g is located, or instantiated in case the feature has not yet been observed. Then $w_{fg}()$ pseudonyms are generated, replacing the respective feature. The more pseudonyms are generated for a feature, the earlier can it be recovered (see Sec. 7).

For an illustrating example we chose some audit records including a simple password guessing attack to demonstrate the record handling (see Fig. 2). We assume a knowledge specification that does not model realistic circumstances of attack scenarios, we rather arbitrarily chose the groups, thresholds and weights. According to that knowledge specification each of the example audit records in Fig. 5 has been augmented with the respective groups and weights for their matching, hence underlined features. Sequence numbers have been assigned to each record such that their original chronological order is preserved.

```
1: identd[22509]: token TWpldDmO2sq65FfQ82zX == uid 1000^{I2,w=1} (deedee^{I1,w=1})
2: su: BAD SU deedee^{I1,w=3} to root^{I1,w=1} on /dev/ttyp1^{I3,w=1}
3: su: BAD SU deedee^{I1,w=3} to root^{I1,w=1} on /dev/ttyp1^{I3,w=1}
4: su: BAD SU deedee^{I1,w=3} to root^{I1,w=1} on /dev/ttyp1^{I3,w=1}
5: su: BAD SU deedee^{I1,w=3} to root^{I1,w=1} on /dev/ttyp1^{I3,w=1}
6: su: deedee^{I1,w=2} to root^{I1,w=1} on /dev/ttyp1^{I3,w=1}
7: postfix/smtpd[22190]: connect from pony.puf^{I4,w=1} [192.168.1.1^{I4,w=1}]
8: postfix/smtpd[22190]: BFF41AD8D: client=pony.puf^{I4,w=1} [192.168.1.1^{I4,w=1}]
9: postfix/cleanup[29752]: BFF41AD8D: message-id=<385D1476.4FDB096B^{I6,w=1}@manda.rk^{I5,w=1}>
10: postfix/qmgr[1519]:BFF41AD8D: from=<dexter^{I6,w=1}@secret.lab^{I5,w=1}>, size=7910 (queue active)
11: postfix/smtpd[22190]: disconnect from pony.puf^{I4,w=1} [192.168.1.1^{I4,w=1}]
12: postfix/local[4864]: BFF41AD8D: to=<deedee^{I6,w=1}@puf^{I5,w=1}>, relay=local, delay=7, ...
```

Fig. 5. *Syslog* audit records from Fig. 2, parsed for features to be pseudonymized

Each of the twelve records in Fig. 5 has been pseudonymized as described above in accordance with the specification. In Fig. 6 pseudonyms are denoted by place-holders indicating the group Ig, the identity's (id_{i_g}) index i_g into I_g, and the running number m_{i_g} of id_{i_g}'s pseudonym. The six tables in Fig. 7 present the states of the feature type groups $I1, \ldots, I6$ after processing all twelve audit records. The column '#' marks the total number of audit records having been processed when the respective id_{i_g} is reidentifiable from its pseudonyms.

Note that the attacker's identity deedee, according to the respective weights in records 2–6, generates more pseudonyms than other identities. With respect to the pseudonyms $I1 : 1.1 - 10$ of the first four records, deedee can be reidentified because the threshold t_1 is reached. Equally the identifying feature /dev/ttyp1 reaches threshold t_3 with respect to the pseudonyms $I3 : 1.1 - 5$ in records 2–6. The identity deedee in record 12 is not associated with $I1$ as the other occurrences of deedee, but with $I6$. The respective pseudonym $I6 : 3.1$ therefore is *not* compatible with the pseudonyms $I1 : 1.1 - 15$.

```
 1: identd[22509]: token TWpldDmO2sq65FfQ82zX == uid I2:1.1 (I1:1.1)
 2: su: BAD SU I1:1.2-4 to I1:2.1 on I3:1.1
 3: su: BAD SU I1:1.5-7 to I1:2.2 on I3:1.2
 4: su: BAD SU I1:1.8-10 to I1:2.3 on I3:1.3
 5: su: BAD SU I1:1.11-13 to I1:2.4 on I3:1.4
 6: su: I1:1.14-15 to I1:2.5 on I3:1.5
 7: postfix/smtpd[22190]: connect from I4:1.1[I4:2.1]
 8: postfix/smtpd[22190]: BFF41AD8D: client=I4:1.2[I4:2.2]
 9: postfix/cleanup[29752]: BFF41AD8D: message-id=<I6:1.1@I5:1.1>
10: postfix/qmgr[1519]: BFF41AD8D: from=<I6:2.1@I5:2.1>, size=7910 (queue active)
11: postfix/smtpd[22190]: disconnect from I4:1.3[I4:2.3]
12: postfix/local[4864]: BFF41AD8D: to=<I6:3.1@I5:3.1>, relay=local, delay=7, ...
```

Fig. 6. Features from Fig. 5 replaced with placeholders for pseudonyms

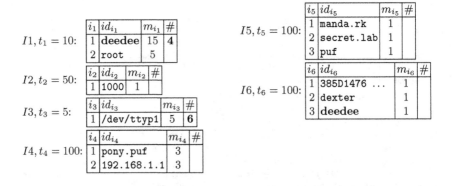

Fig. 7. State of the feature type groups $I1, \ldots, I6$ after pseudonymizing all audit records from Fig. 5

7 An Approach Based on Secret Sharing

Basically our approach to pseudonymization should live up to the following requirements. Different pseudonyms can be issued for each transaction involving a given identity, that is we have transaction-based pseudonyms. Pseudonyms issued for transactions of a given identity within a given attack scenario can be used to reveal that identity only if t or more of these pseudonyms are known. Knowledge of less than t pseudonyms does not enable identity recovery.

We can use secret sharing threshold schemes to split an identity into shares, which then are the pseudonyms, fulfilling above requirements. For this purpose we chose Shamir's threshold scheme [26], which is perfect, ideal, and allows generation of new shares independently from preceding shares. Prioritization of transactions is possible by issuing a different number of shares for identities in the context of some kinds of transactions.

For our approach we apply Shamir's threshold scheme somewhat differently than in other applications of secret sharing, such as key splitting. Since the reidentifiers in our approach receive all shares generated by the pseudonymizer, and since each reidentifier is a potential adversary, it is not required to protect the confidentiality of shares during distribution. We also generate shares on demand, i.e. whenever specific events occur. Due to this stepwise generation of shares we pair the value of ordinate and abscissa, and we can't take advantage of an optimization specific to Shamir's scheme. To avoid inferences wrt. abscissa values, we have to use unique x-coordinates for all shares related to a given attack scenario.

To be independent of the size and characteristics of identities to be shared, we assign secrets to identities. These secrets are unique within an attack scenario. We then use Shamir's scheme to share these secrets. We have to fulfill some security requirements for the mapping of secrets to identities. First, reidentifiers need to know the mapping, but are controlled by SSOs. Then Unix access control cannot protect the confidentiality of the mapping. We thus use cryptograms of identities, considering the respective decryption keys as sharable secrets. Secondly, a user reidentified once in a given attack scenario cannot act anonymously in further transactions that occur in that attack scenario, but don't complete it. We therefore consider expiring valid shares after an epoch, trading anonymity off against accountability.

Both, pseudonymizer and reidentifier know which shares belong to which attack scenario, but the shares, merely being ordinate-abscissa-pairs, provide no information, which of them belong to the same identity. If they did, they weren't transaction-based pseudonyms. A reidentifier thus can only guess, which shares stem from the same identity, i.e. are *compatible*. When guessing combinations of shares, a reidentifier sometimes will interpolate a value, which matches nowhere in above mentioned mapping. In other cases the reidentifier hits a secret. Unfortunately this match is *valid* only, if all involved shares are compatible. In case not all shares stem from the same identity, the match is considered a *mismatch*, which would result in holding an identity accountable for events it did not cause.

We propose some straightforward approaches to handle mismatches. We can mark compatible shares with identical labels, but these labels effectively are relation-based pseudonyms for identities within a given attack scenario. To retain the advantages of transaction-based pseudonyms, we could defer the issuing of the labels of compatible shares, until t of the shares have been distributed.

We can also avoid mismatches without marking shares. To confirm a match, we have to provide a verifier for each identity cryptogram, which is the value of a secure one-way hash function, applied to the respective decryption key, i.e. the shared secret. The pseudonymizer can test for matches using all combinations of t incompatible shares, including the newly generated share to be issued. Since a match in this case is a mismatch, the new share must not be issued and a new one is to be chosen and tested. Although mismatches then will not occur at reidentifiers, they too have to search a match in combinations of t shares, including the new incoming share.

Note, that depending on t and the number of shares issued in the context of an attack scenario, the number of combinations to test grows very large. While reidentifiers could reside on machines dedicated to this task, pseudonymizers are located on the machine in use, to be able to protect the user's anonymity. If we need to avoid high computational cost at pseudonymizers, we let them issue unmarked shares without filtering mismatches. Reidentifiers then have to verify the validity of matches with the issuing pseudonymizer. In an online-protocol the reidentifier provides the pseudonymizer with information enabling validation of the compatibility property of the shares involved in the match, such as a reference to I_g, the shares and the match. Note, that we sacrifice the ability to perform offline identity recovery to reduce the pseudonymizer's performance costs.

Considering the unlinkability of shares, the ability for offline validation, and computational costs, the approach using deferred marking of shares seems most desirable.

To be able to take full advantage of transaction-based pseudonyms, it is necessary to hide or at least coarsen the number of actually involved users. This obviously cannot be achieved when shares are marked, but labels are not deferred. An approach to coarsen the number of actors is the introduction of dummy entities in the secret-to-identity mapping. The issues to be considered concerning dummy entities include how many dummies are needed for a certain degree of security, the upper bound for a useful number of dummies, the choice of the dummy identity string, and concealment of replacements of dummies with real identities.

The useful number of dummies, which from the viewpoint of attackers determines the number of potential actors, is clearly bounded by the known total number of identities of the kind under consideration. Since this number may be large, it may be more storage-efficient to restrict the number of dummies to the product of the estimated number of actors and the estimated number of shares generated per actor. The identity string for dummies should be chosen to be indistinguishable from real identity strings, but if mismatches are not handled, dummies should be distinguishable from real identity strings. When a yet unknown real actor has to be added to the secret-to-identity mapping, we have to conceal which dummy is replaced with the new real identity. A simple way to achieve this, is to completely change the appearance of all entries, all exhibiting the same size. Since the updated mapping needs to be distributed to the reidentifiers, we also have to conceal the number of these transmission, e.g. by means of dummy traffic.

8   Open Issues and Further Research

There are a number of open issues to be investigated, such as the probability of mismatch occurrence, the transition from an epoch of share validity to the next epoch, as well as concerns mentioned above regarding dummy handling. Areas of interest wrt. to dummies are further methods for reducing the granularity of reidentifications, and potential benefits and required properties of dummy audit records. If we can do without the decoupling of identities and secrets, we don't need to solve the problems associated with the secret-to-identity mapping. Another important point is the correlation and reidentification of pseudonyms issued by distributed pseudonymizers for the same user.

Some desired properties wrt. reidentification are automation, technical purpose binding and infrequent involvement of a TTP. Also adversaries should not be able to link pseudonyms to the identities. This obviously is not the case if pseudonyms are introduced within the system while the SSOs can observe the pseudonyms and the identities. As a result, we have to preclude SSOs from observing user identities in the monitored system. This is hard to accomplish if the IDS is local to the system under surveillance, or if IDS personnel has to perform tasks on that system (see Sect. 4.1, 4.3). Approaches such as ANIDA (Sect. 4.4), [20], [21] and [22] solve this problem by introducing pseudonyms external to the monitored system by means of a TTP, or by using a protocol that does not disclose the real identities. Since in these approaches the monitored system uses the pseudonyms for access control, damage can be avoided, even if pseudonyms are invalid, i.e. the identity will not be recoverable. Thus, users may generate the pseudonyms without involving a TTP.

We assume, that reasonable use of a complex system requires fine-grained access control. There are basically two different implementations of access control. Capabilities bestow the right to execute certain known operations on certain known objects upon subjects, which hold the capability. Since for the use of capabilities the identifier of the subject is irrelevant[4], we can use all kinds of pseudonyms. Unfortunately the Unix systems we use do not support capabilities. Alternatively access control lists (ACL) bound to objects can be used to assign to certain known subjects the right to execute certain known operations. If the system trusts in the authenticity of a subject identifier, it just compares the identifier with entries in the ACL to determine the subject's rights. The subject then can use entity-based pseudonyms only, though the pseudonyms stored in the ACL can be relation-based[5]. This basically is, what Unix allows for, if you consider user names being entity-based pseudonyms. Alternatively, if the system authenticates the subject in advance to each access using proofs as described in [20] and [21], there is no need for entity-based pseudonyms to be used by subjects. Then, even if transaction-based pseudonyms are used, the system needs to know against which property to authenticate. It seems advisable to authenticate group memberships, while the cardinality of the groups should be sufficiently large. Unfortunately, the Unix systems we use don't support this kind of access control. Pragmatism led us to the trust model we propose in Sect. 5. We seek to support transaction-based pseudonyms for IDS, but since off-the-shelf Unix only supports entity-based pseudonyms, we introduce pseudonyms independently from access control. Decoupling pseudonyms from access control is dangerous, because we can not avoid illicit accesses in the presence of invalid pseudonyms. We propose a TTP, known to generate valid pseudonyms, allowing identity recovery. If users were to generate pseudonyms on their own, the pseudonyms would have to comprise a proof vouching for pseudonym validity.

Assuming we have valid pseudonyms, i.e. reidentification is possible, then we have to decide, whether SSOs are trusted to respect the privacy of users. In case they are, adherence to purpose binding is expected when identity recovery information is used, thus recovery information may always be available to SSOs. Since primary tasks of SSOs in some environments may inherently conflict with user privacy, we may not be able to afford this kind of trust. We have to make sure, identity recovery information is usually not available to SSOs. In the ap-

---

[4] Here we ignore the intricacies involved in implementing secure capabilities.

[5] The ACL-pseudonyms could be implemented as a one-way function of the concatenation of subject, object and operation.

proaches described in Sect. 4.1, 4.2 and 4.3, isolation of that information from SSOs would require extra tamper-proof hardware.

It is easy to achieve manual purpose binding for reidentification by placing the information needed for identity recovery at a TTP, which most of the time lays dormant. Only if accountability wrt. policy violations requires identity recovery, and upon good cause shown, the TTP makes use of the recovery information (see the approaches in Sect. 4.5).

Manual purpose binding impedes automatic reidentification. To achieve automatic identity recovery, which is a desired property of IDS, technical purpose binding is required. Note, that it is not sufficient to merely trust the IDS analysis component to adhere to purpose binding, for it is controlled by SSOs (see Sect. 4.2). Our approach provides for technical purpose binding independently of the IDS components controlled by SSOs, but it does so at the cost of always involving a TTP (here the PPO) to ensure generation of valid pseudonyms.

References

1. Birgit Pfitzmann, Michael Waidner, and Andreas Pfitzmann. Rechtssicherheit trotz Anonymität in offenen digitalen Systemen (in German). *Datenschutz und Datensicherheit*, 14(5-6):243–253, 305–315, 1990.
2. Kai Rannenberg, Andreas Pfitzmann, and Günther Müller. IT security and multilateral security. In Müller and Rannenberg [27], pages 21–29.
3. Joachim Biskup and Ulrich Flegel. Transaction-based pseudonyms in audit data for privacy respecting intrusion detection. In Hervé Debar, Ludovic Mé, and S. Felix Wu, editors, *Proceedings of the Third International Workshop on Recent Advances in Intrusion Detection (RAID 2000)*, number 1907 in LNCS, pages 28–48, Toulouse, France, October 2000. Springer.
4. Directive 95/46/EC of the European Parliament and of the Council of 24 october 1995 on the protection of individuals with regard to the processing of personal data and on the free movement of such data. Official Journal L 281, October 1995. http://europa.eu.int/eur-lex/en/lif/dat/1995/en_395L0046.html.
5. Erster Senat des Bundesverfassungsgerichts. Urteil vom 15. Dezember 1983 zum Volkszählungsgesetz - 1 BvR 209/83 u.a. (in German). *Datenschutz und Datensicherung*, 84(4):258–281, April 1984. http://www.datenschutz-berlin.de/gesetze/sonstige/volksz.htm.
6. Michael Sobirey, Simone Fischer-Hübner, and Kai Rannenberg. Pseudonymous audit for privacy enhanced intrusion detection. In L. Yngström and J. Carlsen, editors, *Proceedings of the IFIP TC11 13th International Conference on Information Security (SEC'97)*, pages 151–163, Copenhagen, Denmark, May 1997. IFIP, Chapman & Hall, London.
7. Emilie Lundin and Erland Jonsson. Privacy vs intrusion detection analysis. In *Proceedings of the Second International Workshop on the Recent Advances in Intrusion Detection (RAID'99)*, West Lafayette, Indiana, September 1999. Purdue University, CERIAS.
8. Emilie Lundin and Erland Jonsson. Some practical and fundamental problems with anomaly detection. In *Proceedings of NORDSEC'99*, Kista Science Park, Sweden, November 1999.

9. Simone Fischer-Hübner and Klaus Brunnstein. Opportunities and risks of intrusion detection expert systems. In *Proceedings of the International IFIP-GI-Conference Opportunities and Risks of Artificial Intelligence Systems ORAIS'89*, Hamburg, Germany, July 1989. IFIP.

10. Simone Fischer-Hübner. *IDA (Intrusion Detection and Avoidance System): Ein einbruchsentdeckendes und einbruchsvermeidendes System (in German)*. Informatik. Shaker, 1993.

11. Michael Sobirey. Aktuelle Anforderungen an Intrusion Detection-Systeme und deren Berücksichtigung bei der Systemgestaltung von AID² (in German). In Hans H. Brüggemann and Waltraud Gerhardt-Häckl, editors, *Proceedings of Verläßliche IT-Systeme*, DuD-Fachbeiträge, pages 351–370, Rostock, Germany, April 1995. GI, Vieweg.

12. M. Sobirey, B. Richter, and H. König. The intrusion detection system AID – Architecture and experiences in automated audit trail analysis. In P. Horster, editor, *Proceedings of the IFIP TC6/TC11 International Conference on Communications and Multimedia Security*, pages 278–290, Essen, Germany, September 1996. IFIP, Chapman & Hall, London.

13. Michael Sobirey. *Datenschutzorientiertes Intrusion Detection (in German)*. DuD-Fachbeiträge. Vieweg, 1999.

14. Michael Meier and Thomas Holz. Sicheres Schlüsselmanagement für verteilte Intrusion-Detection-Systeme (in German). In Patrick Horster, editor, *Systemsicherheit*, DuD-Fachbeiträge, pages 275–286, Bremen, Germany, March 2000. GI-2.5.3, ITG-6.2, ÖCG/ACS, TeleTrusT, Vieweg.

15. Emilie Lundin and Erland Jonsson. Anomaly-based intrusion detection: privacy concerns and other problems. *Computer Networks*, 34(4):623–640, October 2000.

16. Roland Büschkes and Dogan Kesdogan. Privacy enhanced intrusion detection. In Müller and Rannenberg [27], pages 187–204.

17. David Chaum. Untraceable electronic mail, return addresses, and digital signatures. *Communications of the ACM*, 24(2):84–88, February 1981.

18. D. Kesdogan, R. Büschkes, and J. Egner. Stop-and-go-mixes providing probabilistic anonymity in an open system. In *Proceedings of the 2nd Workshop on Information Hiding (IHW'98)*, number 1525 in LNCS, pages 83–98. Springer, 1998.

19. Teresa F. Lunt, R. Jagannathan, Rosanna Lee, Sherry Listgarten, David L. Edwards, Peter G. Neumann, Harold S. Javitz, and Al Valdes. IDES: The enhanced prototype, a real-time intrusion-detection expert system. Technical Report SRI-CSL-88-12, SRI Project 4185-010, Computer Science Laboratory SRI International, 1988.

20. Joe Kilian and Erez Petrank. Identity escrow. In *Proceedings of the Conference on Advances in Cryptology (CRYPTO'98)*, pages 196–185, 1998.

21. Dan Boneh and Matt Franklin. Anonymous authentication with subset queries. In *Proceedings of the 6th ACM Conference on Computer and Communications Security*, pages 113–119, Kent Ridge Digital Labs, Singapore, November 1999. ACM SIGSAC, ACM Press.

22. Yuen-Yan Chan. On privacy issues of internet access services via proxy servers. In Rainer Baumgart, editor, *Secure Networking – CQRE[Secure]'99*, number 1740 in LNCS, pages 183–191, Düsseldorf, Germany, November 1999. secunet, Springer.

23. David Chaum, Amos Fiat, and Moni Naor. Untraceable electronic cash. In S. Goldwasser, editor, *Proceedings of the Conference on Advances in Cryptology (CRYPTO'88)*, LNCS, pages 319–327, Santa Barbara, CA, August 1988. Springer.

24. National Computer Security Center. US DoD Standard: Department of Defense Trusted Computer System Evaluation Criteria. DOD 5200.28-STD, Supercedes CSC-STD-001-83, dtd 15 Aug 83, Library No. S225,711, December 1985. `http://csrc.ncsl.nist.gov/secpubs/rainbow/std001.txt`.

25. National Computer Security Center. Audit in trusted systems. NCSC-TG-001, Library No. S-228,470, July 1987.
    `http://csrc.ncsl.nist.gov/secpubs/rainbow/tg001.txt`.

26. Alfred J. Menezes, Paul C. van Oorschot, and Scott A. Vanstone. *Handbook of Applied Cryptography*. Discrete Mathematics and its Applications. CRC Press, Inc., Boca Raton, Florida, 1997.

27. Günter Müller and Kai Rannenberg, editors. *Multilateral Security in Communications*. Information Security. Addison Wesley, first edition, 1999.

Protection Profiles for Remailer Mixes

Giovanni Iachello[1] and Kai Rannenberg[2]

[1] Telematics, IIG, Freiburg University
g.iachello@iol.it
[2] Microsoft Research Cambridge, UK
kair@microsoft.com

Abstract. In the past independent IT security evaluation according to published criteria has not realized its potential for the assessment of privacy enhancing technologies (PETs). The main reason for this was, that PETs were not covered appropriately in the evaluation criteria. This situation has changed somewhat, and therefore this paper reports on a case study, in which we developed Protection Profiles for remailer mixes. One reason for the development of these Protection Profiles was to test the privacy related components in the new Evaluation Criteria for IT Security – Common Criteria (International Standard 15408, ECITS/CC) and to develop improvements. Another reason was to contribute to an independent evaluation of privacy enhancing technologies. The experiment shows, that the ECITS/CC enable PPs for remailer mixes, but that there are still improvements necessary. The paper presents the Protection Profiles and the structured threat analysis for mixes, on which the Protection Profiles are based.

1 Introduction

Independent IT security evaluation can be very useful for privacy enhancing technologies (PETs), as PETs very often aim at the protection of individual users, and this is exactly the user group that usually does not have the resources to assess IT on its own. Of course evaluations and criteria then have to cover privacy aspects properly. This is not trivial, and early IT security evaluation criteria like the TCSEC and the ITSEC caught much criticism for their lack of coverage of privacy-related requirements, and for their tendency towards ever increasing data storage and centralization of trust. Meanwhile, evaluation criteria, like the recent Evaluation Criteria for IT Security – Common Criteria (International Standard 15408, ECITS/CC) contain components assigned to privacy. Therefore we used them to specify a number of Protection Profiles for remailer mixes. One reason for the development of these Protection Profiles was to test the privacy related components in the ECITS/CC and to develop improvements. Another reason was to contribute to an independent evaluation of privacy enhancing technologies.

The paper commences with an introduction into IT security certification and evaluation criteria (Chapter 2) and an overview of their problems regarding privacy and multilateral security (Chapter 3). It then describes the new ECITS/CC

H. Federrath (Ed.): Anonymity 2000, LNCS 2009, pp. 181–230, 2001.
© Springer-Verlag Berlin Heidelberg 2001

and their privacy components (Chapter 4). Chapters 5 and 6 describe the approach of writing PPs for remailer mixes and give a short introduction into mix technology. Chapter 7 presents the Protection Profiles and their rationales. Chapter 8 summarizes the experiences gained by writing the Protection Profiles. Chapter 9 proposes changes to the ECITS/CC. Chapter 10 gives a summary and conclusion. The Annex provides not only the references (Chapter 11) but also the three proposed functional families in a notation conformant with the prescriptions of the ECITS/CC (Chapter 12).

2   IT Security Certification and Evaluation Criteria

The complexity of today's information technology (IT) makes it impossible to evaluate its security by simple "examination". However, it is scarcely possible for many users to conduct more detailed checks, which are necessary for a qualified evaluation, as they cannot afford the expenditure this would entail. Thus, more and more users are faced with the problem of knowing very little about the technique they use for important transactions (e.g. processing sensitive patient data, signing documents, or making payments).

One way to enable confidence in IT is to evaluate and certify products and systems by neutral and competent institutions on the basis of published IT security evaluation criteria. Related certification schemes exist since the mid 80's, for example, in the USA, the UK, and Germany. There are differences between the schemes, but typically a sponsor asks (and pays) for an evaluation that is conducted by an accredited (commercial or governmental) IT Security Evaluation Facility (ITSEF) and monitored and certified by a (governmental or commercial) Certification Body (CB), cf. Figure 1. In most cases the sponsor of an evaluation is the manufacturer of the Target of Evaluation (TOE). An overview of Certification Schemes and more details can be found in [19].

To enable comparisons of evaluation results, criteria catalogs have been developed, which structure the IT security requirements. Some examples are given in Table 1.

While the TCSEC [22] had a rather fixed security model aiming at the confidentiality of military information, subsequent criteria e.g. the ITSEC [6] had a broader scope. These criteria are frameworks that IT manufacturers, vendors, or users can use to specify what security functions (Functionality) they wish to have evaluated and to what depth, scope, and rigor the evaluation should be performed (Assurance).

Functionality refers to the behavior of the product with regard to security concerns, while assurance allows stating requirements on e.g. the development process, the evaluation of the compliance to the requirements documents, the preservation of security during installation and maintenance, and the documentation. In practice, these requirements specify a series of actions, which the developer, the writers of documentation and the evaluators must complete.

Independent evaluation can be very useful for privacy enhancing technologies, as those very often aim at the protection of individual users, and this is exactly

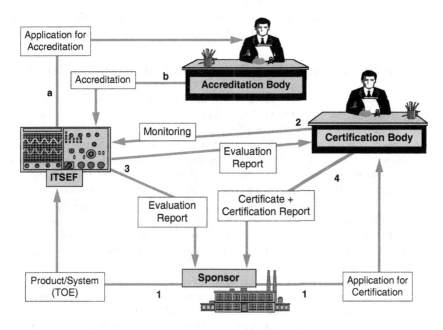

Fig. 1. Evaluation and certification of a TOE (1-4) and accreditation of an ITSEF (a-b)

Table 1. Some IT security evaluation criteria and their editors

Publication / Project Dates	Editors	Criteria Name Current Version
1983/85	USA Department of Defense (DoD)	Trusted Computer System Evaluation Criteria (TCSEC - "Orange Book")
1990/91	Commission of the European Communities (CEC)	Information Technology Security Evaluation Criteria (ITSEC) Version 1.2
1990-99	International Organization for Standardization / International Electrotechnical Commission ISO/IEC JTC1/SC27/WG3	Evaluation Criteria for IT Security (ECITS) International Standard 15408: 1999
1993-99	Common Criteria Project Govt. Agencies from CDN / D / F / GB / NL / USA	Common Criteria (CC) Version 2.1

the user group that usually does not have the resources to assess IT on its own. Of course evaluations and criteria then have to be comprehensive, especially regarding privacy. As the next chapter shows, this was not the case.

3   Problems Regarding Privacy and Multilateral Security

Various aspects of security certification and the underlying early criteria have been criticized, for example thebalance of the criteria and the meaningfulness and use of results (cf. e.g. [10,18,19]).

A main point of criticism from the application side was that the criteria were too biased towards hierarchically administered systems and the protection of system operators. The criteria seemed to not consider the fact that dangers are caused not only by users and outsiders, but also by operators and manufacturers of the systems. So there was a lack of *multilateral security*, i.e. taking the security requirements, not only of operators, but also of users and customers into account. Especially privacy aspects of telecommunication transactions were not covered, e.g. unobservability of calls to help lines or anonymous access to patent information on the Internet.

From a technical point of view systems with distributed organization and administration were only insufficiently covered. Also data-collecting functionality was overemphasized, while data economical functionality was ignored.

The following example illustrates how this lack of consideration for user protection in the criteria affects evaluation results. It also shows that the evaluation, which is described, was focused on the protection of the operators and neglected the protection of users or customers. A function for the selective logging of activities of individual users was classified as a non-critical mechanism that did not need evaluation. In the opinion of the evaluators, failure of this mechanism would not create weaknesses because if the function was not active, the activities of all users were logged [8]. From the operator point of view no real security risk existed, because no audit data would be lost - only perhaps more data than planned would be collected. However, from the users' point of view this is a considerable risk, because excessive logging and the resulting data can lead to substantial dangers for users and customers, e.g. when this data is misused.

4   The New ECITS/CC and Their Privacy Components

Since 1990 two initiatives aim at globally uniform evaluation criteria, mainly to enable the mutual acknowledgement of evaluation results. A joint committee of ISO and IEC (JTC1/SC27/WG3) developed the "Evaluation Criteria for IT Security" (ECITS), which are being finished as IS 15408 [16]. In parallel to the ISO/IEC standardization, North American and European government agencies developed the "Common Criteria" (CC). Since CC Version 2.0 [3] there is a large convergence with the ISO ECITS, and CC Version 2.1 [4] and IS 15408 are fully aligned. After the problems with earlier criteria had also been brought up in ISO/IEC the new criteria contain a section aiming at privacy protection (cf.

Chapter 4.2). At the moment there are no plans for another version of the CC, but the ECITS will undergo the usual periodic revision of ISO/IEC standards, which will probably be done by JTC1/SC27/WG3 in 2003.

4.1   Overview of the ECITS/CC

The ECITS/CC share the goals and general approach of other evaluation criteria, as briefly introduced in Chapter 1, but provide a more flexible structure regarding functional and assurance requirements. In fact, they provide a catalogue of *functional requirements components*, which is a modular, structured library of customizable requirements, each of which tackles one specific aspect of the security requirements for the TOE. The Criteria provide also a catalogue of *assurance requirements*, which are grouped in seven ordered subsets, of increasing depth, scope and rigor.

On the one hand, these modifications create more liberty for the formulation of security targets, but on the other hand, they make the comparison of evaluation results more complicated. In order to resolve this problem and still give users the opportunity to formulate their own requirements, the CC introduced the concept of the "Protection Profile" (PP). A PP describes the functionality and assurance requirements for a certain application (e.g. health care administration) or technique (e.g. firewalls). Ideally, several products will be evaluated against a single PP, so that the results can be compared. ISO is setting up a regulated registry for PPs and the CC project is maintaining a PP list [5].

The ECITS/CC also provide a catalog of seven Evaluation Assurance Levels (EALs). These are an ordered set of packages of assurance components. Each EAL contains the lower level EAL and adds to it some other assurance requirements. The EALs are largely derived from the ITSEC. PP authors, who wish to concentrate on the functional requirements of their PP, can simply choose an EAL.

In most cases the ECITS/CC model the properties and behavior of a TOE by specifying a set of relevant entities and imposing constraints on the relationships between such entities. For this purpose, the following four entities are defined:

- Subject: *"An entity within the TSC[1] that causes operations to be performed"*; this can be, for example, a UNIX process;
- Object: *"An entity within the TSC that contains or receives information and upon which subjects perform operations"*; for example a file, a storage medium, a server system, a hardware component;
- Operation: a process initiated by a subject or user, which employs a subject to interact with one or more objects or subjects; this term is not directly defined in the criteria's' glossary.

---

[1] TSC = TSF Scope of Control: The complete set of interactions that are under the control of the TOE to satisfy its security requirements and to implement its security features.

− User: *"Any entity (human user or external IT entity) outside the TOE that interacts with the TOE"*. It is necessary to clearly distinguish between "Subject" and "User". "User" is the physical user with all its attributes (name, role ...), or an external IT entity (i.e. another system interacting with the TOE), that initiates operations on the TOE, which are carried out, on its behalf, by "Subjects" operating in the TOE.

4.2   The ECITS/CC Privacy Families

The ECITS/CC contain four *Functional Families* directly related to privacy and organized in a privacy *Class*. Some of their components were inserted late in the criteria development process (for example, some of the Unobservability components were not present in version 1.0 of the CC). Most components have several levels, which sometimes are organized in hierarchies. A hierarchical level contains extra requirements. The following description of the components sticks close to that in the ECITS/CC.

Anonymity (FPR_ANO). Anonymity ensures that a user may use a resource or service without disclosing the user's identity. The requirements for Anonymity provide protection of the user identity, but Anonymity is not intended to protect the subject identity. There are two hierarchical levels:

> *FPR_ANO.1 Anonymity* requires that other users or subjects are unable to determine the identity of a user bound to a subject or operation.
> *FPR_ANO.2 Anonymity without soliciting information* enhances the requirements of FPR_ANO.1 by ensuring that the TSF does not ask for the user identity.

Applications include the ability to make inquiries of a confidential nature to public databases, respond to electronic polls, or make anonymous payments or donations.

Pseudonymity (FPR_PSE). Pseudonymity ensures that a user may use a resource or service without disclosing its user identity, but can still be accountable for that use. There are three partially hierarchical levels.

> *FPR_PSE.1 Pseudonymity* requires that a set of users and/or subjects are unable to determine the identity of a user bound to a subject or operation, but that this user is still accountable for its actions.
> *FPR_PSE.2 Reversible pseudonymity* requires the TSF to provide a capability to determine the original user identity based on a provided alias. FPR_PSE.2 is hierarchical to FPR_PSE.1.
> *FPR_PSE.3 Alias pseudonymity* requires the TSF to follow certain construction rules for the alias to the user identity. FPR_PSE.3 is hierarchical to FPR_PSE.1.

Applications include the ability to charge callers for premium rate telephone services without disclosing their identity, or to be charged for the anonymous use of an electronic payment system.

Unlinkability (FPR_UNL). Unlinkability ensures that a user may make multiple uses of resources or services without others being able to link these uses together.

FPR_UNL.1 Unlinkability requires that users and/or subjects are unable to determine whether the same user caused certain specific operations in the system.

Applications include the ability to make multiple use of a pseudonym without creating a usage pattern that might disclose the user's identity.

Unobservability (FPR_UNO). Unobservability ensures that a user may use a resource or service without others, especially third parties, being able to observe that the resource or service is being used. There are four partially hierarchical levels.

FPR_UNO.1 Unobservability requires that users and/or subjects cannot determine whether an operation is being performed.
FPR_UNO.2 Allocation of information impacting unobservability requires that the TSF provide specific mechanisms to avoid the concentration of privacy related information within the TOE. Such concentrations might impact unobservability if a security compromise occurs. FPR_UNO.2 is hierarchical to FPR_UNO.1.
FPR_UNO.3 Unobservability without soliciting information requires that the TSF does not try to obtain privacy related information that might be used to compromise unobservability.
FPR_UNO.4 Authorised user observability requires the TSF to provide one or more authorized users with a capability to observe the usage of resources and/or services.

Applications include technology for telecommunications privacy, especially for avoiding traffic analysis to enforce constitutional rights, organizational policies, or defense requirements.

5   Experimenting by Writing Protection Profiles for Mixes

As the ECITS/CC aim at covering security requirements also for untraditional applications that were not covered in earlier criteria, it seemed useful to experiment with the new criteria by using it. Actually, during the development of the CC a number of example PPs had been produced on the basis of CC V1.0 for testing purposes (see [5]), but there was no (published) PP aiming at privacy requirements. To gain more experience as to whether the ECITS/CC are complete and adequate enough to express requirements on privacy friendly functionality, some example PPs were written.

The mix application (cf. Chapter 6) was chosen because it is a prime example of a distributed application where multilateral security concerns involving operators and users come into existence. The availability of an extensive literature on the subject, of real world implementations and the interest that anonymous and untraceable communication have gained recently, are also all favorable reasons which make this kind of application an ideal testing ground.

The development of the PPs started with an initial survey of the mix literature and implementations to get acquainted with the underlying concepts and technology. A mix implementation was installed and operated in a controlled manner for a couple of weeks. This process resulted in the enumeration of a set of threats that were then used as the basis of the PPs (cf. 7.2).

6   Short Introduction into Mixes

A mix is a remailer system with the objective of hiding the correspondence between sender and recipient of a message. The concept was introduced by D. Chaum in 1981 [7] and has been subsequently refined and applied to other applications besides email, such as ISDN telephony and WWW access (e.g. [21, 17,24]). This basic functionality allows achieving unlinkability of communicating partners, but anonymity can also be achieved if the sender does not explicitly state its identity in the message. As a further development also pseudonymity can be implemented using a mix remailer system, using so-called "return addresses".

There are at least two working implementations of mixes: the first one, is a free software called Mixmaster [9], which evolved from a first-generation plain anonymizing remailer to a complete mix system in 1994. The software is now in use at various sites, but is generally administered by volunteers and thus not apt for widespread commercial use.

A commercial pseudonym-based mix system is being produced by Zero Knowledge Systems [24], which offers a client product for sending email through a set of independently administered nodes. Some of these nodes are administered by ZKS, which also produces the remailer software.

A mix system achieves untraceability of messages essentially by deploying a distributed architecture, where each node is independently administered. The sender selects a path in the mix network to reach the receiver, and each node resends the message to the next one according to instructions present in the message itself. The message is encrypted in such a way that each relay node only gets to know the node from which it received the message and the node to which it forwarded the message.

7   The Protection Profiles Written

Several Protection Profiles were written to cover the features and threats regarding mixes and to test the Common Criteria privacy components. Section 7.1 documents the development history of the PPs and their versions, Section 7.2 gives an overview of the threats considered. The remaining sections in this chapter document the three PPs:

- "Single Mix PP" (7.3);
- "Protection Profile for an Unobservable Message Delivery Application Using Mixes" (or "Multiple Mix PP") (7.4);
- "User-oriented PP for Unobservable Message Delivery Using Mix Networks" (7.5) This PP is described in most detail giving a mapping from threats and other assumptions to security objectives and functional components.

7.1   Development History of the Protection Profiles

The development history of the Protection Profiles already shows some of the issues coming up and is therefore documented here. The following figure gives an overview of the development history; the boxes represent PPs and are positioned in a temporal order (temporal axis from top to bottom); the arrows connecting the PPs represent a "flow of knowledge" (i.e. e. addressed threats, security objectives) from one PP to the other.

Initially, a choice was made to write two PPs following an "architectural" subdivision suggested also by the criteria, i.e. writing a PP for a single mix node ("Single Mix Protection Profile"), and then one for the whole mix network ("Protection Profile for an Unobservable Message Delivery Application Using Mixes", or "Multiple Mix PP" [12]). This represents a rather traditional way of subdividing security problems into manageable pieces, and derives from the "secure each part to secure the system" paradigm.

In the case of the mix network, however, this path resulted in a dead-end, because the second PP, which stated requirements for the whole network, actually tried to make a compromise between the security requirements of the network, and those of the user of the network. For example, a standard option for protecting the mix network from some kinds of flooding attacks is that of keeping audit logs. This clearly endangers the potentially anonymous users, because corrupt administrators or others gaining access to the logs could use the information contained therein to trace back the messages to their original senders.

After unsuccessfully following this path we decided for an alternative approach. This was to divide the security requirements documents based on the so-called "multiple interests" paradigm, i.e. writing one document for each of the involved parties, which in the mix system are the administrators and the users, and each time taking into account the security needs and concerns of the focused party. This approach again led to the writing of two documents: the "Single Mix Protection Profile" [11], which was largely rewritten from the first PP with the same title, and the "User-Oriented Protection Profile for unobservable message

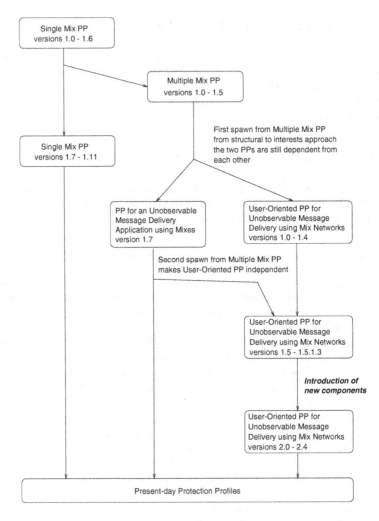

Fig. 2. PP Development history

delivery using Mix networks" [13], which incorporated parts of the "Multiple Mix PP".

The former document states the security requirements of a single node, which overlap largely with the requirements as felt by the administrator of such node (e.g. resistance to attacks, secure operating environment, physical protection . . .), while the latter addresses the needs of the user with respect to the whole network, and includes requirements of anonymity, unlinkability of communicating parties, etc.

Eventually, it was found that the main challenges for the expressive power of the Criteria were posed by this second document, because some of the security requirements related to fundamental privacy-enhancing properties were not to be found in the stock ECITS/CC components (cf. Chapter 8).

Choosing an EAL (see section 4.1) was easier than formulating the functional requirements. The choice is influenced by many external factors, which include the intended use and operational environment of the TOE, policies of the organization that will deploy the TOE, and the will of the sponsor to let the product be evaluated at a high level (which rises the evaluation costs).

Two rather different choices were made: for the "Single Mix PP" and the "Multiple Mix PP" a relatively low level (EAL 3) of assurance was requested; this choice was justified by the fact that the mix is a rather simple system, where the architectural security strengths derive not from the single system, but from the fact that multiple systems operate together.

The "User-Oriented Mix PP" follows another approach. The idea in this case is that the user wants to gain full assurance that the single mix systems were correctly developed, and that the architecture and project, as a whole, were examined by independent organizations. EAL 5 was chosen because it is the first EAL that introduces *complete independent testing* of the TOE.

It is however to be noted that an independent test of the TOE is not sufficient to assure the user that the system will not be malevolently administered after deployment. The ECITS/CC assurance requirements did not aim at evaluating the operation of deployed systems. Closer to this task are risk management standards like IS 13335 [15] or BS7799 [1] and related certification schemes like c:cure [2].

7.2   The Threats Considered in the Protection Profiles

Considering and documenting threats to a TOE is the basis of a PP. The threat list must be *complete* and *relevant*. Obviously, there is no guarantee, that a list of threats is complete. Therefore peer review and multiple incremental cycles are necessary. Each PP was rewritten many times before reaching a stable state for the time being. Additionally, the threats must be stated in a manner to ease the formal demonstration of correspondence with the security objectives, to the degree mandated by the choice of the EAL.

The threat lists are summarized in Table 2, where they are subdivided according to the three Protection Profiles written for the mix system. The threats are briefly described in terms of implementation, effects and countermeasures, and ordered by type. The threat type isone of:

- Active: the threat requires an attacker to actively interfere with the operation of the mix or network, e.g. by blocking communications,
- Passive: this kind of threat is limited to passive operation (e.g. observing traffic through a mix),
- Error: these threats derive from erroneous operation of the mix, due to e.g. bad configuration, etc.

Table 2. Threats used as basis for the Protection Profile (part 1)

Name	Type	Implementation	Permits Analysis ...	(Potential) Effects	Counter-measure(s)
Single mix threats (threats to a single mix system, as seen by the mix operator, and basis for the Single mix PP)					
Logical access	Active	Gain access to the TSF data and algorithms	Of administrative logs Of mix operation	Total failure of mix security functions	Trusted OS, Limit remote administration
Physical access	Active	Gain access to the TSF physical location	Of administrative logs Of mix operation	Total failure of mix security functions	Trusted site
Administrator corruption	Active	Corrupt the administrator	Of administrative logs Of mix operation	Total failure of mix security functions	Organizational policies, Operation review
Replay attack	Active	Intercept and resend a message many times	Of outgoing traffic	Leak of (partial) information	Replay detection on message paths
Flooding attack (DoS)	Active	Flood mix with dummy messages	n/a	Interruption of service	Flooding resistant mix and OS, Origin check
Flooding attack (traffic analysis)	Active	Flood mix with known messages	Of outgoing traffic	Leak of information on singled-out	Origin check message path
Size analysis	Passive	Intercept messages and record their sizes	Of ingoing and outgoing traffic	Leak of information on message paths	Standard and fixed message size
Timing analysis	Passive	Intercept messages and record their transmission times	Of ingoing and outgoing traffic	Leak of (partial) information on message paths	Random delay strategies
Order analysis	Passive	Intercept messages and record their order	Of ingoing and outgoing traffic	(Partial) information on message paths	Random reordering strategies
Content-based traffic analysis	Passive	Intercept messages and read their content	Of ingoing and outgoing traffic	Leak of complete information on message paths	Encryption of message traffic
Mismanagement	Error	Mismanagement of some TSF	n/a	Loss of TOE security properties	Documentation, Design for manageability, Organizational policies
Processing error	Error	Accidental processing error resulting in truncation, loss, alteration of messages	n/a	Unreliable service	Redundancy assurance techniques

Table 2. Threats used as basis for the Protection Profile (part 2)

Name	Type	Implementation	Permits Analysis ...	(Potential) Effects	Counter-measure(s)
Multiple mix threats (**threats to the entire mix network, or related to the network connections, and basis for the Multiple mix PP**)					
Network block	Active	Block the network connections to part of the TOE	n/a	Interruption of service, Degraded service	Organizational policies, distribution of the TOE
Impersonation	Active	Intercept and redirect the network connections to part of the TOE	Of requested traffic in the impersonated network	Degraded service, Leak of information on message paths	Encryption, Sound key distribution policy
Message interception	Passive	Intercept and read messages	Message content exchanged by parts of the TOE	Leak of information on message paths	Encryption
Network unreliability	Error	Accidental damage of messages (truncation, loss, alteration)	n/a	Unreliable service	Redundancy (multiple path ...), Error detection and report
Mismanagement of network security functions	Error	Erroneous configuration of the TSF	n/a	Loss of security properties	Documentation, Design for manageability, Organizational practices
User mix threats (**Threats as seen by the User and basis of the User-oriented mix PP**)					
Untrusted mix	Active	A mix in the network may be compromised and reveal tracing information	Of transiting messages	Exposure of linking information	Division of trust
Mix conspiracy	Active	Some mixes in the network may conspire to share and analyze traffic information	Of transfer logs and TSF operation	Loss of expected security functionalities	Organizational policies, Independent administration
Forgery	Active	An attacker may send forged messages using a user's origin credentials	n/a	Loss of accountability properties	Use of digital signatures
Intercept	Passive	Messages are intercepted while transiting from user to a mix	Of incoming and outgoing traffic	Information on use patterns	Generation of dummy messages by the users
Misuse	Error	Erroneous use of the TSF by the user	n/a	Loss of expected security functionalities	Documentation, Ease of use
Unreliability	Error	The connecting network may be unreliable, resulting in message loss, truncation or alteration	n/a	Unreliable service	Redundancy, Error detection

The threats in the preceding list are then stated in each Protection Profile as formal threats, adhering to the requirements imposed by the PP structure as described in the CC, as shown in the following sections.

The complete text of the PPs [11,12,13] is freely available and also contains extensive justifications for the selection of threats and countermeasures.

7.3   Single Mix Protection Profile

The Single Mix Protection Profile was written to address the security problems of a single mix system, without consideration towards the necessities of the user (who wants to send anonymous mail) and also ignoring all the security threats, which may derive from the connection of the system with other mixes. The threat list of this Protection Profile includes items such as *flooding attacks, logical access to the TOE, replay attacks, traffic size analysis*, as shown in Table 3. The last two threats (marked with "TE") are intended to be countered not only by the mix itself but also by the environment (operating system, etc.).

At this point a general observation regarding the following lists of threats is necessary. These threat lists derive from a detailed analysis of the operation, and risks, of mix networks, both from a practical point of view and from a theoretical one. Afterwards, an informal threat list is produced (see the previous section), which is then used to build a more structured threat list, which complies with the structural requirements (ease of correspondence demonstration, avoiding overlapping threats, etc.) needed by the PP.

The lists must be, obviously, considered together with assumptions, which are also included in separate tables. The idea behind this structure is that the PP should aim at *completeness* in addressing the security issues, either by stating assumptions, or by indicating possible threats. However, the decision of how to subdivide assumptions and threats is a very delicate one, because assumptions clearly do not need to be addressed by the PP, but may hide some major security issues, thus causing the PP to be ineffective.

Table 4 lists the assumptions related to the previous threat list.

Table 5 shows the list of functional components used by the PP to address the shown threats. All the functional components are taken from the ECITS/CC catalog. Each of the selected components listed in the table introduces into the PP a number of atomic requirements that can be tailored by the author.

The selected EAL (Evaluation Assurance Level) is 3. This EAL was selected because it is commonly considered the highest attainable EAL through current not security oriented development practices. Moreover EAL 3 was considered as a good compromise between the TOE analysis complexity and the intended use of the TOE. Recall that a single mix is to be used in a network, and the real strength of the system relies upon the existence of a large number of independent systems.

Table 3. Threats in the Single Mix Protection Profile

Threat Label	Description
T.DenialOfService	An attacker may try flooding the mix with a great amount of messages, thus causing an overload on the mix and possibly leading to Denial of Service by the mix.
T.FloodingAttack	An attacker may try flooding the mix with a great amount of messages, to single out only one unknown message and discover its destination.
T.ForgeOrigin	An attacker may send to the mix messages with a forged origin field. *This can be done for various reasons, for example to hide a flooding attack.*
T.InterceptMessages	An attacker may intercept and read the content of the messages (including the message origin and final destination, arrival and departure order and time) exchanged by users and the mix or between mixes. *The attacker may use intercepted messages to perform a traffic analysis to reveal input/output message flow patterns.*
T.LogicalAccess	An attacker (this includes unauthorized users of the host system) may gain access to the mix. *This may cause the complete failure of the mix.*
T.ReplayAttack	An attacker may intercept an incoming message and feed it to the mix many times, and, by checking the outgoing messages, discover where it is directed.
T.SizeAnalysis	An attacker may track the sizes of incoming and outgoing messages, thus linking origin and destination.
T.WrapAndImpede	An attacker may completely wrap the mix, thus selectively or totally impeding exchange of messages with the users or other mixes.
TE.Untrustworthy Administrator	The mix administrator may abuse his trust and compromise completely the operation of the mix. *Possible actions include: recompiling the mix application and modifying its behaviour, so to trace messages, and impairing the mix and causing DoS.*
TE.Proper Administration	The mix may be administered by the mix administrator in an insecure or careless manner. *This includes both the administration of the mix itself, such as unintentionally disclosing the confidential security attributes of the mix, and the administrative practice, such as not using a trusted channel when remotely administering the mix.*

Table 4. Assumptions in the Single Mix Protection Profile

Assumption Label	Description
A.Environment	The mix works in a networked environment, on a single host.
A.Spam	In case of a spam attack, the mix may not be able to satisfy ist goal.
A.DedicatedHost	The mix is the only process on its host system. Its administrator coincides with the host's system administrator. *This assumption, and the following, is one possible formulation of the main relevant assumption: that the host operating system will not allow or cause security breaches against the TOE. Having the mix as the only application of the host system greatly reduces the complexity of the host's analysis.*
A.OS	The Operating System of the host of the mix identifies authorized users and protects the mix operation and its data with regard to confidentiality, integrity, availability, and accountability.

7.4 Multiple Mix Protection Profile

The "Protection Profile for an Unobservable Message Delivery Application Using Mixes" (or Multiple Mix Protection Profile) was written initially to complement the previous, and to take into account both the entire network of mixes, and the requirements set by the user, which sees the mix network as one homogeneous and opaque entity. Thus, the threats this PP addresses include threats like *message interception* and *denial of service*, as shown in Table 6.

Some of the threats may appear to be too obvious to be included in the threat list (as the T.MixPeek threat, which states the possibility of a mix to read the information contained in a message which is not encrypted.) However, such a statement is necessary exactly to make sure that all messages which transit through the mix system are encrypted in such a way that each mix will not be able to read the content of the message apart from the information of the next node where to send it.

The list of related assumptions follows (Table 7). Some of the assumptions are stated only to simplify the PPs, like the A.DedicatedHost, which excludes other processes on the same host of each mix, and are really not essential. However, there are assumptions, like the A.MinimalTrust, which are very important, because they state explicitly when the entire mix network fails.

This document tries to conciliate the needs of the operators of the mixes on the network with those of the users, and this leads to a conflict, which is difficult to solve using the standard CC components. Table 8 shows the components used to specify the requirements for this PP.

Unless otherwise indicated, the components are described and commented on similarly to the corresponding components of the Single Mix PP (cf. Table 5).

The selected EAL is 3, because the higher EALs are mainly focused on the enhancement of the development process, while in the case of the PP the development is of secondary importance with respect to the installation and operation of the system.

7.5 User-Oriented Protection Profile for Unobservable Message Delivery Using Mix Networks

The "User-Oriented Protection Profile for Unobservable Message Delivery Using Mix Networks" was developed with in mind only the needs of the user of the mix network, and thus addresses threats like *untrusted mix, misuse, key forgery*, as shown in Table 9. The table also includes two Organisational Policies (marked with an "O." label) that state supplementary requirements for the TOE and that do not derive directly from some threat. The policies are however treated like threats in the following steps that lead to the formal requirements statement.

A set of assumptions for the User-Oriented PP follows in Table 10.

The second step of writing a PP is that of specifying a set of security objectives, which state the objectives that the TOE should reach to be able to counter all the threats. Table 11 shows the Security Objectives that were stated for this PP. As for the threats table, the Security Objectives are also divided in two categories, namely, objectives which are to be achieved solely by the TOE, and objectives for which the surrounding environment (Operating System, Administration, etc.) are partly or wholly responsible.

A correspondence between objectives and threats must be demonstrated (the rigor of this analysis depends on the EAL selected for the PP), but such demonstration is omitted here due to space constraints. However, the correspondence between threats and objectives is shown in Table 12.

As written above (section 7.2), the problems encountered during the development of this PP because of expressive deficiencies of the CC components led eventually to the writing of the proposed families. After the development of the new components, a second version of the PP was written; this new PP maintains the same threats and objectives of the previous PP, and simply uses also the new components to express its requirements, accordingly to the recommended top-down practice for PP development. The new version of this PP is decidedly simpler, more effective, and more precise in the requirements definition for the considered application. Table 13 shows the functional components used by this new version of the PP, which also employs the new proposed components (marked in the third column). Where relevant, a short description of the component and its use is provided in the fourth column.

The correspondence table between components and Objectives follows (Table 14). The tables provided in this section allow the reader to trace a single ECITS/CC component selected for inclusion in the PP to a specific threat or policy the TOE must counter or satisfy. Security Objectives that are not "covered" by any component must be addressed either by Assurance requirements, or by additional requirements on the environment, which are however not relevant at this point, and are here omitted.

Table 5. Functional Components in the Single Mix Protection Profile (part 1)

Short name	Unique name	Component Description and Comments
FAU_ARP.1	Security alarms	This family defines the response to be taken in case of detected events indicative of a potential security violation. *This requirement states what the mix should do when a security violation is detected (e.g. Spam attack, Access to the security functions ...) For example, the TOE may inform the administrator of potential attacks, and possibly switch to a secure fail mode upon detection of security violations.*
FAU_GEN.1	Audit data generation	Audit data generation defines the level of auditable events, and specifies the list of data that shall be recorded in each record. *This component requires the TOE to generate an audit trail, which can then be used by an automated or manual attack analysis and by an attack alarm system.*
FAU_SAA.3	Simple attack heuristics	Simple attack heuristics, the TSF shall be able to detect the occurrence of signature events that represent a significant threat to TSP enforcement. This search for signature events may occur in real-time or during a post-collection batch-mode analysis. *This component is used to require the TOE to provide some means for automatic detection of (and thus reaction to) potential attacks.*
FAU_SAR.1	Audit review	Audit review provides the capability to read information from the audit records. *This component ensures that the audit trail is readable and understandable.*
FAU_STG.1	Protected audit data trail storage	Protected audit trail storage, requirements are placed on the audit trail. It will be protected from unauthorized deletion and/or modification. *This component is chosen to ensure that the audit trail is protected from tampering. Only the authorized administrator is permitted to do anything to the audit trail.*
FAU_STG.4	Prevention of audit data loss	Prevention of audit data loss specifies actions in case the audit trail is full. *This component ensures that the authorized administrator will be informed and will be able to take care of the audit trail should it become full. But this component also ensures that no other auditable events as defined in FAU_GEN.1 occur. Thus the authorized administrator is permitted to perform potentially auditable actions though these events will not be recorded until the audit trail is restore to a non-full status.*
FCS_CKM.1	Cryptographic key generation	Cryptographic key generation requires cryptographic keys to be generated in accordance with a specified algorithm and key sizes that can be based on an assigned standard. *This and the following two requirements are included in the PP but left unspecified, since cryptographic standards evolve rapidly.*
FCS_CKM.2	Cryptographic key distribution	Cryptographic key distribution requires cryptographic keys to be distributed in accordance with a specified distribution method that can be based on an assigned standard.
FCS_CKM.4	Cryptographic key destruction	Cryptographic key destruction requires cryptographic keys to be destroyed in accordance with a specified destruction method that can be based on an assigned standard.
FCS_COP.1	Cryptographic operation	Cryptographic operation requires a cryptographic operation to be performed in accordance with a specified algorithm and with a cryptographic key of specified sizes. The specified algorithm and cryptographic key sizes can be based on an assigned standard. *The type and strength of the cryptographic functions is also left unspecified, and must be determined in accordance to the intended use of the TOE, and the perceived threats.*
FDP_IFC.1	Subset information flow control	Subset information flow control requires that each identified information flow control SFP be in place for a subset of the possible operations on a subset of information flows in the TOE. *This requirement (and the following) identifies the security attributes (e.g. routing information) and the allowed information flows through the mix.*

Table 5. Functional Components in the Single Mix Protection Profile (part 2)

Short name	Unique name	Component Description and Comments
FDP_IFF.1	Simple security attributes	This component requires security attributes on information and on subjects that cause that information to flow or that act as recipients of that information. It specifies the rules that must be enforced by the function, and describes how security attributes are derived by the function.
FDP_IFF.4	Partial elimination of illicit information flows	Partial elimination of illicit information flows requires the SFP to cover the elimination of some (but not necessarily all) illicit information flows. *Information about the correlation of origin with destination may reach the attacker through a covert timing or storage covert channel, if care is not used in to blocking such information leakage; this information may help timing, order, and size analysis attacks, and flooding attacks. This requirement ensures that such leakage does not take place.*
FDP_RIP.2	Full residual information protection	Full residual information protection requires that the TSF ensure that any residual information content of any resources is unavailable to all objects upon the resource's allocation or deallocation. *This component requires the TOE not to retain data that could be used by an unauthorized user of the security attributes management functions or by a malevolent administrator to trace messages. (According to the ECITS/CC, this component only relates to "residual" data - storage space that is not overwritten after use, etc.)*
FDP_SDI.2	Stored data integrity monitoring and action	Stored data integrity monitoring and action adds the additional capability to the first component by allowing for actions to be taken as a result of an error detection. *This component is needed for the correct operation of the TOE. If a message is modified while out of TSF control (e.g. by an attacker), this component shall ensure that the message will be discarded as invalid prior to processing.*
FDP_UCT.1	Inter-TSF user data confidentiality transfer protection	Basic data exchange confidentiality, the goal is to provide protection from disclosure of user data while in transit. *This component ensures the data confidentiality during transport of the user data (namely, messages) between separate TSFs and between user and TSF. The FDP_UCT.1 and the FCS_COP.1 components work together (that is, the former requires messages to be confidential (e.g. by using encryption), the latter sets requirements on the cryptographic functions.)*
FMT_MSA.1	Management of security attributes	Management of security attributes allows authorized users (roles) to manage the specified security attributes. *Nobody may modify or change the security attributes associated with messages, as they are integral part of the data needed by the mix to operate correctly. The mix does not store user data other than the transiting messages, so there is no further data to manage.*
FMT_MSA.2	Secure security attributes	Secure security attributes ensures that values assigned to security attributes are valid with respect to the secure state. *This component requires the TOE to perform validity checks on the security attributes used by the TOE itself, such as (local) origin and destination addresses of messages, message signatures and keys, and the like.*
FPR_ANO.2	Anonymity without soliciting information	Anonymity without soliciting information enhances the requirements of FPR_ANO.1 by ensuring that the TSF does not ask for the user identity. *This component (and the following) ensures that the TOE can be used without the user being required of disclosing his own identity.*

Table 5. Functional Components in the Single Mix Protection Profile (part 3)

Short name	Unique name	Component Description and Comments
FPR_UNL.1	Unlinkability	Unlinkability requires that users and/or subjects are unable to determine whether the same user caused certain specific operations in the system.
FPT_FLS.1	Fail with preservation of secure state	Failure with preservation of secure state requires that the TSF preserve a secure state in the face of the identified failures. *This component is used to force the TOE into biasing its operations towards a more secure than reliable operation. The rationale behind this is that a user is more interested in using a safe mix, rather than reliable one, since the TOE is anyhow intended to be used in an environment where multiple mixes are in operation.*
FPT_RCV.1	Manual recovery	Manual recovery, allows a TOE to only provide mechanisms that involve human intervention to return to a secure state. *This component allows for administrators to restore mix operation after a failure; prior to reactivating the mix, however, the administrator shall analyze the audit records, understand the reason that caused the failure, and remove its cause.*
FPT_RPL.1	Replay detection	Replay detection requires that the TSF shall be able to detect the replay of identified entities.
FPT_STM.1	Reliable time stamps	Reliable time stamps requires that the TSF provide reliable time stamps for TSF functions. *This component (and the following) is selected to satisfy dependencies by other components.*
FPT_TST.1	TSF testing	TSF testing provides the ability to test the TSF's correct operation. These tests may be performed at start-up, periodically, at the request of the authorized user, or when other conditions are met. It also provides the ability to verify the integrity of TSF data and executable code.
FTP_ITC.1	Inter-TSF trusted channel	Inter-TSF trusted channel requires that the TSF provide a trusted communication channel between itself and another trusted IT product. *This component is selected to ensure the presence of a trusted channel in inter-TSF communication. The channel provides for confidential and untampered communication between trusted IT products, namely, mixes; such channel might not be reliable, nor does it provide for party identification.*
FTP_TRP.1	Trusted path	Trusted path requires that a trusted path between the TSF and a user be provided for a set of events defined by a PP/ST author. The user and/or the TSF may have the ability to initiate the trusted path. *This component is selected to ensure the presence of a trusted path between the TSF and the user; such a path might not be reliable, nor does it provide for identification of the communicating party.*

The selected EAL level for this PP is EAL 5. The high assurance level is selected to gain a high level of assurance that the TOE will be developed, delivered, and evaluated following rigorous commercial practices. A formal model of the TOE security policies must be provided and evaluated, and the system must be independently tested. EAL 5 is the lowest level providing assurance components that impose the aforementioned tasks.

8   The Experiences Gained

The process of writing PPs is supposed to be top-down. The author identifies a set of threats, devises a set of security objectives that should counter all the

Table 6. Threats in the Multiple Mix Protection Profile

Threat Label	Description
T.DenialOfService	The TOE may be isolated from the users by blocking the network connections, and causing DoS. *This threat applies to the TOE as well as to the surrounding environment. The PP will however only address if from the TOE point of view.*
T.Message Interception	The network and physical layer connections between mixes are not trusted. *This means that an attacker may manage to intercept messages transiting over the network and read their origin and destination fields.*
T.Misuse	Users may improperly use the TOE and produce traceable messages, while thinking the message was correctly sent and delivered. The administrators may inadvertently mismanage or badly configure parts of the TOE as to loose the security properties of that part of the TOE.
T.MixPeek	A subverted mix may be able to gain knowledge of the origin and destination of a message by reading its content while processing it.
T.OneStepPath	A mix may gain information linking origin and destination if the path from the origin user to the destination user contains only one mix.
T.TOESubstitution	An attacker may block messages sent by some user and act as the TOE, or a part thereof. Inadvertent users may send messages to the attacker instead of to the TOE, and the attacker may then read origin and destination data and forward the message to the destination.
T.UnreliableNetwork	The connecting network may not be reliable on correctly delivering messages between parts of the TOE. Specifically, messages may be lost, altered or truncated accidentally.
TE.MixConspiracy	Subverted mixes may share input/output information with the goal of linking origin and destination of a message.

Table 7. Assumptions in the Multiple Mix Protection Profile

Assumption Label	Description
A.Independent Administration	The mixes forming the TOE are assumed to be independently administered from each other.
A.MinimalTrust	The TOE may not be able to reach its goal if all nodes (mixes) are subverted.
A.OpenEnvironment	The mix network works in an open networked environment; each mix is operated on a single host.
A.UserCooperation	Users cooperate actively at the enforcement of the security policy of the TOE. *Users are trusted to use in a correct manner the services made available by the TOE to reach their anonymity goals.*
A.DedicatedHost	The mix is the only process on its host system. Its administrator coincides with the host's system administrator.
A.SecureLocation	The mixes forming the TOE are located at secure sites and physically protected from access by unauthorized users.

Table 8. Functional Components in the Multiple Mix Protection Profile (part 1)

Short name	Unique name	Component Description and comments
FCS_CKM.1	Cryptographic key generation	
FCS_CKM.2	Cryptographic key distribution	
FCS_CKM.4	Cryptographic key destruction	
FCS_COP.1	Cryptographic Operation	
FDP_IFC.1	Subset information flow control	This component requires that each identified information flow control SFP be in place for a subset of the possible operations on a subset of information flows in the TOE. *This component defines the policy of operation of the TOE and the subjects, information and operations controlled by the TOE.*
FDP_ITT.1	Basic internal transfer protection	Basic internal transfer protection requires that user data be protected when transmitted between parts of the TOE.
FDP_ITT.3	Integrity monitoring	Integrity monitoring requires that the SF monitor user data transmitted between parts of the TOE for identified integrity errors. *This component is required to allow safe delivery of messages through the mix network.*
FDP_RIP.2	Full residual information protection	
FMT_MSA.1	Management of security attributes	
FMT_MSA.2	Secure security attributes	
FMT_MSA.3	Static attribute initialisation	Static attribute initialisation ensures that the default values of security attributes are appropriately either permissive or restrictive in nature. *The security attributes (hash values, signatures ...) of the data stored and transferred throughout the TSF are generated automatically by the TOE. This data is not discretionary in nature, but must obey specific rules and may not be changed by users, or by the mix administrator.*
FPR_ANO.2	Anonymity without soliciting information	

Table 8. Functional Components in the Multiple Mix Protection Profile (part 2)

Short name	Unique name	Component Description and comments
FPR_UNL.1 (1)	Unlinkability of origin and destination	Unlinkability requires that users and/or subjects are unable to determine whether the same user caused certain specific operations in the system. *This component is introduced here to make sure that the network actually will grant the unlinkability of origin and destination of a message.*
FPR_UNL.1 (2)	Unlinkability/ untraceability	*This requirement is stated to make sure that an observer may not be able to link two observed messages transiting through the mix network, as being steps of the same message chain. This somewhat awkward formulation of the unlinkability requirements simply states that a mix shall not be able to bind messages exchanges between other nodes together into a single mix chain.*
FPR_UNO.2	Allocation of information impacting unobservability	Allocation of information impacting unobservability requires that the TSF provide specific mechanisms to avoid the concentration of privacy related Information within the TOE. Such concentrations might impact unobservability if a security compromise occurs. *Particularly, this requirement states that routing information may be accessible to mixes only when strictly necessary, e.g. to identify the following step in the mix chain as described for example in [7]. This functional component provides protection both to the mix network, by minimizing the exposure of information to attackers, which may be used to exploit covert channels, and to the user, to guarantee that the network will continue to operate securely even when some, unless not all, nodes are compromised.*
FPT_FLS.1	Failure with preservation of secure state	*If some nodes in the network fail or are subverted, the remaining nodes shall continue to work properly, in a secure manner.*
FPT_ITT.1	Basic internal TSF data transfer protection	Basic internal TSF data transfer protection, requires that TSF data be protected when transmitted between separate parts of the TOE. *This component (and the following) protect the data produced and used by the TSF, and transferred between parts of the TOE, such as dummy messages, mix public keys updates transmitted between mix nodes, etc.*
FPT_ITT.3	TSF data integrity monitoring	TSF data integrity monitoring requires that the TSF data transmitted between separate parts of the TOE is monitored for identified integrity errors.
FTP_TRP.1	Trusted path	

Table 9. Threats in the User-Oriented Mix Protection Profile (part 1)

Threat Label	Description
O.Anonymity	The TOE shall provide for an anonymous message delivery service; that is, the recipient of a message shall not be able to know the origin of the message, unless the author expressly inserts this information in the message body.
O.Untraceability	The TOE shall provide for an untraceable message delivery service; this means that, taken any message transiting through the system at any time, it shall not be possible to obtain enough information to link its origin and destination users.
T.ContentDisclosure	An attacker might intercept transiting messages between parts of the TOE and read their content, thus disclosing it, together with any related information. *This is a threat not only to the operation of the TOE (as discussed in [12]), but also for the user, whose communications might be traced. In particular, this threat relates to messages transiting from the user client to a node on the network and refers to both the original message content (written by the user), and also to the routing information and other auxiliary information carried by the message.*
T.EndPointTraffic Analysis	An attacker might intercept transiting messages between parts of the TOE (user client and mix node), and use the related information to perform traffic analysis on a user. *This threat relates to the concepts of sender anonymity and receiver anonymity. As viewed traditionally, main goal of the mix network is to hide the relation between receiver and sender of a message (this property also known as sender/receiver anonymity). However, once a suspect on a possible communication between two users is established, it may be possible to monitor the end points of message chains for a statistical correlation between transmission and reception times, especially if the traffic on the network is low, the users few, and the per-user traffic low. A similar discussion, related to Web transactions, may be found in [20].*
T.KeyForgery	An attacker might generate forged keys, simulating the activity of a given mix, distribute them, and make the user employ them to encrypt message in the belief that such messages are only readable by the replaced mix. *This is a threat to the originating user, who will send messages readable to an attacker, and might not be warned about it. A trust scheme (implemented for example by a certification authority) is required to counter this threat.*

Table 9. Threats in the User-Oriented Mix Protection Profile (part 2)

Threat Label	Description
T.Misuse	The user might install, configure or use the TOE interaction functions in an insecure manner, hence compromising the expected security properties offered by the TOE. *This threat is particularly relevant when considering the "human" element when this is the user, because the user is not expected to have as deep a knowledge about the TOE functions and about the security concerns as, for example, a system administrator, who represents the human element in the case of an administered mix node.*
T.OneStepPath	A mix may gain information linking origin and destination if the path from the origin user to the destination user contains only one mix.
T.UntrustworthyMix	Some mix(es) in the network may be compromised and hold, process and/or disclose information useful to trace, and/or reveal the content of, communications.
TE.MixConspiracy	Some mixes in the network may be compromised and share information useful to trace, and/or reveal the content of, communications. *This threat represents an extension to the T.UntrustworthyMix threat, in that it introduces the concept of information sharing between parts of the TOE.*
TE.PartialNetwork Block	An attacker might block the connection between parts of the TOE and the user. *This is a typical DoS attack, where part or the entire TOE is rendered unusable.*
TE.Redirection	An attacker might redirect the connections between parts of the TOE and act as to replace that part seamlessly, thus effectively acting as a compromised mix subset.

threats, and finally expresses these objectives through a set of formal requirements taken from the ECITS/CC catalog. This methodology has many advantages, the main one being that the development process of the PP is clean, and the formal demonstration of correspondence between the various threats, objectives and requirements is simple.

The problems arise when the PP author needs to express requirements for security objectives not covered by ECITS/CC components. During the development of the User-Oriented Protection Profile, three such issues were identified:

1. Requirements on the distribution of the TOE: although it may be viewed as a purely architectural requirement, it is worthy to note that many secure systems are based explicitly on a distributed system to perform the security relevant tasks. Mixes are an example, but also digital payment systems, etc. show such pattern.
2. Requirements on the policies requiring the minimization of knowledge: clearly information that has been disposed of cannot be disclosed. Deleting information as soon as it is not essential to the operation of the system anymore is thus always a safe practice.

Table 10. Assumptions in the User-Oriented Mix Protection Profile

Assumption Label	Description
A.SecurityGoals	The TOE is assumed to be used to achieve unlinkable and anonymous or pseudonymous communication. Other security properties, as unobservability of TOE use are not contemplated.
A.LogicalSec	The TOE will perform as long as the user takes care of securing the logical access to their computing environment. *This assumption requires some explanatory text. As logically securing mainstream operating systems and environments, especially when networked, is close to impossible[2], the assumption should be taken rather loosely, provided that if the risk analysis leads to the conclusion that an attack on the user's workstation is likely, then the user should adopt a safer operating environment.*
A.OS	The single parts of the TOE run on operating system platforms that are assumed to be trusted and not to expose privacy related information belonging to the TOE.
A.PhysSec	The TOE will perform as long as the users take care of securing their physical access to the message traffic handled by the TOE. *This is a point that cannot be over-stressed; an insecure physical user location may be easily exploited against the user who mistakenly believes that his or her communications are unobserved.*
A.Minimal Connectivity	The TOE might not be able to reach its goal if an attacker is able to block all access points of the user to the mix network.
A.MinimalTrust	The TOE might not be able to reach its goal if all nodes (mixes) of the network are subverted.
A.OpenEnvironment	The mix network works in an open networked environment.
A.UnreliableNetwork	The connecting network might not be reliable on correctly delivering messages between parts of the TOE. Specifically, messages may be lost, altered or truncated accidentally. *The TOE is however not required to provide reliable service. A high degree of reliability may be achieved by sending multiple copies of a message through different paths.*
A.UserCooperation	Users cooperate actively at the enforcement of the security policy of the TOE. *Users are trusted to use in a correct manner the services made available by the TOE to reach their anonymity goals.*

Table 11. Security Objectives in the User-Oriented Mix Protection Profile (part 1)

Security Objective Label	Description
SO.Adequate Documentation	The TOE shall provide the user with adequate, readable documentation on the correct use of the security functions.
SO.Anonymity	The TOE shall accept and process messages without requiring that the processed data may be in any way linked to the origin user.
SO.Conceal Message Content	The TOE shall enforce that the content of all messages transiting on the network be inaccessible to all third parties, in whatever point of the network the messages are intercepted.
SO.Counter Traffic Analysis	The TOE shall be constructed as to counter traffic analysis techniques specifically aimed at analyzing the communications between user client software and the mix network.
SO.Divide Security Information	The TOE shall be constructed as to provide the user the ability, and enforce the correct use of such ability, of determining the allocation of unlinkability-relevant data among different parts of the TOE.
SO.Divide Security Processing	The TOE shall provide to the user the ability, and enforce the correct use of such ability, of freely choosing a combination of mix nodes among which to allocate the processing activities achieving unlinkability.
SO.Enforce Proper Use	The TOE (and especially the user interface part of the TOE) shall enforce the proper and secure use of the security functions of the TOE. *For example, require secure pass phrases, encryption, and minimum message chain length.*
SO.Enforce Trust Distribution	The TOE shall be constructed to enforce the user's choice of information and processing distribution.

3. Requirements on unlinkability properties to be enforced by the TOE: the statement of unlinkability of operations is possible through the stock ECITS/CC components, but not so for unlinkability of users, which is precisely what the mix network provides.

To solve the expressive deficiencies of the ECITS/CC a number of options may be considered, and the following three are worthwhile to mention:

1. Restate the security objective differently, (i.e. "fit" the objective to the requirements),
2. Try to force the criteria components to cover the objective (i.e. "fit" the requirements to the objective),
3. Develop new functional components.

The first two options show to be not viable in the long run. In fact, the first one breaks the top-down paradigm, and distorts the PP to state what is expressible by the criteria, necessarily avoiding all security issues which are not simply stateable by the ECITS/CC. The second option "overloads" the ECITS/CC

Table 11. Security Objectives in the User-Oriented Mix Protection Profile (part 2)

Security Objective Label	Description
SO.Identity	The TOE shall uniquely identify the single mix nodes and users and provide means to transmit data to a specific mix while preserving the confidentiality of such data.
SO.Key Trust Assurance	The TOE shall provide the user the ability, and enforce the correct use of such ability, of validating any public key used for encryption purposes against some trusted mechanism, to gain confidence that the communicating partner is actually who he claims to be.
SO.Minimize Security Information	The TOE shall be constructed as to minimize the use, distribution and availability time frame of information impacting unlinkability.
SO.Untraceability	The TOE shall also ensure that no subject (user, administrator, threat agent) has the possibility to gain sufficient information as to track back the origin of a message.
SOE.Antagonistic Management	The TOE shall be independently and antagonistically managed. *The main problem with this security objective to be fulfilled by the environment is that it is nearly impossible to enforce it without some form of post-deployment assurance evaluation control and maintenance.*
SOE.Distributed Network	The TOE shall rely on a topologically distributed network. *This is required to maximize the resources that an attacker must deploy in the attempt to "cut off" part of the network from the rest. Apart from requiring specific design choices, this requirement can only be met by implementing a sound collective administration policy, and by providing means to assure the users of the effects of such a policy.*

components to express requirements for which they were not thought. This has many drawbacks; for one thing, it may simply be not always possible. Moreover, the requirements tend to become unclear, and ineffective, and the PP evaluation process becomes more complicated because of the non-straightforward use of the components.

The third option has undoubtedly many formal and theoretical advantages, and some drawbacks. On the one hand, the requirements may be stated in a simple fashion, and the top-down structure is preserved. On the other hand, while the ECITS/CC allow for expansion of the base requirements sets, one of their main advantages (i.e. mutual recognition) is not guaranteed for PPs that use such novel components.

The full discussion of the various problems encountered, and of how it was decided to write new components is too lengthy to be included here, but it can be said that each of the previous issues arose when trying to express specific objectives through the criteria, and an effort was made to approach the problem

Table 12. Security Objectives to Threats and Organizational Policies mapping

	O.Anonymity	O.Untraceability	T.ContentDisclosure	T.EndPointTrafficAnalysis	T.KeyForgery	T.Misuse	T.OneStepPath	T.UntrustworthyMix	TE.MixConspiracy	TE.PartialNetworkBlock	TE.Redirection
SO.AdequateDocumentation						*					
SO.Anonymity	*										
SO.ConcealMessageContent			*								
SO.CounterTrafficAnalysis				*							
SO.DivideSecurityInformation							*	*			
SO.DivideSecurityProcessing							*	*			
SO.EnforceProperUse						*					
SO.EnforceTrustDistribution							*	*	*	*	
SO.Identity								*			*
SO.KeyTrustAssurance					*						
SO.MinimizeSecurityInformation								*			
SO.Untraceability		*									
SOE.AntagonisticManagement									*		
SOE.DistributedNetwork										*	*

by using all three strategies [14]. In each case, the conclusion was found that the technically best way to proceed was that of developing new components.

The decision might have been different in the situation of a concrete evaluation. There resource constraints (getting an evaluation through without spending too much time discussing novel approaches) and easier mutual recognition (therefore staying with the standard set of components) might have got priority. However, with respect to improving the ECITS/CC two new families and one largely revised family are proposed in the next chapter.

9 Proposals for New and Revised Functional Families

Three new functional families were devised, in a general enough formulation, and in a suitable format to be included in the ECITS/CC set. The new families are summarized inTable 15. Each family is discussed in a separate section below. The formal statement of the three families, which follows the typographical, layout and content standards of the ECITS/CC, can be found in the Annexes (Chapter 12).

Table 13. Functional Components in the User-Oriented Protection Profile for unobservable message delivery using mix networks (part 1)

Sort name	Unique name	New?	Component Description and Comments
FCS_CKM.1	Cryptographic key generation		Cryptographic key generation requires cryptographic keys to be generated in accordance with a specified algorithm and key sizes that can be based on an assigned standard.
FCS_CKM.2	Cryptographic key distribution		Cryptographic key distribution requires cryptographic keys to be distributed in accordance with a specified distribution method that can be based on an assigned standard.
FCS_CKM.4	Cryptographic key destruction		Cryptographic key destruction requires cryptographic keys to be destroyed in accordance with a specified destruction method that can be based on an assigned standard.
FCS_COP.1	Cryptographic operation		Cryptographic operation requires a cryptographic operation to be performed in accordance with a specified algorithm and with a cryptographic key of specified sizes. The specified algorithm and cryptographic key sizes can be based on an assigned standard.
FDP_ACC.2	Complete access control		Complete access control requires that each identified access control SFP cover all operations on subjects and objects covered by that SFP. It further requires that all objects and operations with the TSC are covered by at least one identified access control SFP. *This access control policy, which is composed of this component and the following, states that:* — *All data produced by subjects covered by the SFP must obey the policy's requirements;* — *Data produced by subjects covered by the SFP must be explicitly addressed to some subject;* — *Data explicitly addressed to some subject must be unreadable by all other subjects;* — *Data produced by a subject may be read by the same subject that originated it.*
FDP_ACF.1	Security attribute based access control		Complete access control requires that each identified access control SFP cover all operations on subjects and objects covered by that SFP. It further requires that all objects and operations with the TSC are covered by at least one identified access control SFP.
FDP_IFC.1	Subset information flow control (CCE)		Subset information flow control requires that each identified information flow control SFP be in place for a subset of the possible operations on a subset of information flows in the TOE. *The CCE (Covert Channel Elimination) SFP, stated in this component and the following, requires the TOE to deploy techniques to eliminate covert channels by which an attacker may gain information about the use of the system by some user, especially with regards to traffic analysis information. (The specific technique to adopt is not specified.)*
FDP_IFF.4	Partial elimination of illicit information flows		Partial elimination of illicit information flows requires the SFP to cover the elimination of some (but not necessarily all) illicit information flows.

Table 13. Functional Components in the User-Oriented Protection Profile for unobservable message delivery using mix networks (part 2)

Sort name	Unique name	New?	Component Description and Comments
FDP_IRC.2	Full information retention control	Yes	Full information retention control requires that the TSF ensure that any copy of all objects in the TSC is deleted when not more strictly necessary for the operation of the TOE, and to identify and define the activities for which the object is required. *This component is used to state a minimization of access to information policy, which we tried to state using the stock CC components with access control requirements. However stating such a policy by means of access control is not satisfying, in that it represents a considerable extension to the intended use of the components, which are, as the name suggests, to be used to state information objects access policies in the traditional sense and do not lend themselves to other applications. For this reason this new component was developed and used in this PP.*
FDP_ITT.1	Basic internal transfer protection		Basic internal transfer protection requires that user data be protected when transmitted between parts of the TOE.
FDP_RIP.2	Full residual information protection		Full residual information protection requires that the TSF ensure that any residual information content of any resources is unavailable to all objects upon the resource's allocation or deallocation.
FIA_ATD.1	User attribute definition		User attribute definition, allows user security attributes for each user to be maintained individually.
FIA_UID.1	Timing of identification		Timing of identification, allows users to perform certain actions before being identified by the TSF.
FMT_MSA.1	Management of security attributes		Management of security attributes allows authorized users (roles) to manage the specified security attributes.
FMT_MSA.2	Secure security attributes		Secure security attributes ensures that values assigned to security attributes are valid with respect to the secure state.
FMT_MSA.3	Static attribute initialisation		Static attribute initialisation ensures that the default values of security attributes are appropriately either permissive or restrictive in nature.
FMT_SMR.1	Security roles		Security roles specifies the roles with respect to security that the TSF recognizes.
FPR_ANO.2	Anonymity without soliciting information		This component makes sure that the TOE does not request identification information regarding the origin and destination of messages it handles, and that nobody may gain information linking a data object (message) to users.

The components were proposed to solve precise problems we incurred in while using the ECITS/CC to state requirements for mix networks, but are devised to be as reusable and general as possible.

9.1   Information Retention Control (FDP_IRC)

The "Information retention control" family addresses a basic need in secure information processing and storage applications, which however appears not to be covered by the ECITS/CC: the need for secure management of data no more needed by the TOE to perform its operation, but still stored in the TOE. The traditional view of IT systems as data storage systems induced naturally into

Table 13. Functional Components in the User-Oriented Protection Profile for unobservable message delivery using mix networks (part 3)

Sort name	Unique name	New?	Component Description and Comments
FPR_TRD.2	Allocation of information assets	Yes	Allocation of information assets requires that the TSF ensure that selected information impacting privacy be allocated among different parts of the TOE in such a way that in no state a single administrative domain will be able to access such information. *This component, and the following one, is needed to implement a trust distribution mechanism, which by the sole use of stock CC components was stated using the FPR_UNO.2 "Allocation of information impacting observability". However, the fact that it refers specifically to "unobservability" has impeded its use for other security properties. Additionally, in the initial version of the PP, which used the stock CC components, the FDP_ACC.2 "Complete access control", and FDP_ACF.1 "Security attribute based access control" were used to implement a mandatory access control policy in the TOE, which would require data:* — *To be explicitly addressed* — *To be not accessible by any subject except the intended addressee.* *However, using access control requirements to state requirements on the distribution of information resulted in stating unclear and ineffective requirements, since the structure of the CC access control components derives from experience in implementing standard access control policies, and does not lend itself well to the requirements needed for the mix.* *Therefore, in the new PP the more general FPR_TRD "Distribution of trust" family replaces all of the cited stock CC requirements components.* *This component divides the TOE (the mix network) in multiple administrative domains (a single mix node), as described in section 9.3.* *A more complete explanation of how this family enhances the PP can be found in section 9.3.3.*
FPR_TRD.3	Allocation of processing activities	Yes	FPR_TRD.3 Allocation of processing activities requires that the TSF ensure that selected processing activities impacting privacy be executed on different parts of the TOE in such a way that no single administrative domain will be able to make use of information gathered from the processing activity.
FPR_UNL.2	Unlinkability of users	Yes	Unlinkability of users requires that users and/or subjects are unable to determine whether two users are referenced to by the same object, subject or operation, or are linked in some other manner. *Originally the FPR_UNL.1 "Unlinkability" component was used to state requirements on the intended purpose of the mix network, i.e. to provide for unlinkable communication between partners. However, the fact that the CC unlinkability component is expressly limited to "unlinkability of operations" has made it difficult to use such a component in a more general way. For this reason it was replaced by the new, more general, FPR_UNL.2 "Unlinkability of users" component.*

Table 14. Functional components to Security Objectives mapping

	SO.AdequateDocumentation	SO.Anonymity	SO.ConcealMessageContent	SO.CounterTrafficAnalysis	SO.DivideSecurityInformation	SO.DivideSecurityProcessing	SO.EnforceProperUse	SO.EnforceTrustDistribution	SO.Identity	SO.KeyTrustAssurance	SO.MinimizeSecurityInformation	SO.Untraceability	SOE.AntagonisticManagement	SOE.DistributedNetwork
FCS_CKM.1										*				
FCS_CKM.2											*			
FCS_CKM.4											*			
FCS_COP.1		*												
FDP_ACC.2							*	*						
FDP_ACF.1							*	*						
FDP_IFC.1			*											
FDP_IFF.4			*											
FDP_IRC.2												*		
FDP_ITT.1		*												
FDP_RIP.2												*		
FIA_ATD.1									*					
FIA_UID.1					*	*								
FMT_MSA.1					*	*								
FMT_MSA.2					*	*	*							
FMT_MSA.3					*	*	*							
FMT_SMR.1					*	*								
FPR_ANO.2	*													
FPR_TRD.2			*				*						*	
FPR_TRD.3						*	*						*	
FPR_UNL.2												*		

Table 15. Proposed new and revised functional families

Label	Name	Purpose
FDP_IRC	Information retention control	Limit the accumulation of non-essential information.
FPR_UNL	Unlinkability	Extend the current unlinkability requirements.
FPR_TRD	Distribution of trust	Allow the user to allocate information and processing activities.

thinking that once entered, data would be seldom deleted from the system, and if so, mainly because of storage exhaustion problems.

But in a multilateral or high security environment it is important to minimize the replication, and temporal time frame in which information is contained in the system. Also, users might want their IT products to avoid retaining data that they consider exploitable by third parties, or threatening their privacy. In this case, such a requirement can help users to gain confidence that the product is secure, as far as it deletes every copy of the data when not needed anymore.

The FDP_RIP "Residual information protection" family addresses one side of this problem[3], but an explicit requirement on the management of no longer needed data is missing.

Of course competing requirements may arise, as data may be needed by the system for more activities over a long period of time. Possible solutions to this problem are:

- Better protecting the information objects stored in the TOE from access,
- Re-requesting the protected information from the user each time it is needed.

Overview of the family. Information retention control ensures, that information no longer necessary for the operation of the TOE is deleted by the TOE. Components of this family require the PP author to identify TOE activities and objects required for those activities, and not to be kept in the TOE, and the TOE to keep track of such stored objects, and to delete on-line and off-line copies of unnecessary information objects.

The suggested class for this family is class FDP "*User Data Protection*", since the main purpose of this family is the protection of user data while in the TOE.

This family sets only requirements on information objects requested for specific activities in the TOE operation, and not on general data gathering. The policies which control the collection, storage, processing, disclosure and elimination of general user data stored on the TOE must be detailed elsewhere, and are domain of the environmental objectives and organizational policies, not of the PP.

Components belonging to this family could be used, for example, when the TOE needs some information from the user, or generates information, which might be easily mismanaged or misused in case of a malicious or inadvertent use or administration of the TOE. This category includes, for example:

- Connecting IP numbers on anonymizing proxy servers;
- One-time cryptographic keys, which if eventually disclosed could allow the decryption of intercepted and stored communications or files;
- TOE usage histories, as interactive command line shell histories, or information presentation tools cache files (i.e. WWW browser caches), which, while

---

[3] Namely, the elimination from the TOE of all traces left behind by objects upon deallocation of resources used to store or manipulate them.

useful to the user and TOE during specific activities, could be used to track user or TOE actions, if preserved across sessions;
- Any information for which security considerations (both of the TOE and of the user) suggest not to keep on the TOE, if not strictly necessary.

When more than one activity requires the presence of a protected object, all activities, which refer to the required object must end before deleting it.

Components. The family has two hierarchical components:

> *FDP_IRC.1 Subset information retention control* requires that the TSF ensure that any copy of *a defined subset of* objects in the TSC is deleted when no longer strictly necessary for the operation of the TOE, and to identify and define the activities for which the object is required.
> *FDP_IRC.2 Full information retention control* requires them same but regarding to *all* objects in the TSC.

FDP_IRC.1 Subset information retention control. This component requires that, for a subset of the objects in the TOE, the TSF will ensure that the objects will be deleted from the TOE when no longer required for some specific action.

The formal description of the component is available in section 12.1. The PP/ST author should specify the list of objects subject to information retention control. He should also specify the list of activities which require specific objects to be stored in the TOE, and whose termination requires the TOE to delete the no more required objects.

FDP_IRC.2 Full information retention control. This component requires that, for all objects in the TOE, the TSF will ensure that the objects will be deleted from the TOE when no longer required for some specific action. In other words, *every* object used by the TOE must be tracked for its necessity, and if not more strictly required, deleted. Therefore this component is hierarchical to FDP_IRC.1.

The assignment can be limited to specifying the list of activities which require specific objects to be stored in the TOE, and whose conclusion requires the TOE to delete the no more required objects.

9.2   Unlinkability (FPR_UNL)

The general model of entities as set up in the ECITS/CC (cf. 4.1) allows specifying various kinds of security requirements, including privacy-related requirements. For example an unlinkability of operations requirement would impose a constraint on the relationship between operations in the TSC relating them to a particular user.

However, the full expressive potential of this model is not described by the standard ECITS/CC components. Figure 3 shows the current situation: The solid arrows indicate a relationship, which is covered by a particular ECITS/CC

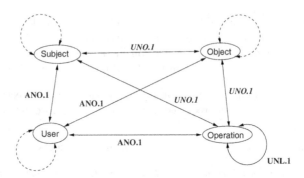

Fig. 3. Unlinkability properties covered (solid arrows) and not covered (dashed arrows) by existing components

component, and the dashed arrows indicate that the link they represent is not expressible using the current ECITS/CC privacy components. With regard to unlinkability, the ECITS/CC provide the FPR_UNL.1 component that provides unlinkability of operations (cf. 4.2.3). Its only functional element reads:

> **FPR_UNL.1.1** The TSF shall ensure that [assignment: *set of users and/or subjects*] are unable to determine whether [assignment: *list of operations*] [selection: *were caused by the same user, are related as follows* [assignment: list of relations]].

Although useful, this family does not cover at least one case, which is of primary importance for mixes: the unlinkability of users, in relation to a specific data object (the mail message). This kind of property is also hard to express through the other families: one could try using the unobservability (FPR_UNO) family, which is however not adequate because the action itself of transmitting a message is not hidden by the mix system. The mix hides only the relation between users, and between email and user.

In conclusion an enhancement of the unlinkability family is necessary to augment the expressiveness of the ECITS/CC to include also the mentioned cases.

Overview of the family. The aim of the unlinkability family is still to ensure that selected entities may refer each another without others being able to observe these references (cf. 4.2.3); the change is that it now applies not only to users operations, but also to subjects and objects.

The components share a common structure and provide the PP author with the possibility of tailoring the following:

1. The users and subjects from which the information should be hidden.
2. A list of specific entities that the requirement protects.
3. A selection or an assignment of a list of relationships to hide.

Components. The family consists of four sibling components:

> *FPR_UNL.1 Unlinkability of operations* requires that users and/or subjects
> are unable to determine whether the same user caused certain specific opera-
> tions in the system, or whether operations are related in some other manner.
> This component ensures that users cannot link different operations in the
> system and thereby obtain information.
>
> *FPR_UNL.2 Unlinkability of users* requires that users and/or subjects are
> unable to determine whether two users are referenced to by the same object,
> subject or operation, or are linked in some other manner.
>
> This component ensures that users cannot link different users of the system
> and thereby obtain information on the communication patterns and relati-
> onships between users.
>
> *FPR_UNL.3 Unlinkability of subjects* requires that users and/or subjects
> are unable to determine whether two subjects are referenced to by the same
> object, user or operation, or are linked in some other manner.
>
> This component ensures that users cannot link different subjects in the sy-
> stem and thereby obtain information on the usage and operation patterns of
> the subjects.
>
> *FPR_UNL.4 Unlinkability of objects* requires that users and/or subjects are
> unable to determine whether two objects are associated to the same user,
> subject or operation, or are linked in some other manner.
>
> This component ensures that users cannot link different objects in the system
> and thereby obtain information on the usage patterns of objects.

9.3   Distribution of Trust (FPR_TRD)

Among the current families in the privacy class of the ECITS/CC no provision is
made to address privacy requirements related to the distribution of trust among
parts of the TOE, except in the FPR_UNO.2 component; the new functional
family is therefore proposed to be integrated into the FPR class.

Trust may be defined, not only in an IT setting, as *"Assured resting of the
mind on the integrity, veracity, justice, friendship, or other sound principle, of
another person; confidence; reliance."* [23]. In a more restrictive definition, one
may define it as *"confidence on the integrity of another person or organization in
the managing of an asset given to him, her or it"*. In this context, trust division
may be described as the process of allocating assets among different trustees
with the aim of minimizing the damage, which one might suffer if one of the
trustees betrays the trust given.

Clearly in IT the main asset is *information*, and the accidental or intentional
loss or mismanagement of it may result in great damages for the owners or
beneficiaries of it. Data may be either supplied directly to an information system,
as inputted files, documents, personal information, or they may be derived from
interaction with the system, such as data regarding on-line time and login times
of a user, requests and destination of email deliveries and WWW accesses, or
called telephone numbers; often the collection of this kind of information is

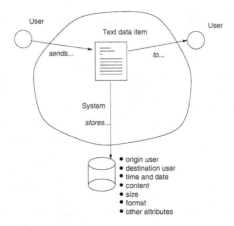

Fig. 4. Hidden activities and information objects involved in sending a data object through a system

not clearly stated in the (contract) terms which bind user and operator of a system. Figure 4 shows the hidden information processed and possibly stored in a system, which provides textual data transmission capabilities to users when such an operation is initiated.

Another related observation is that the processing itself produces information, whose existence or content may not even be known to the user that requested the processing activity to be initiated. For example, in large WWW sites which employ distributed, redundant, servers requests are redirected to one of the servers in a pool, and such mechanism, and also the identity of the server which actually executes the request is not visible to the end user, neither is the server choice known.

The proposed *"Distribution of trust"* family addresses both aspects of the trust issue, i.e. the distribution of information, and the distribution of processing activities, which may produce privacy-relevant information themselves.

Overview of the family. This family describes specific functions that can be used to allocate information and processing activities on the TOE with the objective of protecting the privacy of users of the system. To allow such allocation, the concept of *"Administrative Domain"* (AD) is introduced to indicate a part of the TOE whose security functions are accessible and usable to access data by a single subject (system user, administrator ...) without requesting any additional authorization or performing additional authentication procedures.

The AD is a formalization of the concept of the more intuitive "part of the TOE", which is also used in the statement of the FPR_UNO.2 component. Moreover, it specifies that administrators of an AD may not access other ADs without gaining rightful permission. In fact, allocating information on different "parts of the TOE" is not very useful, if the different parts are accessible by the same administration. If all the parts are administered by the same user or organization, a subverted administrator or an attacker gaining administrator privileges may as well access such information even if it is distributed. Instead, it is necessary to provide for independent administration and separate access domains for different parts of the TOE; this means that an administrator of one part will not be able to access as such also other parts of the TOE.

As an example, consider a monolithic TOE (i.e. a UNIX operating system environment), where only one administrative domain exists, and the administrator may access the security functions of the whole TOE. As a result, if users store both their sensitive data, even in an encrypted form, and their private keys on the same system, the administrator (or an attacker gaining administrator privileges) will be able to access the data.

To avoid this problem, the TSF could be designed to allocate data and keys on different, independently administered systems, and to require that the decryption be done on a third system when the owner needs to access it. This obviously raises the common chicken and egg problem of whether the system where the cryptographic functions take place is trusted or not. Many solutions can be applied in this case, e.g.:

1. Performing a two-phase en/decryption in separate administrative domains (which is, in essence, what the mix system does),
2. Personally administering the system where cryptographic functions take place (for example, a smartcard with cryptographic capabilities, which stores the keys and communicates with the outside only with the input and output of cryptographic algorithms; the card is always carried by the owner of the data, which trusts the issuer of the card, or a certificate regarding the card[4].)

Components. The family is structured in three components, one of which is a base component defining the concept of administrative domain, while the other two express the requirements on information and operations allocation:

FPR_TRD.1 Administrative domains requires that the TOE be divided in distinct administrative domains (AD), with separate authentication and access control procedures; administrators of one administrative domain may not access other ADs.

FPR_TRD.2 Allocation of information assets requires that the TSF ensure that selected information impacting privacy be allocated among different parts of the TOE in such a way that in no state a single administrative domain will be able to access such information.

FPR_TRD.3 Allocation of processing activities requires that the TSF ensure that selected processing activities impacting privacy be executed on different parts of the TOE in such a way that no single administrative domain will be able to make use of information gathered from the processing activity.

---

[4] Of course a secure administration would also require secure input (e.g. keyboard) and output (e.g. display) facility for the user.

The derivate components (FPR_TRD.2 and FPR_TRD.3) let the PP author tailor the following:

1. A list of objects or operations which should be subject to allocation in different ADs,
2. In the case of objects, the form of allocation (e.g. distribution, encryption ...),
3. A set of conditions that should always be maintained by the TOE with regard to assets allocation.

The formal component descriptions are available in section 12.3.

The effect of using the new components. In the previous chapters, we stated that the introduction of the new privacy-oriented components in the User-Oriented Mix PP greatly simplified the statement of the requirements and enhanced their effectiveness. To support this assertion, we now show in detail how the new components perform. To avoid lengthening the paper excessively we will limit the example to only one of the new functional families (FPR_TRD "Distribution of Trust").

The introduction of the new components has a twofold advantage. First of all, it allows requirements to be specified in a more clear and simple manner compared to using the stock components, which had to be overloaded to express certain requirements for which they were not intended. Secondarily, it also allows expressing more complete and precise requirements, and reduces the number of unmet Security Objectives.

Table 16 shows the subset of security objectives in which the new FPR_TRD family is used. For each Security Objective, the table lists the stock functional components that were used in the first version of the PP (second column), and the components used in the final version (third column).

The new components do not only replace some of the old ones, but also provide for a better coverage of the security objectives stated in the PP. The following list shows this in detail for every security objective:

- SO.DivideSecurityInformation "The TOE shall be constructed as to allow the user the ability, and enforce the correct use of such ability, the allocation of unlinkability-relevant data among different parts of the TOE."
  Before the introduction of the new families, this objective was reached by adopting a set of three requirements. Essentially, an access control policy would control the enforcement part of the requirement, while the security attribute management components would allow the user to divide the allocation of security-relevant information. Finally, the "Allocation of information impacting unobservability" component was used in an "overloaded" manner, which proved to be ineffective. Thus, the initial PP addressed this Security Objective by using the following components:
    - FPR_UNO.2 "Allocation of information impacting unobservability"

Table 16. How the FPR_TRD family helps to fulfill Security Objectives

Security Objective	Initial PP	Final PP
SO.Divide Security Information	FDP_ACC.2 "Complete access control (MUDAC)" FDP_ACF.1 "Security attribute based access control (MUDAC)" FMT_MSA.1 "Management of security attributes" FMT_MSA.2 "Secure security attributes" FMT_MSA.3 "Static attribute initialisation" FPR_UNO.2 "Allocation of information impacting unobservability"	FMT_MSA.1 "Management of security attributes" FMT_MSA.2 "Secure security attributes" FMT_MSA.3 "Static attribute initialisation" FPR_TRD.2 "Allocation of information assets"
SO.Divide Security Processing	FMT_MSA.1 "Management of security attributes" FMT_MSA.2 "Secure security attributes" FMT_MSA.3 "Static attribute initialisation"	FMT_MSA.1 "Management of security attributes" FMT_MSA.2 "Secure security attributes" FMT_MSA.3 "Static attribute initialisation" FPR_TRD.3 "Allocation of processing activities"
SO.Enforce Trust Distribution	FDP_ACC.2 "Complete access control (MUDAC)" FDP_ACF.1 "Security attribute based access control (MUDAC)"	FDP_ACC.2 "Complete access control (MUDAC)" FDP_ACF.1 "Security attribute based access control (MUDAC)" FPR_TRD.2 "Allocation of information assets" FPR_TRD.3 "Allocation of processing activities"
SOE.Antagonistic Management	Previously no component available to cover this objective	FPR_TRD.2 "Allocation of information assets" FPR_TRD.3 "Allocation of processing activities"

This is the only component in the CC/ECITS that expressly provides for allocation of information. However, the fact that it refers specifically to "unobservability" causes problems to its use for other security properties. The "trick" for overloading the stock component was that of requiring the operation of transmitting a message between users to be unobservable. However, this results in an ambiguous requirement because nothing can be said about the *link* between communicating partners, which a mix network also aims at hiding (Unlinkability).

- FDP_ACC.2 "Complete access control (MUDAC)", and FDP_ACF.1 "Security attribute based access control (MUDAC)"

  These two components were introduced into the initial PP to implement a mandatory access control policy. This policy requires data to be explicitly addressed and access to be strictly controlled and limited to the intended recipient. The components remain in the new PP to enforce the SO.EnforceTrustDistribution and SO.Identity objectives, but are superseded by the FPR_TRD.2 "Allocation of information assets" component with regard to the SO.DivideSecurityInformation objective.

  In this case, the access control requirements allow the PP author to define requirements on which subjects may access the information that flows through the mix network. However, they fail completely at specifying requirements on how such information flow must be structured to achieve unlinkability and unobservability (the distributed nature of message processing in the mix network).

In the final version, the division of trust component takes the place of both the access control components and the allocation of unobservability information component.

- SO.DivideSecurityProcessing "The TOE shall provide to the user the ability, and enforce the correct use of such ability, of freely choosing a combination of mix nodes among which to allocate the processing activities achieving unlinkability."

  In this case the objective was not fully satisfied in the initial version of the PP, because the CC/ECITS do not provide a functional component for allocating *processing activities* in different parts of the TOE.

  This previously not satisfied objective can now be fully covered by using one of the new components. The new FPR_TRD.3 "Allocation of processing activities" component provides for distribution of processing among different, independently administered, parts of the TOE, while the ability for the user to specify some of the security attributes (which is how routing information is considered in this PP) allows to actually make use of distributed processing.

- SO.EnforceTrustDistribution "The TOE shall be constructed to enforce the user's choice of information and processing distribution."

  This requirement was only partially covered in the initial PP, because the access control requirements do not allow stating requirements on the TOE structure. Adding the FPR_TRD components complements the access control requirements and results in a fully covered objective.

- SOE.AntagonisticManagement "The TOE shall be independently and antagonistically managed."

  This objective that was not at all covered in the first version of the PP is now partially covered, as the TOE is now built to allow for independent administration, at least from a technical point of view. Obviously adequate environmental procedures and policies are still necessary for the correct operation of the TOE.

To ease analyzing the relationship between security objectives and functional components, Table 17 splits the objectives in atomic assertions and shows how each assertion is covered by one or more components.

Table 17. Overview of coverage of the TOE distribution objective

Requirement name	Single component statements	Satisfied by ...
SO.Divide Security Information	TOE shall be distributed	Administrative domains FPR_TRD
SO.Divide Security Processing	User ability of choosing a distributed use pattern	Management of security attributes FMT_MSA
SO.EnforceTrust Distribution	Enforce users' choices	Mandatory access control FDP_ACF, FDP_ACC
	Construction of the TOE as to allow information and processing distribution	Administrative domains FPR_TRD
SOE.Antagonistic Management	Independent management	Administrative domains FPR_TRD

Note that objectives and functional components do not match exactly, i.e. more than one component is necessary to meet a security objective, and a single component may address more than one objective. This is a common situation when both the objectives and the components state complex requirements with multiple, independent assertions.

As a final note one may observe that in the old PP, without the trust division components, the partial objectives marked in Table 17, as "construction of the TOE" and "TOE shall be distributed" were simply not covered.

10   Summary and Conclusion

The experiences gained while writing the Protection Profiles include the following major issues:

1. In general the ECITS/CC provide much more flexibility than their predecessors. They also contain much better instruments to describe privacy friendly functionality. However as shown above, the ECITS/CC components do not offer a complete solution to all the issues which characterize privacy-related objectives.
2. The greatest challenges to the expressive capacity of the functional components appear in the Multiple Mix PP and in the User-Oriented Mix PP, where a point of multilateral security is raised (security of the TOE vs. security of the user).

3. For some applications, architectural choices and objectives (i.e. distributed vs. centralized system) influence the security properties of the system. This applies to mixes, but holds also for other "secure" applications, as digital money, information handling and storage, etc.

4. The probably most relevant evidence is that simply trying to force the application's requirements or the functional components to "fit" is not a sustainable solution, because it results in an unclear and ineffective requirements definition.

5. The proposed components aim at forming a useful start-up for enhancing future versions of the ECITS/CC, even when the respective part of the criteria becomes slightly longer. Privacy oriented functionality covers only a small part (ca. 10 percent) of the criteria, so there should be space for the improvements.

6. Especially in the area of communication the evaluation of service security becomes important for users. While the ECITS/CC provide some help for this further work is needed.

Annexes

References

1. British Standards Institution: Code of practice for information security management (BS 7799-1: 1999); Specification for information security management systems (BS 7799-2: 1999)

2. c:cure scheme; http://www.c-cure.org

3. Common Criteria Implementation Board: Common Criteria for IT Security Evaluation, V. 2.0, May 1998; http://csrc.nist.gov/cc

4. Common Criteria Implementation Board: Common Criteria for IT Security Evaluation, V. 2.1, August 1999; www.commoncriteria.org and http://csrc.nist.gov/cc

5. Common Criteria Project: List of Protection Profiles; http://csrc.nist.gov/cc/pp/pplist.htm

6. European Commission: IT Security Evaluation Criteria, V. 1.2; 1991-06-28; Office for Official Publications of the EC; also www.itsec.gov.uk/docs/pdfs/formal/ITSEC.PDF

7. Untraceable electronic mail, return addresses, and digital pseudonyms. Communications of the ACM, 1981, Vol. 24, No. 2, pp. 84-88

8. Chris Corbett: ITSEC in Operation - an Evaluation Experience, Proc. 4th Annual Canadian Computer Security Conference, May 1992, Ottawa, Canada, pp. 439-460

9. Lance Cottrell: Mixmaster & Remailer Attacks; http://www.obscura.com/~loki/remailer/remailer-essay.html

10. Privacy Protection and Data Security task Force of the German Society for Informatics: Statement of Observations concerning the Information Technology Security Evaluation Criteria (ITSEC) V1.2; 24 February 1992, edited in Data Security Letter, No 32, April 1992

11. Giovanni Iachello: Single Mix Protection Profile, Revision 1.11, May 1999; http://www.iig.uni-freiburg.de/~giac

12. Giovanni Iachello: Protection Profile for an Unobservable Message Delivery Application using Mixes, Revision 1.7, June 1999; http://www.iig.uni-freiburg.de/~giac

13. Giovanni Iachello: User-Oriented Protection Profile for an Unobservable Message Delivery Application using Mix networks, Revision 2.4, June 1999; http://www.iig.uni-freiburg.de/~giac

14. Giovanni Iachello: IT Security Evaluation Criteria, and Advanced Technologies for Multilateral Security - The Mix Example; Tesi di Laurea; Universität Freiburg, Institut für Informatik und Gesellschaft, Abt. Telematik and Università degli Studi di Padova; June 1999; http://www.iig.uni-freiburg.de/~giac

15. ISO/IEC: Guidelines for the management of IT security (GMITS); Parts 1-5; Technical Report 13335 (part 5 still under development)

16. ISO/IEC: Evaluation Criteria for IT Security (ECITS), Parts 1-3; International Standard 15408;1999-12-16

17. Anja Jerichow, Jan Müller, Andreas Pfitzmann, Birgit Pfitzmann, Michael Waidner: Real-Time Mixes: A Bandwidth-Efficient Anonymity Protocol; IEEE Journal on Selected Areas in Communications 16/4 (May 1998) 495-509

18. Kai Rannenberg: Recent Development in Information Technology Security Evaluation - The Need for Evaluation Criteria for multilateral security; in Richard Sizer, Louise Yngström, Henrik Kaspersen und Simone Fischer-Hübner: Security and Control of Information Technology in Society - Proceedings of the IFIP TC9/WG 9.6 Working Conference August 12-17, 1993, onboard M/S Ilich and ashore at St. Petersburg, Russia; North-Holland, Amsterdam 1994, pp. 113-128; ISBN 0-444-81831-6

19. Kai Rannenberg: What can IT Security Certification do for Multilateral Security? pp. 515-530 in Günter Müller, Kai Rannenberg: Multilateral Security in Communications - Technology, Infrastructure, Economy; Addison-Wesley-Longman, München, Reading (Massachusetts) ... 1999; ISBN 3-8273-1360-0

20. M. K. Reiter and A. D. Rubin. Crowds: Anonymity for web transactions. ACM Transactions on Information and System Security 1(1):66-92, November 1998.

21. Paul F. Syverson, David M. Goldschlag, Michael G. Reed: Anonymous connections and onion routing; in: Proceedings of the 1997 IEEE Symposium on Security and Privacy; IEEE Pres, Piscataway NJ

22. USA Department of Defense Trusted Computer System Evaluation Criteria; December 1985, DOD 5200.28-STD, http://www.radium.ncsc.mil/tpep/library/rainbow/5200.28-STD.html

23. Webster's Revised Unabridged Dictionary, 1913, ftp://ftp.dict.org/pub/dict/

24. The Freedom Network Architecture, Version 1.0, Zero-Knowledge Systems, Inc., http://www.zks.net/products/whitepapers.asp

11 Proposed Criteria Components

The three proposed families are included in a notation conformant with the prescriptions of the ECITS/CC. Specifically, this means that **bold facing** in components or in parts of components indicates an additional requirement compared with a hierarchical lower component.

11.1   Information Retention Control (FDP_IRC)

Family behaviour

This family addresses the need to ensure that information no longer necessary for the operation of the TOE is deleted by the TOE. Components of this family require the PP author to identify TOE activities and objects required for those activities, and not to be kept in the TOE, and the TOE to keep track of such stored objects, and to delete on-line and off-line copies of unnecessary information objects.

Component levelling

FDP_IRC.1 Subset information retention control requires that the TSF ensure that any copy of a defined subset of objects in the TSC is deleted when not more strictly necessary for the operation of the TOE, and to identify and define the activities for which the object is required.

FDP_IRC.2 Full information retention control requires that the TSF ensure that any copy of all objects in the TSC is deleted when not more strictly necessary for the operation of the TOE, and to identify and define the activities for which the object is required.

Management: FDP_IRC.1, FDP_IRC.2

There are no management activities foreseen for this component.

Audit: FDP_IRC.1, FDP_IRC.2

There are no events identified that should be auditable if FAU_GEN Security audit data generation is included in the PP/ST.

FDP_IRC.1 Subset information retention control

Hierarchical to: No other components

FDP_IRC.1.1 The TSF shall ensure that [assignment: *list of objects*] required for [assignment: *list of activities*] shall be eliminated immediately from the TOE upon termination of the activities for which they are required.

Dependencies: No dependencies.

FDP_IRC.2 Full information retention control

Hierarchical to: FDP_IRC.1

FDP_IRC.2.1 The TSF shall ensure that **all** objects required for [assignment: *list of activities*] shall be eliminated immediately from the TOE upon termination of the activities for which they are required.

Dependencies: No dependencies.

11.2   Unlinkability (FDP_UNL)

This family ensures that selected entities may be linked together without others being able to observe these links.

Component levelling

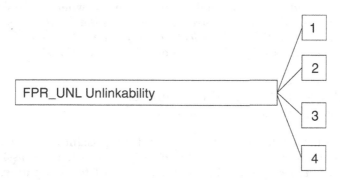

FPR_UNL.1 Unlinkability of operations requires that users and/or subjects are unable to determine whether the same user caused certain specific operations in the system, or are related in some other manner.

FPR_UNL.2 Unlinkability of users requires that users and/or subjects are unable to determine whether two users are referenced to by the same object, subject or operation, or are linked in some other manner.

FPR_UNL.3 Unlinkability of subjects requires that users and/or subjects are unable to determine whether two subjects are referenced to by the same object, user or operation, or are linked in some other manner.

FPR_UNL.4 Unlinkability of objects requires that users and/or subjects are unable to determine whether two objects are associated to the same user, subject or operation, or are linked in some other manner.

Management: FPR_UNL.1,   FPR_UNL.2,   FPR_UNL.3, FPR_UNL.4

The following actions could be considered for the management functions in FMT:

a) the management of the unlinkability function.

Audit: FPR_UNL.1, FPR_UNL.2, FPR_UNL.3, FPR_UNL.4

The following actions shall be auditable if FAU_GEN Security audit data generation is included in the PP / ST:

a) Minimal: The invocation of the unlinkability mechanism.

FPR_UNL.1 Unlinkability of operations

Hierarchical to: No other components

FPR_UNL.1.1 The TSF shall ensure that [assignment: *set of users and/or subjects*] are unable to determine whether [assignment: *list of operations*] [selection: *were caused by the same user, are related as follows* [assignment: *list of relations*]].

Dependencies: No dependencies.

FPR_UNL.2 Unlinkability of users

Hierarchical to: No other components

FPR_UNL.2.1 The TSF shall ensure that [assignment: *set of users and/or subjects*] **are unable to determine whether** [assignment: *list of users*] [selection: *are referenced by the same operation, are referenced by the same object, are referenced by the same subject, are related as follows* [assignment: *list of relations*]].

Dependencies: No dependencies.

FPR_UNL.3 Unlinkability of subjects

Hierarchical to: No other components

FPR_UNL.3.1 The TSF shall ensure that [assignment: *set of users and/or subjects*] **are unable to determine whether** [assignment: *list of subjects*] [selection: *act on behalf of the same user, are referenced by the same object, are referenced by the same operation, are related as follows* [assignment: *list of relations*]].

Dependencies: No dependencies.

FPR_UNL.4 Unlinkability of objects

Hierarchical to: No other components

FPR_UNL.4.1 The TSF shall ensure that [assignment: *set of users and/or subjects*] **are unable to determine whether** [assignment: *list of objects*] [selection: *are associated to the same user, are associated to the same subject, are associated to the same operation, are related as follows* [assignment: *list of relations*]].

Dependencies: No dependencies.

11.3   Distribution of Trust (FPR_TRD)

This family addresses the need to ensure that privacy-relevant information referring to a user of a TOE is divided among different parts of the TOE, or stored in such a manner (as with encryption) to make it impossible that a part of the TOE under a single administrative domain is able to access such information.

Component Levelling

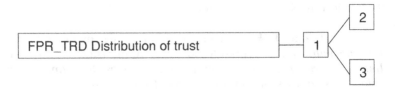

FPR_TRD.1 Administrative domains requires that the TOE be divided in distinct administrative domains (AD), with separate authentication and access control procedures; administrators of one administrative domain may not access other ADs.

FPR_TRD.2 Allocation of information assets requires that the TSF ensure that selected information impacting privacy be allocated among different parts of the TOE in such a way that in no state a single administrative domain will be able to access such information.

FPR_TRD.3 Allocation of processing activities requires that the TSF ensure that selected processing activities impacting privacy be executed on different parts of the TOE in such a way that no single administrative domain will be able to make use of information gathered from the processing activity.

Management: FPR_TRD.1

There are no management activities foreseen for this component.

Management: FPR_TRD.2

The following actions and definitions could be considered for the management functions in FMT:

1. The FMT_SMR.1 component could define a new security role "information owner" with regard to a specific data object or operation; this role represents the originator, and main user and beneficiary of such object or operation, and is the only subject or user allowed to specify distribution policies as security attributes for these entities;
2. An information owner could define default object security attributes;
3. An information owner could define and change security attributes on objects he or she owns.

Management: FPR_TRD.3

The following actions and definitions could be considered for the management functions in FMT:

1. The FMT_SMR component could define a new security role "information owner" with regard to a specific data object or operation; this role represents the originator, and main user and beneficiary of such object or operation, and is the only subject or user allowed to specify distribution policies as security attributes for these entities;
2. An information owner could define default operation security attributes;
3. An information owner could define and change security attributes on operations it initiates.

Audit: FPR_TRD.1, FPR_TRD.2, FPR_TRD.3

There are no events identified that should be auditable if FAU_GEN Security audit data generation is included in the PP/ST.

FPR_TRD.1 Administrative domains

Hierarchical to: No other components

FPR_TRD.1.1 The TOE shall be divided in separate, independent, intercommunicating parts (administrative domains) governed by distinct access control and authentication configurations.

FPR_TRD.1.2 The distinct administrative domains of the TOE shall explicitly request access to data stored on other parts of the TOE to be granted access to it.

Dependencies: No dependencies.
FPR_TRD.2 Allocation of information assets
Hierarchical to: FPR_TRD.1

FPR_TRD.2.1 The TOE shall be divided in separate, independent, intercommunicating parts (administrative domains) governed by distinct access control and authentication configurations.

FPR_TRD.2.2 The distinct administrative domains of the TOE shall explicitly request access to data stored on other parts of the TOE to be granted access to it.

FPR_TRD.2.3 The TSF shall ensure that [assignment: *list of objects*] shall be stored [selection: *on different administrative domains of the TOE, in a form unreadable by a single administrative domain of the TOE*] as to maintain the following conditions: [assignment: *list of conditions on objects*].

Dependencies: No dependencies.
FPR_TRD.3 Allocation of processing activities
Hierarchical to: FPR_TRD.1

FPR_TRD.3.1 The TOE shall be divided in separate, independent, intercommunicating parts (administrative domains) governed by distinct access control and authentication configurations.

FPR_TRD.3.2 The distinct administrative domains of the TOE shall explicitly request access to data stored on other parts of the TOE to be granted access to it.

FPR_TRD.3.3 The TSF shall ensure that [assignment: *list of operations*] shall be performed by different administrative domains of the TOE, so that the following conditions are maintained: [assignment: *list of conditions on operations*].

Dependencies: No dependencies.

Author Index

Lecture Notes in Computer Science

For information about Vols. 1–1920
please contact your bookseller or Springer-Verlag

Vol. 1952: M.C. Monard, J. Simão Sichman (Eds.), Advances in Artificial Intelligence. Proceedings, 2000. XV, 498 pages. 2000. (Subseries LNAI).

Vol. 1953: G. Borgefors, I. Nyström, G. Sanniti di Baja (Eds.), Discrete Geometry for Computer Imagery. Proceedings, 2000. XI, 544 pages. 2000.

Vol. 1954: W.A. Hunt, Jr., S.D. Johnson (Eds.), Formal Methods in Computer-Aided Design. Proceedings, 2000. XI, 539 pages. 2000.

Vol. 1955: M. Parigot, A. Voronkov (Eds.), Logic for Programming and Automated Reasoning. Proceedings, 2000. XIII, 487 pages. 2000. (Subseries LNAI).

Vol. 1956: T. Coquand, P. Dybjer, B. Nordström, J. Smith (Eds.), Types for Proofs and Programs. Proceedings, 1999. VII, 195 pages. 2000.

Vol. 1957: P. Ciancarini, M. Wooldridge (Eds.), Agent-Oriented Software Engineering. Proceedings, 2000. X, 323 pages. 2001.

Vol. 1960: A. Ambler, S.B. Calo, G. Kar (Eds.), Services Management in Intelligent Networks. Proceedings, 2000. X, 259 pages. 2000.

Vol. 1961: J. He, M. Sato (Eds.), Advances in Computing Science – ASIAN 2000. Proceedings, 2000. X, 299 pages. 2000.

Vol. 1963: V. Hlaváč, K.G. Jeffery, J. Wiedermann (Eds.), SOFSEM 2000: Theory and Practice of Informatics. Proceedings, 2000. XI, 460 pages. 2000.

Vol. 1964: J. Malenfant, S. Moisan, A. Moreira (Eds.), Object-Oriented Technology. Proceedings, 2000. XI, 309 pages. 2000.

Vol. 1965: Ç. K. Koç, C. Paar (Eds.), Cryptographic Hardware and Embedded Systems – CHES 2000. Proceedings, 2000. XI, 355 pages. 2000.

Vol. 1966: S. Bhalla (Ed.), Databases in Networked Information Systems. Proceedings, 2000. VIII, 247 pages. 2000.

Vol. 1967: S. Arikawa, S. Morishita (Eds.), Discovery Science. Proceedings, 2000. XII, 332 pages. 2000. (Subseries LNAI).

Vol. 1968: H. Arimura, S. Jain, A. Sharma (Eds.), Algorithmic Learning Theory. Proceedings, 2000. XI, 335 pages. 2000. (Subseries LNAI).

Vol. 1969: D.T. Lee, S.-H. Teng (Eds.), Algorithms and Computation. Proceedings, 2000. XIV, 578 pages. 2000.

Vol. 1970: M. Valero, V.K. Prasanna, S. Vajapeyam (Eds.), High Performance Computing – HiPC 2000. Proceedings, 2000. XVIII, 568 pages. 2000.

Vol. 1971: R. Buyya, M. Baker (Eds.), Grid Computing – GRID 2000. Proceedings, 2000. XIV, 229 pages. 2000.

Vol. 1972: A. Omicini, R. Tolksdorf, F. Zambonelli (Eds.), Engineering Societies in the Agents World. Proceedings, 2000. IX, 143 pages. 2000. (Subseries LNAI).

Vol. 1973: J. Van den Bussche, V. Vianu (Eds.), Database Theory – ICDT 2001. Proceedings, 2001. X, 451 pages. 2001.

Vol. 1974: S. Kapoor, S. Prasad (Eds.), FST TCS 2000: Foundations of Software Technology and Theoretical Computer Science. Proceedings, 2000. XIII, 532 pages. 2000.

Vol. 1975: J. Pieprzyk, E. Okamoto, J. Seberry (Eds.), Information Security. Proceedings, 2000. X, 323 pages. 2000.

Vol. 1976: T. Okamoto (Ed.), Advances in Cryptology – ASIACRYPT 2000. Proceedings, 2000. XII, 630 pages. 2000.

Vol. 1977: B. Roy, E. Okamoto (Eds.), Progress in Cryptology – INDOCRYPT 2000. Proceedings, 2000. X, 295 pages. 2000.

Vol. 1978: B. Schneier (Ed.), Fast Software Encryption. Proceedings, 2000. VIII, 315 pages. 2001.

Vol. 1979: S. Moss, P. Davidsson (Eds.), Multi-Agent-Based Simulation. Proceedings, 2000. VIII, 267 pages. 2001. (Subseries LNAI).

Vol. 1983: K.S. Leung, L.-W. Chan, H. Meng (Eds.), Intelligent Data Engineering and Automated Learning – IDEAL 2000. Proceedings, 2000. XVI, 573 pages. 2000.

Vol. 1984: J. Marks (Ed.), Graph Drawing. Proceedings, 2001. XII, 419 pages. 2001.

Vol. 1987: K.-L. Tan, M.J. Franklin, J. C.-S. Lui (Eds.), Mobile Data Management. Proceedings, 2001. XIII, 289 pages. 2001.

Vol. 1989: M. Ajmone Marsan, A. Bianco (Eds.), Quality of Service in Multiservice IP Networks. Proceedings, 2001. XII, 440 pages. 2001.

Vol. 1991: F. Dignum, C. Sierra (Eds.), Agent Mediated Electronic Commerce. VIII, 241 pages. 2001. (Subseries LNAI).

Vol. 1992: K. Kim (Ed.), Public Key Cryptography. Proceedings, 2001. XI, 423 pages. 2001.

Vol. 1993: E. Zitzler, K. Deb, L. Thiele, C.A.Coello Coello, D. Corne (Eds.), Evolutionary Multi-Criterion Optimization. Proceedings, 2001. XIII, 712 pages. 2001.

Vol. 1995: M. Sloman, J. Lobo, E.C. Lupu (Eds.), Policies for Distributed Systems and Networks. Proceedings, 2001. X, 263 pages. 2001.

Vol. 1998: R. Klette, S. Peleg, G. Sommer (Eds.), Robot Vision. Proceedings, 2001. IX, 285 pages. 2001.

Vol. 2000: R. Wilhelm (Ed.), Informatics: 10 Years Back, 10 Years Ahead. IX, 369 pages. 2001.

Vol. 2003: F. Dignum, U. Cortés (Eds.), Agent Mediated Electronic Commerce III. XII, 193 pages. 2001. (Subseries LNAI).

Vol. 2004: A. Gelbukh (Ed.), Computational Linguistics and Intelligent Text Processing. Proceedings, 2001. XII, 528 pages. 2001.

Vol. 2006: R. Dunke, A. Abran (Eds.), New Approaches in Software Measurement. Proceedings, 2000. VIII, 245 pages. 2001.

Vol. 2009: H. Federrath (Ed.), Designing Privacy Enhancing Technologies. Proceedings, 2000. X, 231 pages. 2001.

Vol. 2010: A. Ferreira, H. Reichel (Eds.), STACS 2001. Proceedings, 2001. XV, 576 pages. 2001.

Vol. 2024: H. Kuchen, K. Ueda (Eds.), Functional and Logic Programming. Proceedings, 2001. X, 391 pages. 2001.